H O L L Y W O R L D

HOLLYWORLD

Space, Power, and Fantasy
in the American Economy

AIDA A. HOZIC

CORNELL
UNIVERSITY
PRESS

ITHACA
&
LONDON

First published 2001 by Cornell University Press

Printed in the United States of America

Library of Congress Cataloging-in-Publication Data

Hozic, Aida A.
    Hollyworld : space, power, and fantasy in the American economy / Aida A. Hozic.
        p. cm.
    Includes bibliographical references and index.
    ISBN 0-8014-3926-4 (alk. paper)
    1. Motion picture industry—United States—History. I. Title.
PN1993.5U6 H68 2001
384'.8'0973—dc21

                                                          2001003646

Cornell University Press strives to use environmentally responsible suppliers and materials to the fullest extent possible in the publishing of its books. Such materials include vegetable-based, low-VOC inks and acid-free papers that are re-cycled, totally chlorine-free, or partly composed of nonwood fibers. Books that bear the logo of the FSC (Forest Stewardship Council) use paper taken from forests that have been inspected and certified as meeting the highest standards for environmental and social responsibility. For further information, visit our website at www.cornellpress.cornell.edu.

Cloth printing   10 9 8 7 6 5 4 3 2 1

To the memory of my father

CONTENTS

ILLUSTRATIONS

PREFACE

"Fall of Babylon," a sketch from the set design book for D. W. Griffith's *Intolerance* (Triangle Productions, 1916) by the famous French artist Georges Rochegrosse. Courtesy of the Museum of Modern Art, New York.

Hollywood," said Budd Schulberg, a screenwriter who grew up in the (in)famous Los Angeles suburb, was "a picture of America run through the projector at triple speed. If the Hollywood party was excessive, it was only because Hollywood had always been an excessive, speeded-up, larger-than-life reflection of the American way."[1]

Several decades ago, Hollywood, this hyperbolic incarnation of America's dreams and nightmares, was a dying company town whose single product—a feature-length motion picture—seemed no longer profitable. In 1963, both in the United States and overseas, box office receipts hit their all-time low. That same year, the number of theaters in the United States was cut in half. Critics openly sided with European and Japanese filmmakers, and America was importing more movies than it was producing. Art houses and drive-ins flourished. Directors such as Godard, Bergman, Fellini, Truffaut, and Kurosawa became familiar names in the United States, while American teenagers learned how to make love by watching low-budget, off-Hollywood movies from their parents' cars. Even the concept of female beauty was no longer a Hollywood monopoly. If, immediately after World War II, Italian communists felt compelled to organize their own beauty pageants in order to counteract the impact of Hollywood's bourgeois aesthetics,[2] by the beginning of the 1960s such a Gramscian response to American cultural imperialism was no longer necessary. The most beautiful actresses at the time had foreign names—Brigitte Bardot, Gina Lollobrigida, Catherine Deneuve, Anna Karina, Liv Ullmann—and lived in Rome, Paris, or Stockholm instead of Beverly Hills. One after the other, Hollywood studios closed down their back lots or transformed them into theme parks and parking lots. What was left of the Dream Factory was quickly turning into rubble and dust. The New Wave, danish porno, and Spaghetti Westerns were IN, Hollywood was OUT, and the future of Hollywood studios seemed uncertain at best.

Thirty-some years later, Hollywood is again the booming center of the global multimedia industry whose products now range from films and TV series to theme parks, special effects, bubble baths, toys, and gated communities. Since 1995, the entertainment industry has been the single largest employer in Southern California, surpassing aerospace and defense industries. American films again dominate world markets. Trade conflicts over popular culture are not just common but the cornerstone of debates about the new intellectual property rights regime. Hollywood is successfully forging alliances with Silicon Valley, the telecommunications industry, and tourism, thus turning itself into the focal point of the highest growth sectors in the American and global, economies. As Ed McCracken, CEO of Silicon Graphics, noted several years ago, at the height of the Clinton era, the entertainment industry replaced the military-industrial complex as the dominant force in the American economy. "Since World War II, the military has driven the advancement of technology," said McCracken. "Now we see that role really moving toward the entertainment industry. They are the ones who push the envelope now. They've got lots of money, very short cycle times, and they want to do things nobody's ever done before."[3] For the first time in its turbulent history, Hollywood is receiving accolades not as a cultural or ideological machine par excellence but as one of the most important strategic sectors in the U.S. and global economy.

The resurrection of Hollywood from the ruins of its studio system to the point of global dominance represents one of the few truly fascinating tales of latter-day capitalism. It is also one of the most telling examples of corporate and industrial change in contemporary world economy. In just a few decades, Hollywood has transformed itself from a factory devoted to the "manufacturing of prefabricated daydreams," as Hortense Powdermaker described it in 1950,[4] into a merchandising emporium of movies, games, and licensed characters. It is quickly moving even further—into the unexplored areas of cyberspace, virtual reality, and digital imaging. The contradictions of Hollywood success, which are most transparent in its old and new architectural constructs, pose important questions about the relationship between contemporary global economy and global (dis)order, industrial and social organization, economic and political change. But they also underscore the fact that industrial change always goes beyond structured worlds of organized interests, regulatory agencies, and economic competitiveness and invades the hidden pockets of our everyday lives. For although we are often reluctant to think about it, Hollywood, much like other industries (or, perhaps, even more so), constitutes its audiences while constituting itself as an industry. Ultimately, therefore, any discussion about Hollywood's economic transformations turns into a discussion about Zeitgeist: about our relationship to ourselves, our fantasies and nightmares, and our most hopeful and most fearful visions of the future.

Therefore, the questions that have guided me in this exploration of industrial and corporate change in the American film industry seek to transcend both the narrow framework of sectoral analyses and the broad horizon of contemporary debates about globalization of culture industries. What I am interested in is not just the process of industrial transformation in Hollywood, or the extent of American influence in the world, but the ways in which Hollywood—insofar as it is a reflection of the American way, and in so far as it is conquering the world—can help us illuminate the nature of the relationship between political, economic, and cultural or moral authority. How does Hollywood produce the political?[5] How do changes in Hollywood's power structures affect and relate to politics outside of Hollywood? What can the changes in Hollywood's internal organization tell us about changes in other industrial sectors, particularly in this age of dot-com economy? What is the nature of political order in which Hollywood—and media industries in general—are quickly becoming the most important strategic sector in the American and world economy? And why is production of ambivalence—and of the boundary—between real and fantastic so critical to the production and reproduction of power? What is it, then, not about Hollywood per se but about the ways in which economic, cultural, and political power manifest themselves that has made Hollywood so important, so interesting, and so paradigmatic of America itself?

In the book, I address these questions by tracing a conflict between two groups of economic actors—manufacturers and merchants—through three distinct periods of Hollywood's history: the studio system between 1915 and 1960 when Hollywood dominated markets with a combination of mass production and vertical organization; a period of dispersed production and centralized distribution which, between 1960 and 1990, gave rise to multimedia companies such as Time Warner, Sony/Columbia and Disney/ABC; and, finally, the most recent digital era in which Hollywood companies have been rapidly fusing with the much larger infotainment complex while gradually losing their once-distinct identities as moviemakers. Each period, I will argue, corresponds to a different mode of spatial organization of production and to a different mode of political and economic organization of everyday life. Each demonstrates how the new industrial architecture shaped battles between manufacturers and merchants and, conversely, how the spatial and temporal choices that actors made in order to assert their own position in the economy created internal contradictions which set a stage for a new cycle of struggle. The book suggests that spatial reorganization of production, in all industrial sectors but Hollywood in particular, changes both material and conceptual boundaries between public and private as well as between real and fantastic and, therefore, transforms our understanding of what is and is not a matter of politics. Consequently, the shifts from manufacturer- to merchant-dominated economy and from centralized to dispersed production, which the book describes in detail, also indicate important shifts in patterns of censorship and surveillance, character of political authority, and the nature of moral and symbolic order.

So, while the focus of the book is on the shifting patterns of control in the entertainment industry, I am equally interested in explaining the peculiar nature of Hollywood's political authority and the complex manifestations of power that it enunciates. Limning the thin line between political economy and cultural studies, geography and political theory, the book describes the ways in which Hollywood reflects changes in the American economy and creates conditions for its political reproduction. Situated on the borders of real and fantastic, of what can and cannot be dreamed, envisioned, and, ultimately, discussed—and simultaneously capable of producing and shifting those boundaries—Hollywood is, I propose, neither a simple propaganda machine nor an epiphenomenon of the American empire. It is, and has frequently been, the economic precursor of the things to come and the political creator of the status quo. Thus, as we shall see, what makes Hollywood so important, so interesting and so paradigmatic—politically and economically—are precisely its ambivalences: the fact that it is and is not like any other industrial sector, that it is and is not just a geographic location, that its product is and is not sheer entertainment. Hollywood's peculiarities do not make it different than other industrial sectors, they just turn it, as Budd Schulberg would say, into an exaggerated—sometimes caricatured—picture of America itself. Now more than ever, since thinking Hollywood increasingly means thinking total entertainment: ahead of us is an empire that stretches from Disneyland to Kosovo, a multimedia arcade that features O. J. Simpson, Rwandan victims, Holocaust deniers, and William Jefferson Clinton. *Welcome to Hollyworld.*

Credits

My own journey into movie-land was made possible by the generous support of the following individuals and institutions (unlike in Hollywood, these credits are listed in no particular order): Roger Haydon, Herman Schwartz, John Echeverri-Gent, Valerie Bunce, Nada Hozić, Eric Lott, Laura Oaksmith, Hector Schamis, Daria Šito, Cheryl Roberts, Brian Schott, Terry Geesken, Aaron Presnall, Mine Eder, Orson Watson, Anna Eliasson, Ralph and Libby Cohen, The Kibbutz Cohen, Slobodan Mišeljić, Boris Vujović, Zillah Eisenstein, Aleksandra Zimonjić, Patti Goff, Srdjan Hrisafović, Jodi Dean, Chip Gagnon, Naeem Inayatullah, Abdulah Šarčević, Libby Eshbach, Susan and Sid Tarrow, Patty Zimmermann, Vicki Birchfield, Stuart Auyash, David

Ost, Petar Ramadanović, Catherine Peebles, Hans Schaeffer, Richard Bondi, Dietmar Schirmer, Sorayya Khan, Len Schoppa, Julie Hemment, Frank Hein, Asma Barlas, Craig Rimmerman, Sanja Mandić, Béla Greskovits, Dorothee Bohle, the University of Virginia, the Thomas Jefferson Memorial Foundation, Hobart and William Smith Colleges, Ithaca College, the Institute for European Studies and the Government Department at Cornell University, the Margaret Herrick Library, the Film Stills Archive at the Museum of Modern Art, the Seaside Public Relations Office, the Kauai Film Office, the Darden School Library, the Bosnian refugee community in Charlottesville, Virginia, and the warmth of Ithaca, New York.

The book is dedicated to the memory of my father whose imagination was infinite but whose integrity could not easily be swayed by the lure of fantasy.

AIDA HOZIC

Ithaca, New York

INTRODUCTION: INTO THE ZONES

And now, we are only five miles up and it becomes increasingly obvious that the great Metropolis is a ghost town, that what was once the world's largest oasis is now its greatest agglomeration of ruins in a wasteland. Nothing moves in the streets. Dunes of sand have drifted across the concrete. The avenues of palms and pepper trees have left no trace.

Aldous Huxley, *Ape and Essence*

The Thief of Bagdad (United Artists, 1924) with Douglas Fairbanks and Lotta Woods enchanted audiences with its special effects, flying carpets and horses in particular. Courtesy of the Museum of Modern Art, New York.

In early evenings, Universal City looms like a mirage over Burbank, a typical Los Angeles suburb. From atop the hill which rests above the Studio's famous theme park, one can assume more than see that somewhere in the distance, beyond glittering tram rides and leaps toward the sky with E.T., far beyond faux Moulin Rouge, medieval castles, and facades of houses that never were, and far, far beyond the limits of simulation, lies an entirely different reality: scattered apartment complexes inhabited by frightened illegal immigrants, clustered suburban houses that once belonged to Lockheed employees, police cars cruising along desolate avenues of endless billboards, car dealerships and semi-deserted office towers. As the bifurcated Los Angeles economy of haves and have-nots takes its toll even on Burbank, one of the more prosperous middle-class suburbs in San Fernando Valley, the entertainment industry prepares itself to outlast the community which hosts it.

Here, on the site of the largest motion-picture shrine in the world where, as *Barron's* magazine once put it, "Southern Californians send their guests for a day's respite,"[1] America's economic past meets its economic future. The old company town, "the Woolworth's of movie production world," in Doug Gomery's words,[2] is gradually being replaced by projects that will turn Universal City into the entertainment metropolis of the world. Universal Studio Tour and Universal

Amphitheater attracted more than seven million visitors per year in the 1980s. Since the addition of Universal CityWalk in 1993, the number of visitors has increased to ten million. CityWalk, the heart of the future entertainment city, inspires political and media praise as the "controlled environment success."[3] The studio backlot, since the 1970s mostly a locus of TV production, tries to attract independent producers and TV companies with a similar slogan. "Control your environment and your costs . . . Universal rents great locations!" urged the studio brochure distributed at the 1994 Location Expo in Santa Monica. But for Universal officials, the production facility is little more than an obstacle to further futuristic developments of their corporation. "My guess is that of the 420 acres, 360 could easily be developed, assuming there was no studio," said Albert Dorskind, president of Universal's real-estate division, a decade ago.[4] *Assuming there was no studio.* The "controlled environment" of the past, focused on production, inclusion of all tangible and intangible assets, and standardization of products and consumers alike, has already given way to the "controlled environment" of the future. In place of the old motion picture studio emerges the new metropolis focused on consumption, exclusion of assets (most visible in subcontracted labor and leased property), and blurred boundaries between public and private space.

According to its own press releases, Universal has always been the company oriented towards the future, the cutting edge of the entertainment industry. When Universal City opened its gates on March 15, 1915, *Photoplay* magazine wrote that the event was celebrated with a lot of fanfare, "like an occupation of a conquered territory."[5] For just a few months before the special train with guests and curious onlookers rolled in from New York for the grandiose opening, added *Photoplay*, a hen ranch and a "great barley field bared its tan face to heaven nine months a year"[6] at the site of the future studio. Carl Laemmle, president of the Universal Film Manufacturing Company, approved the location in the middle of nowhere and conceived the City after having come to the conclusion that "the best way of having men, women, birds, beasts, buildings, lakes, rivers, mountains, and so forth in pictures was to build a city and put some of each in it."[7] The result was the city whose plentiful picturesque sites included

Egyptian pyramids, a zoo full of African lions, leopards, lizards, and all sorts of domestic animals, a Mississippi steamboat, and an entire tribe of "Redmen", as Native Americans were called by Universal, "paid and cared for by the Universal Film Manufacturing Company with the special permission of the United States Government."[8] For the purposes of cinematographic verity, the purchased "Redmen" were discouraged from "assimilating modern progress or adopting any modern customs and costumes."[9] The City was so versatile that it could be changed "within three days to conform to any nationality, style of architecture, color or scheme or state of preservation which any of the twenty producing directors who use this metropolis as their base of operations call for."[10]

But in spite of this chameleon appearance which ignited the fantasy of moviegoers, Universal City was nothing but an ordinary company town, one of the thousands incorporated across the United States in the beginning of this century. Planned to be a habitat for over 15,000 people, Universal City of 1915 had its own City Hall, police department and jail, fire department, post office, school, and bank. All of these services were, naturally, tied to employment at the Universal Film Manufacturing Company and vice versa. Two misdemeanors, if viewed as such by Mr. McRea, director general, assistant mayor, and a magistrate in lieu of the magistrate, were sufficient to throw someone off the property. By "unifying control in the hands of the employer"[11] and building a City whose sole purpose was to crank "pictures like Model Ts off the assembly line,"[12] Universal was simply, as its own weekly journal described, "obeying the law of Progress":

> It is one of the laws of nature that there is no such condition as rest. Life itself is founded up in movements in the purport of Progress. This movement must be either forward or backward. There is no such thing as standing still. The Universal is obeying the law of Progress in carrying out its plans in Universal City, without the slightest fear of any contraction of business or of any stagnation in the motion picture industry.[13]

These prophetic words continue to resonate even today. At the 1993 press conference, where Lew Wasserman, chairman of Universal's former parent company, MCA, announced that the company had "decided to move forward with a planning concept for future development" of the three-billion-dollar "Entertainment City," Los Angeles technocratic mayor Richard Riordan praised MCA for its "obvious commitment to the City of Los Angeles."[14] "At a time when Los Angeles is rebuilding not only its city but also its image," said Riordan evidently referring to the damage done to the city by the 1992 riots, "MCA's announcement sends all the right signals to the world that Los Angeles is the place to visit, live and do business in."[15] The company's future City, according to Riordan, was "exactly the type of program which will bring about the positive change to Los Angeles."[16]

The glimpse of this positive change can already be caught in Universal CityWalk, a $100-million "unique entertainment, dining, and shopping promenade featuring more than three dozen specialty restaurants and retail shops,"[17] the "prototype for controlled entertainment Meccas around the globe."[18] According to its authors, the promenade links Universal Studios-Hollywood, Universal Amphitheater, and the Universal City Cinemas. But, in actuality, it is an inevitable walkway through the maze of stores leading from a parking lot the size of a football stadium to the gates of the Universal Studios Tour. As Sam Grogg, a former dean of the North Carolina School of the Arts, once said, "all the movies now lead to the Gift Shop."[19] In spite of all its pretenses of being the "urban village which tries to address the needs of everybody who would have the need for a center, a community, an emotional place to relate to,"[20] Universal CityWalk, like the movies that its parent company produces these days, is nothing but a highly successful gateway to enforced consumption.

And yet, as a cross between a theme park and a mall, Universal CityWalk is also more than both. Unlike theme parks, it is not a clearly delineated area of make believe, for it aims at being the reality itself, the public space that Los Angeles has never had. Unlike malls, it is admittedly not open and available to everyone. Jon Jerde, the architect of this allegedly communal place, openly states that Universal CityWalk "will be safer than most public places in Los Angeles because this is private property."[21] Echoing the architect's words, Wendy Armstrong, of suburban Sherman Oaks, adds: "I feel great here. There's no panhandlers, no graffiti." However, some stylized graffiti were scrawled on the walls, to make the place a bit more believable, and street entertainers were carefully screened and auditioned to lend authenticity to the urban environment cleansed of crime, poverty, homelessness and trouble. In fear of racial violence, both John Singleton's *Poetic Justice* (1993) and Mario Van Peebles's black western *Posse* (1993) could not be shown in the eighteen-screen Cineplex Odeon, half owned by Universal and located on the CityWalk entry plaza. Universal CityWalk, built after years of consultations with local homeowners' associations, prides itself on being "safely chaotic."[22]

The elimination of realities that do not belong in this "safe chaos" marks the essential difference between a motion picture studio, the quintessential controlled environment of the past, and CityWalk, its contemporary counterpart. Born at the very end of the nineteenth century, the motion picture studio was much more than a place where movies were being made. It was the epitome of the new industrial architecture and of the novel social and economic organization of production. Its creator, Thomas Alva Edison, strongly believed—much like his contemporaries Henry Ford and Frederick Winslow Taylor— that "the future of race depends on quantity production"[23] and constructed a building that could maximize his movie output. "Black Maria," as Edison's first studio came to be known, was a small building, painted black from both inside and outside, rotated on a graphite center, and equipped with a movable roof to allow for maximization of sunlight. Production levels, though limited to vignettes from everyday life, staged sports events, and dances, were very high by the standards of its time. The studio inspired the idea of an enclosed space in which circumstances could not only be controlled but created from scratch—like an empirical resolution to the famous Russell's logical problem, the motion picture studio became the sum of all sums which did contain itself. Within its walls lived wind and fire, light and darkness, the Roman Empire and the streets of Brooklyn, oceans and deserts, earthquakes and meadows. By the end of the 1920s, every country in the world with any desire to make movies embarked on building a studio of its own—the world that contained all other worlds, the place that would make any demiurge envious.

The outdoor sets used for the Babylonian sequence of D. W. Griffith's *Intolerance* (Triangle Productions, 1916) were the most grandiose sets of their time. Courtesy of the Museum of Modern Art, New York.

CityWalks, too, are mushrooming around the globe. The Japanese have built an enclosed beach in Seagaia—complete with an artificial horizon, waves perfect for surfing, and the recorded chirping of birds—that "does not look like Japan" and where "water is really wonderful and really clean."[24] Disney has "CityWalked" New York's Times Square and 42nd Street. Universal and its parent company Seagram are building CityWalk replicas in Florida and Japan. MGM hotel in Las Vegas even has a tour of a fake movie studio—where no films have been or will be produced—while its parent company in Santa Monica has all but ceased to produce or even distribute motion pictures. Themed retail stores and restaurants are in vogue; future malls are expected to incorporate medical facilities, education centers, hotels and virtual reality travel (including such options as mountain climbing, skiing, and artificial beaches). The architects of The Forum Shops, an integral part of Caesar's Palace hotel and casino in Las Vegas and the mall that experts most often compare to Universal CityWalk, "began with a dream of making shopping a convenient and enjoyable experience."[25] Therefore, as their promotional materials boast, "storefront facades and common areas resemble an ancient Roman streetscape," and on a "barrel-vaulted ceiling, a painted sky feature emulates the beauty of the Mediterranean sky." In the Fountain Plaza, Bacchus "hosts a party with Apollo, Plutus, and Venus who join in an astoundingly realistic, animated robotic feature that includes lasers, music, and sound effects."[26] And then there is Celebration, a pre-war look-alike town built and designed by Disney corporation on Disney property in central Florida, which attempts to revive the sense of neighborly camaraderie and community that Americans have allegedly lost since World War II.[27]

However tacky or fascinating, though, the spectacles that are included in these new "controlled environments" do not capture their essence. In fact, the emblematic places of our time are defined, first and foremost, by what they exclude—not just labor but production in general, not just inner-city problems but widespread economic and political disarray.[28] If the motion picture studio, almost literally, gobbled the world in order to control it, CityWalks of the world are now spitting it back out. Their safety and their prosperity depend, both symbolically and economically, on the chaos in their surroundings.

There may be no better parable for this century of hope and disillusionment than the architectural transformations of the film industry. To the extent to which "controlled environments" have, throughout this century, been the model for all social engineers, the motion picture industry has become the material representation of their failed ambitions. Stefan Zweig once wrote that Honoré de Balzac's main ambition was to become Napoléon. But, once the future famous writer realized that he could never become the ruler of the world, he created a world—thirty-something volumes of *The Comedy of Human Life*—in which he could be the sole ruler.[29] Similarly, the motion picture industry appropriated and realized the illusion of societal control, never fully attainable in the real world—from the time when the first motion picture studio was built as the embodiment of the world that contains all other worlds to the present, a time in which theme parks, motion-picture-inspired towns and interactive technologies represent the attempt to replace communities forever lost. The new zones of entertainment now clearly embody the faith of their developers that particular spatial arrangements can condition the development of particular social and economic relations; self-consciously construed as zones of exclusion, they reflect a new form of power that no longer requires territorial acquisition and surveillance of production forces as the industrial age did. It is, therefore, the main contention of the following pages that the spectacular growth of the American and global film industry and its off-springs in other entertainment sectors cannot be fully understood without looking at its spatial representations. And, similarly, that the careful examination of the changes in the entertainment industry—one of the fastest growing industrial sectors in the world—may help us get new answers to the enduring questions of political economy—control by whom, over whom, and for whom.

Who Controls Hollywood?

The "thick description" of the Universal CityWalk and its predecessor, Universal City, directs our attention to an inextricable link between space, power, and fantasy: elements of economic and political control embedded in social imagining; the intimate relationship between power and architecture; and possible pitfalls and advantages of attempts to transcend the limitations of here and now through fantasy and its realization. But analyzing the metamorphosis of "controlled environments" and theoretically disentangling the bundle of space, power, and fantasy is much more difficult than moving in parables and allegories. Literary figures, much like architecture, to paraphrase Fredric Jameson, allow us to relate differences and conceptualize the social totality that, otherwise, may seem unintelligible.[30] By contrast, the extant social theories—both economic and cultural—leave us strangely inept to comprehend the essence of this emerging socio-economic system in which the spheres of production and consumption appear to be tragically divorced but whose existence, while precarious, may not be nearly as transient as the much too consumed prefix "post" in its numerous descriptions would imply. As Sharon Zukin has written in her penetrating account of the postmodern "landscapes of power," neither the pessimistic accounts of de-industrialization nor the optimistic panegyrics to the post-industrial age can capture the "simultaneous advance and decline of economic forms, or the sense that as ground shifts under our feet, taller buildings continue to rise."[31]

This book is built around a simple premise and a series of nested arguments. The premise, as the CityWalk tale has already illustrated, is that contradictions of Hollywood's transformations are nowhere as visible as in its social geography, real estate investments, and places created by the new entertainment economy. As we shall see repeatedly throughout the book, space, landscapes, and architecture oppose the vagueness of Hollywood's power lines and the transient nature of success and failure in the entertainment industry. Thus, an easy path through Hollywood history simply follows the trail of its architectural remnants: abandoned studio buildings, old and new mansions of Hollywood moguls, bulldozed studio lots turned into shopping malls, forgotten makeshift studios in places as far-flung as Spain, Egypt, and Morocco. Similarly, a quick look at recent entertainment constructions across the country—from Fox's *Titanic* (1997) studio in Baja California to new hotels in Las Vegas, or from I. M. Pei's building of the Creative Artists Agency in Beverly Hills to the Disneyfied 42nd Street in New York—clearly shows where the industry is heading. Driving through LA's sprawled economy, it also becomes obvious that Hollywood's architecture is nothing but an exaggerated reflection of places and spaces produced by American industrialization and de-industrialization. Much like in other industrial sectors, power struggles and profit aspirations determined where Hollywood corporations would locate their film production. More often than not, Hollywood choices mimicked the architectural and spatial choices of other successful sectors and industrial leaders. At the same time, however, Hollywood's ability to produce space and place according to its own fantasy—and, thus, seemingly transcend the natural limitations that geography often imposed on other sectors—has made its industrial zones more exuberant, more excessive, and easier to read as valuable documents on social and economic change than steel plants or contemporary silicon fabs.

Still, and here is where the more complex, nested, arguments begin, it would be a mistake to treat architecture only as a text.[32] Reading space as a sheer reflection of particular economic periods in Hollywood's history underestimates the role of space in the creation and sustenance of power relations in the entertainment industry, and the role of the entertainment industry in both the American and global economy. Instead, to paraphrase Henri Lefebvre, space should be viewed both as an inscription of particular social relations and as the arena of their change.[33] Thus, more than a record of things past, space, landscapes, and architecture are products of conflicts and tensions between various economic and political actors and, consequently, preconditions of their change. In this book, I perceive them as objects of struggle between two groups of actors, manufacturers and merchants, and their two distinct modes of capital accumulation, *economies of space* and *economies of time*. Following Gary Gereffi's distinction between "producer-driven" and "buyer-driven" commodity chains, I argue that changes in contemporary Hollywood are not just a result of the shift from vertical to horizontal integration, or from mass production to flexible specialization, but a historical process of resurgence and consolidation of merchant power in the American and global economies.[34]

On a more abstract level, the book explores links between the spatial organization of production and the moral and symbolic organization of the society. From Bentham's Panopticon to Foucault's analysis of spatial ordering as social ordering in the history of prisons to the most recent writings of social geographers, Mike Davis in particular, it is evident that spatial relations of power are inextricably entwined with patterns of surveillance, subjugation, and moral construction of society. In fact, space is not just an objective category, a material given that determines power relations as the long history of geo-strategic thinking would imply, but is itself a product of our imaginary. The changes in spatial organization of the economy reconfigure the discursive boundaries between public and private, real and fantastic, which serve as the ideological foundation of economic and political power. And vice versa: the way in which space is envisioned usually determines where the physical boundaries between these spheres would be erected. Thus, spatial reorganization of production in the American entertainment industry entails far more than relocation of production: it brings to surface a close relationship between economic interests and politics of everyday life as well as the extent to which the conceptualization of space has always been closely entwined with power relations in the world economy. By examining the links between economic and moral space more closely, it is possible to portray industrial change as the process of making and unmaking of the boundaries between reality and fantasy, public and private—the process much more similar to the creation of hegemonic blocks in the Gramscian sense than to the evolutionary theories of social change which dominate our current economic thought.

Finally, such complex representations of industrial change make it possible to suggest that establishment of hegemony within the American film industry has had its counterparts in the establishment of American hegemony abroad, revealing an interesting continuum in power relations inside and outside of Hollywood. If the power of merchants and manufacturers in Hollywood itself has mostly depended on particular spatial arrangements and their moral interpretation, the power of Hollywood within the American economy and the power of the American economy in the world have also been highly dependent on the construction of new social and moral spaces and of new fantasies. In both cases, imagination and fantasy were not just fellow travelers of economic power but constitutive of its force. Indeed, one could argue, power is nothing but the ability to organize fantasies, and it is precisely for this reason that the film industry appears to be inherently and profoundly political: not only because it is related to the well-known loci of power—state, presidency, war machine, or because it is capable of producing first-rate propaganda, but because it is itself sitting on the fence of real and fantastic, because it is itself capable of producing alternate spaces and histories, and because it is itself nothing but the organized public fantasy.

Economic Analysis of Hollywood

Throughout history, one issue has implicitly or explicitly dominated economic studies of Hollywood, due to its tremendous bearing on the social status of the industry: the relationship between the film industry and other industrial sectors. Both Hollywood moguls and film historians have always been perfectly aware of this relationship's dual relevance: stressing the similarities between the film industry and other industrial sectors could greatly enhance Hollywood's legitimacy and, by default, the study of film; and emphasizing its uniqueness justified some of Hollywood's peculiar business practices and, quite obviously, allowed film scholars to venture into the analysis of text and representation unthinkable in other sectoral studies.[35] This ambivalence could not but leave its trace on the study of industrial change in Hollywood. The attempt of economists to make the film industry fit into the existent economic models has led to a neglect of its cultural and social aspects. Conversely, as Tom Gunning has written, the long hegemony of narrative cinema and textual analysis among film scholars have brought about not just a neglect of the economic aspects of the film industry but of its interaction with the world of consumption and consumer culture in general.[36] In a somewhat simplified version of these extreme views, we could say that film has usually been understood either as a "business as usual," or as a self-enclosed and self-sufficient narrative universe.

An important omission stemming from this polarization has been the lack of attention paid to the intra-industrial struggle between manufacturers, or film producers, and merchants, or film distributors and exhibitors. Namely, while the majority of film historians regard the tensions between Hollywood's manufacturers (producers) and merchants (distributors and exhibitors) as the principal source of conflict and the generator of change within the film industry, the lack of any general economic theory which could explain or even acknowledge the relevance of this phenomenon has left the issue relatively under-theorized and under-examined.[37] For despite tedious works of economic historians who have always acknowledged the importance and distinct features of merchant capitalism, neither neoclassical nor Marxist theories of economic change have had much of an understanding for the special role of merchants in the development of American and the world economy.[38] Not surprisingly, the students of film industry have mostly emphasized just one group of economic actors—producers (manufacturers) or distributors (merchants)—and their emphasis was usually guided by their perceptions of Hollywood's business practices as, respectively, exemplary or perverse. The static view of power relations in Hollywood, which such analyses presumed, has helped place the study of film under the umbrella of traditional economic theory, but has done little to contribute to our understanding of the changing relations between culture, power, and space in contemporary global economy; subtle mechanisms of control—including control over leisure and everyday life—that economic actors use in order to establish their positions of dominance within and outside of Hollywood; and complex ways in which the spatial organization of production and the organization of fantasy influence an exercise of economic power. Failing to see that the film industry is a complex and porous social institution, they have perpetuated the division between production and consumption, filmmakers and their audiences, manufacturers and merchants and have neglected the more subtle aspects of their tenuous, co-dependent, and tremendously important relationship.

Consequently, two different portraits of Hollywood have emerged over the decades, yet both, as we shall see, share similar views of social and economic change and similar limitations in its portrayal. The first view places emphasis on the production side of the industry and is, at least in the contemporary film studies, mostly associated with a group of scholars who had initially gathered at the University of Wisconsin. In late 1970s, in response to the so called *auteur* theory and the growing significance of textual analysis of film, the Wisconsin School initiated a study of the Hollywood studio system as a mass production industry or, as Janet Staiger had put it, "a factory system akin to a Ford plant."[39] Their research relied on works of neo-Marxists like Harry Braverman, Paul Baran, and Paul Sweezy on monopoly capital and mass production, and of the business historian Alfred Chandler on the rise of managerial capitalism in America to shed light on division of labor, standardization of technology and production, and vertical integration in the Hollywood studio system. Apart from the wealth of historical information that they had uncovered, the studies of the studio system as a mass production system by the Wisconsin School opened doors for further works on Hollywood based on its similarities to other industrial sectors, and reinstated the focus on production as the critical activity in the film industry.

The research of the Wisconsin School has significantly influenced more recent studies by economic geographers Michael Storper and Susan Christopherson, who have argued that organization of production in Hollywood greatly resembles the model of the Third Italy—that Hollywood functions as a flexible, regionally concentrated network of firms whose main competitive advantages are swift adaptation to market uncertainties and continuous product innovation.[40] Basing their arguments on the theory of "flexible specialization," developed by Charles Sabel and Michael Piore of MIT, Storper and Christopherson have made a compelling case that Hollywood's dominance in global markets is mostly due to its successful, albeit neither predetermined nor linear, transition from the mass production system of the 1930s and 1940s to the system of flexible specialization in the 1980s.[41] According to Christopherson and Storper, Hollywood's Golden Age came to an end due to two exogenous shocks—the famous anti-trust suit *United States vs. Paramount* which ordered Hollywood majors to divest themselves of their theater chains, and the emergence of television. The ensuing market instability forced the Hollywood majors into aggressive product differentiation and increased the need for specialized inputs which the studios themselves were not able to provide. A number of independent producers and firms offering specialized services emerged to fill the gap. Over time, they developed a greater variety of products and services "than the independent firms which existed in 1950s or the specialized departments in the major studios which once carried similar phases of the production process."[42] The studios maintained control over distribution, but were "unable to compete against the independent production companies and specialized contractors they had helped to create, in the very markets they had hoped to retain."[43] The process of industrial reorganization continued with "a wave of horizontal integration" into other areas of entertainment, creating a complex web of inter-related companies and products and spreading the collective risk embedded in the production process. In the resultant industrial structure, internal economies were supplanted by the external ones, allowing for an increase in the economies of scale and Verdoorn effects from a "continually differentiating and uneven roundabouts in the economy as a whole."[44]

The second, alternative, view emphasizes the power of distributors and is associated with the work of Mae Huettig who wrote the most significant study of Hollywood in the pre-war period.[45] Based on the research that she conducted in Hollywood between 1939 and 1941, Huettig challenged the prevalent view of Hollywood as the "glamour factory" by claiming that the real power in the industry actually rested in distribution and the control of Hollywood majors over the best first-run theaters in the United States. As their own "best customers"—that is, as the principal buyers and sellers of movies in the United States—Hollywood majors, argued Huettig, amassed enormous economic power which effectively excluded both independent producers and independent exhibitors from the industry's playing field. Although majors did not account for "more than 50 percent of the total number of features nor for more than approximately 15 percent of the total number of theaters," they controlled nearly all the profits.[46] The control, wrote Huettig, worked from two directions: "by their ownership of key theaters they [the majors] are able to skim the cream of the market and influence a much larger number of theaters than they own; second, by virtue of this same ownership they can prevent films other than those released by them from reaching the market, thereby enhancing the value of their product to the independent theater owners who are left with no alternative but to buy the majors' films if they are to continue operations."[47] Huettig's study was a precursor to the similar findings by the Justice Department several years later, and it played a significant role in the above mentioned Supreme Court's *Paramount*

Decision from 1947 which charged Hollywood studios with violation of anti-trust laws and ordered them to divest from their theaters.

Huettig's views continue to resonate in the works of contemporary cultural studies theorists and critical political economists who view Hollywood as the prototype of an economy completely divorced from its production side and paradigmatic for the age of speculative, postmodern capitalism. Since the early '80s, "the cream of European postmodernists," as Mike Davis once called them—Umberto Eco and Jean Baudrillard—have reinvigorated the old European fascination with Hollywood with new forays into America's hyperreality of theme parks, Trump Towers, global media industries, and Frank Gehry's houses in Los Angeles.[48] On the surface, their primary objective may have been to contrast the European, or high-brow, culture with the presumed American lack thereof ("American imagination demands the real thing and to attain it must fabricate the absolute fake," wrote Eco[49]) but behind that was a genuine, and often ingenious, fascination with the society of "organized consumption." Both Baudrillard's simulacri and Eco's hyperreality represented moments of the "virtual world" where perpetual symbolic exchanges were taking place but nothing was being produced anymore. Critical political economists, relying on Huettig's study of distribution, have also stressed the oligopolistic structure of global media industries and argued that Hollywood's key learning economies were not in production but in consumption. According to Kevin Robins and Asu Aksoy, who have engaged in a lively debate with Michael Storper, the success of Hollywood films owes little to the genius of its independent producers. Rather, it is a product of Hollywood's ability to anticipate, nurture and channel consumer preferences or, in other words, of the ability of its giant media companies to build the audiences and structure their choices.[50] An unintended consequence of the "bonfire of the vanities" of the 1980s, this preoccupation with consumption—its objects, places, and processes—in contemporary cultural and economic studies has become the landmark of postmodern thinking. At one point, the proliferation of studies on consumption was such that it led Fredric Jameson to conclude that "culture has now become a product in its own right; the market has become a substitute for itself and fully as much a commodity as any of the items it includes within itself. . . . Postmodernism is the consumption of sheer commodification as a process."[51]

Seemingly, these contrasting views of Hollywood, which have, combined, elevated the American film industry into the paradigm of contemporary capitalism, could not be further apart. The former focuses on flexible production and liberation of creativity from the limited world of mass production; the latter is concerned with the emerging world of "disorganized capitalism" and "organized consumption" whose very flexibility transforms goods and people from durables into disposables.[52] Yet, interestingly enough, they both share similar assumptions regarding the process of social and economic change. The theory of flexible specialization presumes that economic change takes place in response to exogenous shocks and that industrial and organizational change, in particular, represent adaptive or innovative, even if not always the most efficient, answers to changes in corporate environment. Cultural theorists and critical political economists implicitly, if not explicitly, perceive change as the result of contradictions of capitalist development and of concealed, but still very much alive, class conflict. The common denominator, however, remains: change is perceived as an objective, evolutionary phenomenon entirely rooted in the *production* side of the economy. For when cultural theorists, such as Baudrillard, claim that political economy has reached its end in this era dominated by "transeconomics of speculation," they simply express the fear of the world economy in which production is no longer the core activity in the global economy.[53] Or when Jameson writes about the "effacement of production" as the precondition of postmodern capitalism in which consumption takes the center stage, he also openly argues that the tragic rift between production and consumption, which such effacement creates, and our loss of relation to the forces of production are nothing but symptoms of utter political and economic impotence.[54] Or, finally, when Askoy and Robins denounce the relevance of flexible production in the contemporary entertainment economy, they also denounce the relevance of change in its organization: by arguing that the entertainment sector is still dominated by the same old oligopolies as forty years ago, they actually deny that any significant change had ever taken place in Hollywood. Their challenge is not directed against the predominant, productionist view of the economy but against Hollywood's perverse monopoly in distribution.

The relative lack of attention paid to the conflicts and tensions between production and distribution in economic and cultural analysis of Hollywood is not surprising. Unlike production, distribution—that core of the merchant economy—has never been granted an autonomous status in economic theory. The implicit emphasis on production—rather than on the relations between the two key economic spheres, production and consumption, has led to other omissions. The first is the portrayal of Hollywood as an isolated and encapsulated institution, rather than as an industry which intrudes deeply and persistently into the most intimate aspects of our daily lives and reflects, or tries to reflect, even the most minuscule changes in social moods and habits. The interaction of Hollywood with its surroundings—while publicly acknowledged when it comes to a discussion of its cultural influence or possible censorship—miraculously disappears in any analysis of its economic performance. And yet, as we shall see by way of a number of examples in this book, the issues of moral and economic regulation have been practically inseparable throughout Hollywood's history. Hence, the reduction of Hollywood, or, for that matter, any other sector to the world which lives within its fixed industrial boundaries seems quite limiting, particularly at a time when permeability of corporate boundaries is a readily acknowledged fact and when the existence of cinema as a distinct form of entertainment is a problematic assumption. As Tom Gunning has put it, in a slightly different context, cinema's constant imbrication with and exploitation by consumer culture does not necessarily diminish its "fascinating and even liberating possibilities," but opens up the possibility for explorations of the hidden pockets of modernity.[55]

The second omission is a somewhat paradoxical lack of precise spatial and temporal coordinates in the existent analysis of the film industry. I say paradoxical, because all of the above analyses of Hollywood have had a significant spatial component—for the Wisconsin School it was the centralization of production within the walls of Hollywood studios; for Storper and Christopherson, it was the issue of industrial districting and regional concentration; for Mae Huettig, it was the zoning of first-run theatres in the best urban areas; for Baudrillard and Eco, it was the architectural manifestations of Americana; for Aksoy and Robins, it was global diffusion of production. Yet, this acknowledgment of spatiality has not been further developed in any of these depictions of Hollywood: there is little analysis as to how Hollywood arrived at these—divergent—modes of spatial organization; there is no explanation as to why some activities within the entertainment complex may still be concentrated while others are diffused; and no attempt is made to relate these changes to the possible shifts in power within the industry. In other words, there is no recognition of the fact that space is both a subjective and an objective category of any economic activity, and that its emphasis or de-emphasis in an industry whose essence is production of alternative spaces and environments has tremendous bearing not just on its economic performance or status within the society but also on the demarcation lines between public and private space, as well as of reality and fantasy themselves.

Thus, while the film industry can obviously be made to fit into the prevailing theories of industrial change, such views neglect some of the most interesting aspects of the film industry and industrial change in general. The emergence of Hollywood as the symbol of success in the American economy in the last decade of this millennium owes as much to this greater acceptance of leisure industries as legitimate participants in the national economy as it does to any objective changes in the entertainment industry itself. At least in part, that legitimacy has been purchased by neglecting the conflict between manufacturers (producers) and merchants (distributors) and retailoring the industry to the standards of economic theory. And yet, some of Hollywood's peculiarities may not be so peculiar at all. The significance of the intra-industrial conflict between producers and distributors, the dependence of industrial performance on the relatively unstructured and chaotic world outside of factory gates, and the nexus of power and knowledge embedded in different visions of economic and moral spaces are not limited to the film industry. Hence, the critical problem in contemporary entertainment economy, and global economy in general, is not a matter of determining whether production or consumption is driving the economy but of clarifying how they relate to each other, what mechanisms of control are employed to mediate between them, and who controls the critical hubs of the economy. Or as Michael Storper himself has put it, the most puzzling element of Hollywood's current market strength is "how did major companies lose competitive edge in production, but nonetheless have asserted control over distribution?"[56] In the global economy in which the volume of trade has been increasing four times faster than the output over the past twenty years, this could be the most puzzling element of latter-day capitalism in general.

Commodity Chains

A combination of insights from the theory of commodity chains and recent works in social geography offers an interesting alternative interpretation of the puzzling relations between manufacturers and merchants and enables us to forge a more complex link between production of space, production of power, and production of fantasy. A subset of the world-systems theory, the theory of commodity chains starts by acknowledging the existence of both flexibility in production and oligopolies in distribution. It also supercedes the rift between production and consumption by drawing our attention to the crucial role played by merchants and commercial capital in historical changes that have recast the relative strength of economic agents in commodity chains and led to the creation of a novel and alternative way of organizing international business.[57] Analogous to the struggle between producers, distributors, and exhibitors in the film industry, the conflict between manufacturers and merchants that comes to the surface in commodity chains analysis indicates that the process of industrial change in contemporary economy may be more profound than the shift from mass production to flexible specialization. Rather, by drawing an analogy with other sectors, it is possible to argue that the contemporary process of industrial change in the American film industry could be and should be viewed as a historical process of resurgence and consolidation of merchant power in the American and global economies.

Immanuel Wallerstein and Terence Hopkins define a commodity chain as "a network of labor and production processes whose end result is a finished commodity."[58] More simply, perhaps, it is possible to think of the chains as routes which goods take from conception to consumption, linking on their way "households, enterprises, and states to one another within the world-economy."[59] According to Gary Gereffi, whose distinction between "producer-driven" and "buyer-driven" commodity chains is particularly applicable to the film industry, "producer-driven" commodity chains characterize industries in which "large enterprises play the central role in controlling the production system."[60] Like old Hollywood studios, they shape the character of demand based on their own production patterns. "Buyer-driven" commodity chains, on the other hand, "refer to those industries in which large retailers, brand name merchandisers, and trading companies play the pivotal role in setting up decentralized production networks in a variety of exporting countries."[61] In such chains, the organization of consumption determines the locus of production. In other words, the control exercised by major companies in "buyer-driven" commodity chains is no longer located at the point of production but at the point of consumption. Much like Hollywood majors these days, key companies in "buyer-driven" commodity chains do not even have any production facilities. Instead, they are "merchandisers that design and/or market, but do not make the branded products that they sell." Hence, the companies that Gereffi describes— such as GAP or Nike—devote an increasing proportion of their investments to market research, advertising, and promotion in the attempt to shape and even create markets for their products. They accumulate their profits by acting as "strategic brokers in linking overseas factories and traders with evolving product niches in their own markets."[62] Consequently, the actual site of production in "buyer-driven" commodity chains becomes secondary to the sites of "deal making," product and finance packaging, distribution, and marketing decision-making.

Aside from the almost uncanny parallels that could be made between Nike and Disney, or GAP and Time Warner, Gereffi's work enunciates—even if it does not elaborate on—several theoretical themes that are, perhaps, worth exploring in more detail. First, unlike most of the economic literature which uncritically adopts an evolutionary and teleological view of social change, the emphasis on dominance and control of commodity chains appears more sensitive to historically contingent aspects of social change and the role which particular economic agents play in it. Namely, as we have just seen on the example of contemporary analyses of Hollywood, traditional economic analysis perceives industrial change as a result of factors either exogenous or endogenous to firm or national economies. Neoclassical economists, wedded to equilibrium analysis, view economic change as a product of factors extraneous to the economic system or a firm. In their view, economic change takes place sporadically, in spurts, as a consequence of adaptation to exogenous technological discoveries or equally exogenous changes in the market place. Radical political economists, on the other hand, while reluctant to admit that any substantive change is indeed possible within capitalism, also tend to view transitions, transformations, and alterations in organizational forms and regimes of accumulation as sporadic events. But, unlike neoclassical economists, they perceive them as results of crisis brought about by internal contradictions of capitalism or, in other words, as results of adaptation to endogenous pressures of class struggle. Both of these views, however, explicitly consider production as the key economic activity and, paradoxically, pay little attention to the question of who governs the economy. Paradoxically, I would say, because even radical political economists, despite their proclaimed interest in power issues—which is explicitly irrelevant to neoclassical economists—remain locked within the logic of the production process and class conflicts.

The analysis of shifting patterns of control over commodity chains reveals, by contrast, that production has not always been the key economic activity, and that the question of who dominates the economy may be more complex than usually assumed. In particular, if observed against the backdrop of longer economic cycles, it becomes obvious that the conflict between manufacturers and merchants and their two distinct modes of capital accumulation—*economies of time* and *economies of space*—predates the industrial era. As we shall see in more detail in the next chapter, merchants dominated American economy at least until the turn of this century. Their power rested on their ability to control vast territories of land and to link geographically dispersed and isolated manufacturers with their equally dispersed and isolated consumers, negotiating tastes and predicting consumer trends along the way. The power of manufacturers, on the other hand, relied on what David Harvey calls "appropriation of space"—tight regulation and "zoning" of space that would ensure that *economies of time* (optimization of production per unit of time)—are being maximized.[63] The rise of manufacturers, thus, reflected itself in the rise of the new industrial architecture which emphasized territorial enclosure, isolation of workplace from home and urban areas, and gigantic factory floors that could accommodate the entire assembly line under one roof. The resurgence of merchant power, by contrast, has brought back the old preoccupation with space and trade routes (what else is the information superhighway? telecommunication lines?), both as key objects of power struggles and as the key concepts of economic theory.

The shift in power from manufacturers to merchants, and the conceptual malleability of space and time serve as warnings that the growing concern with space in contemporary political economy should not go unquestioned. The way in which space and time are conceptualized and embedded within economic structures has a tremendous impact on actors' perceptions of economic activities and on the economy itself. For instance, David Harvey has persuasively argued that different forms of spatial representation directly affected the distribution of power within modern capitalist societies.[64] The conquest and control of space, Harvey says, first require that the space be conceived as something usable, malleable, and therefore capable of domination through human action. Thus, Renaissance cartography and mapping techniques were critical to the territorial expansion of capitalism from the fifteenth century on.[65] Objective and scientifically constructed maps embedded the idea of spatial domination and became an integral part of the modernization project. Likewise, the ability of capitalists to convince workers that "space is an open field for capital but a closed terrain for labor" resulted in workers conceding a greater power of mobility to capital.[66] Thus, although Harvey declines to argue for a "complete dissolution of the objective-subjective distinction" in the conceptualization of space and time, he is apparently quite willing to accept that time and space are social constructs. According to Harvey, it is very "important to challenge the idea of a single and objective sense of time or space" and to accept the possibility that "each distinctive mode of production or social formation will embody a distinctive bundle of time and space practices and concepts."[67] In this Harvey comes fairly close to John Urry who also writes that "there is really no space as such—only different spaces," and that time and space should be seen "as produced and producing, as contested and determined, and as symbolically represented and structurally organized."[68]

Similar arguments have been made about time too. Far from being just an objective, external category which governs our lives, time has also been differently imagined and represented throughout modern history. Thus, it is now fairly well established that the development of interchangeable hours, the mechanical clock, and homogenous time were preconditions for the development of modern capitalism. As Moishe Postone has written following the works of E. P. Thompson and French historian Jacques Le Goff, the entire evolution of capitalism can be viewed as the evolution of "abstract" time, and progress as a succession of attempts to conquer this "ultimate capitalist tyrant," as Marx used to refer to time.[69] According to Postone, the creation of standard time between the fourteenth and the seventeenth centuries reflected the development of increasingly commodified social relations in early capitalism and of the need to control, regulate, and discipline wage-labor in sectors such as textiles where large-scale production for exports had become a norm. Variable length of the work day and subjective interpretations of time could no longer satisfy either the "employers" (merchants) or "employees" (outwork labor) because the arbitrary definitions of time only opened the door for constant haggling, manipulation, and cheating on both sides. Thus, wide-spread adoption of work-bells and, later on, of standard hour became the precondition for quantity production and translated labor into exchange value. Ever since, all the major economic theories—David Riccardo's theory of competitive advantage, Adam Smith's and Karl Marx's labor theory of value, and the neoclassical notion of efficiency—have been expressed in temporal terms, whereas the compression of time—the increase in output per unit of time—became the main indicator of productivity, growth, and progress.

Therefore, in the evolution of modern capitalism, the emphasis and de-emphasis of space and time as economic categories has often served as the way of legitimizing or de-legitimizing the power of manufacturers and merchants and of assigning different degrees of political and economic importance to the production or distribution of goods. Still, though I shall be coming back to these issues later in the book, the significance of these discussions about space and time lies less in the specifics of their arguments and more in the possibilities they create for further analysis. Spatial analysis and the analysis of different modes of spatial representation provide the framework for a simultaneous inquiry into the disparate aspects of economic life, linking economics of household to changes in the global economy, and changes in the basic categories of economic thought to our daily experiences of self and the world. What these analyses convey is the idea that concepts and material manifestations of space, much like the more elusive notion of "structure" in social theory, represent both an inscription of social relations and the arena of their change. The common thread among these varied lines of inquiry is the trust that even the slightest changes in power relations get recorded in the spatial and temporal organization of the economy and reinforced—or challenged—by the way in which space and time are conceptualized. In addition, thanks to the fact that space also defines the boundaries of what is private and what is public, of what is visible and what is concealed, of what is imagined and what is real, spatial analysis also defines the boundaries of what can and cannot to be discussed and, therefore, in some respects, delineates the boundaries of politics itself. The complexities of this intimate relationship between space, power, and fantasy really come to the fore in discussions about censorship and in Hollywood's battles and skirmishes over the moral regulation of everyday life on and off the screen.

Moral Space and Hegemonic Power

As a framework for economic and political activity, space operates on both macro and micro levels. On a macro level, space delineates a historical and territorial playground for economic actors. It defines boundaries of capitalist expansion, determines distances at which economic activity can be successfully mastered, and creates constraints and opportunities for economic actors depending on their mobility and ability to subsume time and space to their own interests. On a micro level, space enters deeply into the sphere of everyday life. It defines the limits of work and leisure, fantasy and reality, private and public space—or, to paraphrase Anthony Giddens, the spheres of what is hidden and what is revealed—and, as such, largely determines power relations within and around both households and work places.[70] The two levels are closely interrelated. Hence, the spatial reorganization of production translates easily into the reorganization of moral space, and the physical appropriation of space often leads to the appropriation of privacy. In Hollywood, in particular, where the spatial organization of production also entails the construction of imaginary worlds, changing patterns of industrial organizations have always led to new patterns of censorship and surveillance as well as to the (re)production of economic power and to the moral regulation of our fantasies.

If economists have rarely studied architecture, they have even more rarely studied fantasies. However, Hollywood's peculiar position as the quintessential "industry of desire" demands from us to take both architecture and fantasies quite seriously. Hollywood-created zones of production and consumption materialize the illusions of societal control and pleasure that could never have been realized in other industrial sectors or in American economy in general. As such, they do not just express the unattainable social ideals or repressed fears: they actively (some would say forcefully) construct the world which they claim to evade. Both politically and economically, Hollywood has long performed the art of "false openings" for its audiences. By presenting alternative histories (entire worlds) that by accident have never happened, and by promising an array of economic opportunities that have always been available only to a select few, Hollywood has, in effect, become the fantasy that makes all other fantasies possible.

The notion of fantasy used throughout this text is more complex than commonly assumed. In a series of his works, Slovenian philoso-

The sets for *The Thief of Bagdad* (United Artists, 1924) were designed by William Cameron Menzies. Note the Bagdad sign on the top of the building on the right. Courtesy of the Museum of Modern Art, New York.

pher Slavoj Žižek attempts to dispel some common myths about fantasies and their relation to ideology.[71] According to Žižek, fantasy is not, as commonly understood, an imagined scenario that represents the realization of our (impossible) desires. Rather, Žižek argues, fantasy provides the coordinates of our desires and constructs the frame which enables us to desire something. Thus, "in the fantasy-scene, desire is not fulfilled, 'satisfied,' but constituted [. . .] *through fantasy, we learn how to desire*."[72] Ideological fantasy, then, often gives shape to an irremediable social lack, or provides an answer to an irreconcilable social antagonism. Instead of an unbearable encounter with some political impossibility (such as the creation of a homogenous and organic social body), fantasy provides us with the object-cause of our desire—an immigrant, a Jew, an Arab, a stranger—with that special "someone" who precludes the constitution of pure community and occludes the fact that such is, in and of itself, improbable. In political terms, then, fantasies both open and close the span of available options. As Žižek puts it, fantasies maintain "the false opening, the idea that the excluded choice could have happened, and does not actually take place only on account of contingent circumstances [. . .] 'Traversing the fantasy,' therefore, involves precisely the acceptance of radical closure: there is no opening, contingency as such is necessary."[73]

In this account, policing of the boundary between reality and fantasy is essential to political success of any ideology or hegemonic power. In contrast to traditional Marxist interpretations of ideology as false consciousness, Žižek's interpretation implies that it is precisely the actors' consciousness of the falsity, of the fantastic quality of ideology, which ensures its wide acceptance. The very statement "It is just a movie!" or "It is just a theme-park" (in other words, "It is just a fantasy!") occludes the fact that the truth is, actually, always "out there." The constitution and reconstitution of the borders between reality and fantasy maintains the hope that beyond the veils of fantasy exists some other, unspoiled, reality that can be reached, attained, materialized. And vice versa, the trust in fantasy as fantasy ensures that the most probing questions about its relation to reality will never be posed. In other words, fantasy itself is not a utopia, but the precondition for a utopian trust in reality that surrounds us. Or, in Žižek's own words, "fantasy is a means for an ideology to take its own failure into account in advance."[74] There, thus, lies the political power of Hollywood's fantasies and the political need to keep them apart from reality itself.

Not surprisingly then, Hollywood's ability to entice the fantasies of its moviegoers has always been the main cause of its ambivalent social and political legitimacy. Along with its industrial transformations and economic ups and downs, Hollywood has continuously faced immense public scrutiny, threats of government oversight of its content, and numerous attacks for its portrayal of sex and violence, women and ethnic minorities, gays and lesbians, priests and lawyers, and nearly everyone else under the sun. In an attempt to ward off this criticism and keep the government at bay, industry leaders have often walked the thin line between the claims that movies were nothing but sheer entertainment and that they could promise life-changing experiences to their audiences. Just as often, Hollywood's producers and distributors have pledged self-regulation and self-censorship in exchange for government permission to expand their businesses. From the days of the Production Code Administration, the famous codex of on-screen and off-screen behavior in the studio era, to contemporary debates about media violence, conflicts over morality have always had a distinct economic component and political message. In most instances, Hollywood has purchased a relaxation of anti-trust regulations in exchange for self-regulation of its content. In other words, and as we shall see on numerous examples throughout the book, industry leaders have consistently traded their control over moral spaces for the size and the expanse of their economic universe.

This trade-off between economic and moral worlds has had a tremendous bearing not just on the economic performance of the industry but also on the production and reproduction of power within Hollywood and on Hollywood's role within the American and global economy. As most Gramscian theorists would suggest, the expansion of private, commercial space has come at the expense of freedom of expression and the size of available public space. Perhaps just as importantly, the expansion has been concealed through discourses of safety and family values, protection of children and anti-violence measures. "Domestication" of power which such discourses have entailed is analogous to Peter Taylor's arguments about the establishment of hegemony via the "domestication of modernity." Namely, in his fresh and innovative re-introduction of Gramsci into the world-system theory, Peter Taylor has recently argued that world hegemons establish their power first and foremost through the construction of "ordinary modernity" in civil society, cultural practices, and everyday life.[75] Rightly, Taylor insists that economic or military preponderance are neither sufficient nor critical for the maintenance of hegemonic power in the world system; rather, it is the particular separation of public and private spheres, focused on the creation of "comfort zones" for ordinary consumers, that has been the key to the sustenance of three modern world-system hegemons—the Dutch, the British, and the Americans. In Taylor's view, the design of home space as "comfort space" separate from the exigencies of public life and the drudgery of work—from Dutch town houses to American suburbia— was a "product of hegemonic civil societies where wealth was accumulated and distributed widely enough to create new domestic worlds."[76] In other words, the domestication of hegemony through the domestication of space constituted the foundation for the spread of bourgeois modernity and the essence of its allure for millions of people around the world. Likewise, the development of art forms intent on celebrating this newly discovered "ordinary modernity" of everyday life—Dutch paintings, British novels, and Hollywood movies—have all been the manifestations of and preconditions for these countries' enduring influence on world affairs.

To summarize this section and foreshadow the rest of the book: just as the power of manufacturers and merchants has depended on emphasis and de-emphasis of time and space; and just as the power of Hollywood has depended on regulation and de-regulation of its own fantasy; the power and the strength of the American hegemony have depended on its relationship with Hollywood. Thus, both inside and outside of Hollywood, the success of hegemonic projects has always been closely related to the ability to reveal what was beyond dispute and to hide what should have been discussed. Once again, Peter Taylor's metaphor is apt: hegemony relies on the production of "comfort zones," be they CityWalks or sanitized fantasies. Consequently, as Hollywood's presence expands throughout the American and global economy, it is not just the economic sphere that is being privatized through the enlargement of commercial media space and the construction of the new "controlled environments;" rather, it is our very notion of politics that is potentially being transformed.

ECONOMIC ANALYSES of film industry have, thus far, mostly attempted to tailor the industry to the requirements of the more traditional economic interpretations of industrial change and corporate transformation. Such views have had a tendency to neglect some of its most interesting aspects: constant tension between its manufacturers (producers) and merchants (distributors and exhibitors), changes in the spatial organization of film production and its relation to self-censorship and regulation of fantasy, and the ways in which Hollywood contributes to the production and re-production of American hegemony. And yet, as the following chapters will demonstrate, transformations of the American film industry in this century can all be traced to this intra-industrial struggle, to the way in which manufacturers and merchants have transposed their own conflict over economic space onto the regulation of moral space, and to the particular cognitive structures which—each one at its time—helped consolidate the prevalent power relations within the industry. In addition, such an alternative explanation of changes in the American film industry, more in tune with Gereffi's theory of commodity chains and the works in social geography, could take advantage of the fact that Hollywood has had an unusual degree of freedom in its choice of spatial and temporal coordinates. The history of Hollywood's production sites—from the reconstruction of the entire world in its backlots in the studio era to the most recent replacement of location shooting by cyberspace—makes apparent, more so than does the history of other industrial sectors, not just the changes in the American film industry but also the relationship between power, space, and fantasy.

The following three chapters explore the specifics of the intra-industrial struggle between manufacturers and merchants in three distinct time periods: the era of mass production in the Hollywood studio system from the 1920s through the 1950s, the era of dispersed production from the 1960s to the late 1990s, and the most recent digital and infotainment age. Each chapter demonstrates how the new industrial architecture, production foci and definitions of public and private have shaped their battles and, conversely, how the spatial and temporal choices that actors made in order to assert their own position in the economy created internal contradictions which set the stage for a new cycle of struggle. Thus, the next chapter, "Hollywood in the Studio," focuses on the period of the manufacturers' dominance in the film industry and explores their dependence on highly centralized production in Hollywood studios. The chapter shows how the construction of increasingly isolated and self-contained production areas not only enabled film manufacturers to achieve economies of scale in production but also deepened the division between public and private space, work and leisure, producers and consumers. In order to consolidate their position over the commodity chain, manufacturers—a.k.a. film producers—had to extend their control beyond factory gates and therefore they created a fascinating set of institutions of censorship and surveillance that lasted until the early 1960s. But internal contradictions in their strategies—*occupation of space* and *occupation of privacy*—eventually brought the studio system to an end.

The second chapter, "Hollywood on Location" examines the relationship between dispersed production—location shooting—and the resurgence of merchants in the film industry. Dispersed production not only undermined the institutions of censorship and surveillance of the studio era but also enabled the merchants to exclude manufacturers from any fair participation in profits and exacerbated conflicts over licensing fees, royalties, and brand names. In order to restore their power, producers have turned to the world of digital technology and animated characters. But the world of cyberspace, which they so wholeheartedly support, has thus far only allowed merchants to consolidate their own power.

Finally, the last, third, chapter, "Hollywood in Cyberspace," shows how Hollywood's investments in digital technology have placed the entertainment industry in a paradoxical position: while praised as one of the most important strategic sectors in the American economy and the generator of growth in high technology sectors, Hollywood is also becoming a part of much larger military-industrial and multi-media complex and losing its distinct identity. Thus, the production of cyberspace brings the relation between space, power, and fantasy out into the open: by contributing to the creation of a space bigger than itself, Hollywood is contributing to the re-creation of American hegemony in the new global economy. But this expansion into the seemingly limitless computer-generated space is also minimizing the livable places that we all inhabit. Although the new world order brings an amazing array of possibilities for all economic actors to overcome the constraints of time and space as well as the dichotomies of private and public or work and leisure, it finds its ultimate expression in simulated environments and gated communities of cyberspace and urban space, changing the nature of politics and leading to new, and, perhaps, as yet unforeseen, forms of social and political conflicts.

Just as the imaginary body of water was a history of civilization in the form of a marine junkyard, the studio lot was one in the form of a dream dump. A Sargasso of the imagination! And the dump grew continually, for there was not a dream afloat somewhere which wouldn't sooner or later turn up on it, having first been made photographic by plaster, canvas, lath, and paint. Many boats sink and never reach Sargasso, but no dream ever entirely disappears. Somewhere it troubles some unfortunate person and some day, when that person has been sufficiently troubled, it will be reproduced on the lot.

Nathanael West, *The Day of the Locust*

Most of us have a fairly accurate mental picture of an English Gothic cathedral or an American colonial country house, but cannot imagine the building where Model T Fords were made.

John Winter, *Industrial Architecture*

Stars' houses are timid and reticent, 'unobtrusive in the extreme,' as one starologist termed it. They suffer a kind of cultural deprivation so complete that it should be disallowed by law even for the very rich.

Charles Jenks, *Daydream Houses of Los Angeles*

Hanging by the Clock. Few shots from Hollywood films in the 1920s exemplify the increasing dependence of everyday life on the mechanical clock as well as this photo of Harold Lloyd from *Safety Last* (Hal Roach Studios, 1923). Courtesy of the Museum of Modern Art, New York.

In the beginning of the twentieth century, Americans were obsessed with time and speed. Film manufacturers were no exception. According to one of the fathers of the motion picture industry, Thomas Alva Edison, the advent of mass production marked the dawn of an age in which humankind would be "making more things cheaper, selling more things faster, and creating more and more jobs."[1] Trying to achieve this goal and fighting against Edison's trust, Hollywood producers established in the 1910s an elaborate corporate system that was to govern the production, distribution, and exhibition of motion pictures in the American film industry for the following five decades. The "studio system," as this governance structure came to be known, successfully adapted Henry Ford's technological and organizational innovations from the automobile industry to the production and sales of motion pictures. The studio system combined elements of mass production with vertical integration and market oligopoly. Production of movies closely resembled the assembly line production of Model Ts, and division of labor in the motion picture industry followed the scientific management methods based on time-motion studies of Frederick Winslow Taylor. The industry was dominated by just eight companies, five of which controlled over 75 percent of the total box office gross.[2] The high volume of production and ingenious overseas distribution network ensured the dominance of Hollywood films in most of the world's markets.[3] Some film historians even contend that the "genius" of the Hollywood studio system created a particular cinematic style: the classic Hollywood cinema based on causal narrative, conventional story lines, glamorous photography, and lavish set designs.[4]

Traditional explanations of the rise and fall of the studio system, much like the explanations of the rise and fall of mass production, perpetuate this obsession with time by focusing, almost exclusively, on temporal advantages and contradictions of the new production and distribution methods. What they often neglect is that spatial control over the economy was the main precondition for all other forms of control in the mass production era, including the dominance over time, and that novel forms of spatial organization frequently brought about contradictions in social organization of everyday life that temporal analysis cannot even begin to elucidate. This section, therefore, complements the standard, temporal interpretations of the studio system by examining the spatial aspects of mass production and their relationship with intra-industrial strife between producers and merchants. It focuses, in particular, on two entwined yet divergent processes—*occupation of space* and *occupation of privacy*—that glued the studio system together and eventually pulled it apart. On the one hand, Hollywood producers tried to achieve a desired quantity and speed of production by minimizing the impact of the outside world onto the inner workings of the industry; and in order to do so they constructed a spatially and institutionally enclosed and self-regulated environment. On the other hand, the producers tried to circumvent the power of local merchants by regulating the private life of their stars and the moral content of their product. By focusing on the moral code of entertainment, manufacturers and merchants transposed their conflict over the speed of production and territories of consumption onto the private life of their employees and their consumers. Paradoxically, however, such politicization of private life eventually exposed the industry to public scrutiny far greater than producers had ever wanted. In the years after World War II, *occupation of space* and *occupation of privacy* collided to such an extent that they brought to an end the studio system itself.

The section is divided into five parts. The first part gives an overview of temporal analyses of mass production systems and emphasizes their key shortcoming—the exclusive focus on the inner workings of the modern factory and of the Chandlerian multi-divisional corporation. The second part examines how a conquest of space—the centralization of film production in Southern California—enabled Hollywood producers to achieve economies of time. The third part focuses on the star system, as a form of branding and social control that producers established in order to circumvent the power of exhibitors and to achieve greater control over their talent and their audiences. The fourth part examines in more detail the key institution of censorship and surveillance of the studio era—The Motion Picture Producers Association, popularly known as the Hays Office. Finally, the fifth part looks at how *occupation of space* and *occupation of privacy* clashed after World War II and culminated in one of the darkest periods in Hollywood history—the era of blacklisting.

PRECIOUS LITTLE of Hollywood's old glory has survived in Los Angeles to our day: a surprising fact for an industry obsessed with its own past and for the city which boosts almost fourteen million visitors a year thanks to Hollywood–related tourism. But Los Angeles real estate developers and film industry personnel have never been particularly kind to the architectural landmarks of Hollywood's Golden Age. Studio backlots that once contained Egyptian pyramids and Dutch villages have given way to shopping malls and office buildings. The Garden of Allah, a residential hotel once known as the "Algonquin Table West" because it hosted the crème de la crème of American screenwriters, is now a bank on Sunset Boulevard. No one protested when, a decade ago, the owners of Culver City Studios on West Washington Boulevard destroyed two glass studios from the silent era. Even the attempts of Hollywood's Chamber of Commerce to constantly produce new stars for its Walk of Fame could not prevent Hollywood Boulevard from deteriorating into a zone of tacky tourism, crime, and prostitution. And as the City Council continues to debate whether or not to redo the Boulevard like New York's 42nd Street, there seems to be little sentiment in the industry for the things long gone and even less understanding of the value of their preservation. "Imagine if Ford Motor Co. was told it had to keep the building where the Model T was produced," said Thomas McGovern, vice president of Raleigh Studios at the time of its renovation. "How would they put out the Ford Taurus or the Probe?"[5]

Stars' homes are the exception to the architectural oblivion of our age that seems intent on destroying the original and preserving the copy. If the relics of Hollywood's Golden Age—including the Garden of Allah—can now be seen only in Universal Studios Florida, the houses of Barbra Streisand, Marlon Brando, Steven Spielberg and Tom Cruise are still scattered through posh neighborhoods of Hollywood Hills, Brentwood, Pacific Palisades and Bel Air. Architecturally insignificant, particularly in the city which prides itself on the finest works of Richard Neutra, Rudolph Schindler, and American Moderne in general, stars' homes attract attention and a kind of voyeurism which would be considered indecent anywhere else but in Hollywood. Every week, *The Los Angeles Times* carries a column about real estate transactions among celebrities: Madonna's purchase of a Spanish-style villa that once served as Bugsy Siegal's casino entertained Angelenos for several months in 1992 as did the construction of Aaron Spelling's 56,000 square-foot manor in Holmby Hills in the late 1980s. Televised accounts of annual mudslides and Santa Anna fires revel in disasters that affect/afflict the houses of Hollywood's rich and famous. Tourist guides, strategically placed in front of Mann's Chinese Theatre, lure visitors into costly tours of the houses that are so well guarded that they cannot, in fact, be seen. And finally, at the tail end of this peculiar commodity chain, Latino kids sell outdated star maps of houses along Sunset Boulevard, which keep the myth of the eternal industry alive. As Frederic Raphael, a writer and an Oscar-winning screenwriter, once said: "For a town with no memory, Los Angeles is remarkably nostalgic."[6]

There is a reason for this continued fascination with the homes of entertainers, alive and deceased. Stars' homes are probably the most vivid material and cultural representation of the Hollywood studio system, a logical counterpart to its hangar-like sound stages and vast backlots. Despite—or, perhaps, thanks to—their obnoxious display of wealth, stars' houses draw attention to an element of social control inherent to mass production that economic interpretations of the Hollywood studio system, and Fordism in general, tend to neglect. As Kevin Robins and Frank Webster have noted, Fordism entailed far more than control over the production process and disciplining of the workforce—it necessitated "a restructuring of the relation between factory and the outside world," and, consequently, "an extensive re-codification of the microstructures of everyday life."[7] Similarly, the Hollywood studio system—in many respects an exaggerated reflection of a typical greenfield factory and a company town—rested as much on the overt control over the institutions of mass production as it did on the more subtle mechanisms of control such as censorship and surveillance as well as the appropriation and commodification of the privacy of its stars.

This recurrent neglect of the intrusions of mass production into everyday life is mostly the consequence of an emphasis on temporal characteristics of mass production. Although a preoccupation with the time and speed of production represented an important element of manufacturers' dominance in the mass production era, it has limited our perceptions of this period to the inner workings of the modern corporation and allowed for an artificial separation of economy from society, of producers from consumers, of work from leisure. Thus, despite a large and rich body of literature on the mass production system, David Harvey is probably right when he notes that our views of this complex and complicated period in the economic history of the United States tend to be relatively simplistic, perhaps even more simplistic than the views of the alleged father of mass production, Henry Ford.[8] In contrast to Ford and his contemporaries who perceived mass production as a dynamic, conflictual process of producing people as much as of producing things, our views of mass production tend to be limited to its temporal advantages and disadvantages and locked, both literally and metaphorically, within factory gates. Temporal analyses treat the emergence of economic and social institutions specific to mass production either as a functional appendix to the production process or as a replica of the relations of dominance and subordination on the factory floor. Not surprisingly, they pay little attention to the issues that, at the time, deeply engaged both critics and proponents of mass production: homogenization and standardization of people both inside and, even more so, outside of the workplace. By excluding the entire sphere of everyday life, temporal analyses perpetuate the artificial separation of producers and consumers and gloss over the tenuous relationship between manufacturers and merchants: as such, they actually act as the cognitive reinforcement of manufacturers' dominance in the mass production economy.

Temporal and Spatial Analyses of Mass Production

Temporal analyses start from the assumption that the compression of time—the increase in the volume of output per unit of time—represents the main indicator of productivity and efficiency and logically conclude that the principal advantage of mass production stemmed from what William Lazonick aptly calls *economies of speed*.[9] Since mass production allowed for more goods to be produced in a shorter period of time, the accelerated pace of production significantly decreased their cost. In addition, the creation of multi-divisional firms—giant corporations such as DuPont, General Motors, Metropolitan Life Insurance, and Ford Motor Company—brought further organizational improvements to the so-called *throughput* time.[10] Integration of production, distribution, and retail within a single corporate unit stabilized the demand for mass-produced goods and services and allowed for more "things" to be both produced and sold per unit of time. Even the explanations for the emergence of the Keynesian state rest on similar, albeit less transparent, temporal assumptions. Mass production required huge, up-front investments in highly specialized machinery. Such investments were impossible without stable and predictable markets.[11] Hence, the overt attempts of producers to dominate time in production created a temporal gap between production and consumption—goods were produced much faster than the market could absorb them. The already mentioned Chandlerian corporation, as the first attempt at micro-regulation of the market, and then the Keynesian state and its macro-economic policies evolved as institutions intent on bridging that temporal gap.

Time plays an equally critical role in explaining the contradictions of mass production, which allegedly brought about its demise. Both exogenous and endogenous approaches to mass production rest on a common set of assumptions. The struggle over the pace of work exacerbated labor-management problems and caused numerous costly

The most famous cinematic depiction of mass production, aside from Fritz Lang's *Metropolis,* was Charlie Chaplin's film *Modern Times* (United Artists, 1936). Courtesy of the Museum of Modern Art, New York.

stoppages of the assembly line. Huge inventories of intermediary parts, considered an imperative for the continuous flow of production, tied up resources that could have been more efficiently used elsewhere.[12] Massive investments and bureaucratic red tape precluded a quick redeployment of resources and fast adaptation to market changes. In short, the attempts of manufacturers to attain full control over the speed of production inadvertently resulted in price and wage disparities, in deeper and deeper time lags between production and consumption and, finally, in an absolute decrease in productivity. According to temporal analysis, an obsession with time and the speed of production created rigidities, which made mass production extremely vulnerable to both endogenous and exogenous shocks.

Explanations of the rise and fall of the studio system do not depart too far from these classical accounts of the mass production era. Hollywood's success in the interwar period is generally ascribed to the ingenious implementation of mass-production techniques which significantly increased the volume of film production, on the one hand, and to the tight control over the market through vertical integration and market oligopoly, on the other. Similarly, it is generally assumed that a system as complex and intricate as the Hollywood studio system could only come to an end due to some major exogenous shocks.[13] The common explanations of the collapse of the studio system usually focus on three such factors. First, in May of 1948, the United States Supreme Court decided that vertical integration in the motion picture industry violated U.S. anti-trust laws and ordered the eight largest motion picture companies to divest from their theater chains.[14] Second, the advent of television and the availability of other, cheaper forms of entertainment in the aftermath of World War II pushed Hollywood producers into fierce competition for audiences. Finally, the difficult economic situation in Europe after World War II and the dearth of foreign currency forced (the cynics would say "allowed") European governments to impose restrictions on the import of American movies. The combination of these three factors seriously undermined the stability of the demand for motion pictures both inside and outside of the United States, made planning and investment in future productions difficult to gauge, and forced Hollywood majors to cut down on their production levels.[15] The alleged impact of these changes was to effectively end the studio era and to initiate a period of major restructuring in the American film industry starting in the 1960s.

Such explanations of the rise and fall of the studio system gloss over some important elements of Hollywood history. The Golden Age of Hollywood was also the period of dramatic intra-industrial power struggles and of serious debates about the purpose and morale of motion pictures. Vertical integration came late to the American film industry and, once accomplished, it did not last very long. While vertical integration streamlined the operations of Hollywood studios, facilitated the sales of their product, and significantly improved their *throughput time*, it also aggravated labor-management relations, alienated independent exhibitors and made Hollywood producers far more susceptible to the whims of the Wall Street bankers who had financed their expansion. The period that film historian Tino Balio calls "the era of mature oligopoly" was both the best and the worst of times in Hollywood.[16] Similarly, the collapse of the Hollywood studio system cannot be fully attributed to "exogenous" shocks. The divestiture from theater chains located in downtown areas coincided with the great American move into the suburbs and the slowdown of economic activity in American urban centers. The Supreme Court decision essentially ordered the Hollywood majors to pull out from the losing—and most labor intensive—branch of their business. The relationship between Hollywood studios and television was also not a zero-sum game. Already in the early 1950s, Hollywood studios became active producers of television shows, TV networks turned into a welcome outlet for the reruns of old movies, and the side of the business particularly hit by the advent of television—theaters—was no longer a part of Hollywood machinery anyway.[17] Finally, Hollywood studios quickly—some would say much too quickly—adjusted to the restrictions and quotas imposed by European governments. The latter retained the earnings from American movies, so Hollywood majors employed ingenious methods to re-appropriate their monies, including schemes of purchasing "wood pulp, whiskey, furniture, and other commodities and selling them elsewhere for dollars."[18] Even more importantly, they engaged in overseas productions—frequently benefiting from subsidies intended to encourage local production—to such an extent that the United States Congress held special hearings on the impact of "runaway production" on Hollywood labor in 1963.[19]

A somewhat different and more complex picture of mass production and, consequently, of the studio era, emerges if we pay closer attention to the spatial reorganization of production at the turn of the century and its relation to the intensification of intra-industrial strife between manufacturers and merchants. According to Alfred Chandler, whose classic works on the rise of the multidivisional firm in the United States tangentially dealt with the conflict between manufacturers and merchants, the turn of the century brought about a shift in power from merchants—wholesalers and retailers—to manufacturers.[20] Because the industrial age came late to America, local merchants and organized wholesalers dominated its economy until the end of the nineteenth century. The power of wholesalers and retailers rested upon dispersion of production, on the one hand, and on their ability to control a trade network among distant places of production and consumption, on the other.[21] In contrast, the rise of manufacturers' capitalism was closely linked to the process of progressive spatial and institutional enclosure.[22] Throughout the nineteenth century, industrial architecture had changed to accommodate an increasing need for control over the production process and to reap the benefits of new machines that could no longer be situated at home. By the beginning of the twentieth century, the trend towards spatial enclosure went a step further as greenfield factories, built on the outskirts of major urban areas, replaced company towns, artisan shops, and outwork practices. Factory walls, tightly secured gates, and enormous glass windows divided workers from their environment, enabling the manufacturers to maximize the speed of production and minimize the impact of extraneous influences on its flow.

It is probably not a coincidence that the architect of Ford's Model T plant—Albert Kahn—is also widely regarded as the father of modern industrial architecture. Kahn's first work—the Pierce plant from 1906—was a vast, enclosed, one-floor, industrial site whose great internal visibility ensured an easy overview of the entire production line and of each worker's behavior. Kahn further elaborated on his initial industrial work in the construction of Ford's Highland Park and Rouge

plants, both of which were considered masterpieces of industrial architecture in their day, the "cathedrals of industrial age." Kahn's insistence on functionalism minimized the influence of extraneous
factors on the assembly line and maximized the potential for an uninterrupted flow of production. The interior design kept factory floors
clear for the machines, placed management's offices on a higher level
to facilitate supervision of the assembly line, and even put toilets close
to the assembly line to minimize the time needed for breaks. By the
end of 1929, Kahn's architectural firm was making millions of dollars
by replicating his innovative approach to industrial architecture across
the United States. Joseph Stalin considered Kahn's design so critically
important to industrialization that he invited him to the Soviet
Union, where Kahn and his brother Moritz built 525 plants in just two
years (between 1929 and 1931). By 1938, it was estimated that Kahn
was responsible for 19 percent of all architect-designed buildings
in the United States.[23] According to architectural historians, what
Albert Kahn and his associates created was the new industrial space
whose main characteristics—elimination of non-essentials and spatial homogenization—were nothing less than "a great step towards an
Architecture, an architecture which will be expressive of a great civilization."[24] Without any doubt, control over space was seen as the precondition for control over time.

Kahn's spatial innovations facilitated control over the assembly line
and dramatically improved the quantity of production, but they also
created new and unexpected contradictions. The new industrial architecture separated, for the first time in history, the workplace from
home and the worker's public performance at work from his private
life. Yet for the employers, the entire edifice of mass production, and
the balancing of production and consumption, increasingly came to
depend on the appropriation of the private life of their employees and
on control over the chaotic world outside the factory—the two aspects
of reality which they had tried so hard to eliminate from the workplace. On the production side, the assembly line—however repetitive
and monotonous—required tremendous discipline and self-control
since even the smallest mistake could halt the entire production process. Thus, the spatial distanciation of workplace and household led,
ironically, to an increased need for the surveillance of workers'

private lives and to the development of institutions that could perform that task—personnel departments, welfare offices, and state-sponsored behavioral regulations such as prohibition.

As usual, Henry Ford was the first to grasp the depth and the relevance of the problem. "We want to make men in this factory as well as automobiles," Ford allegedly said to Reverend Dr. Samuel S. Marquis, head of the Ford's Sociological Department.[25] The Department, set up in 1914, had the sole purpose of elevating Ford's employees to the standards of the five-dollar-a-day wage rate—no smoking, no drinking, a healthy diet, and, preferably, a pious adherence to the Christian faith. Ford's welfare workers examined the houses of his employees on regular basis, and organized "Americanization" classes for immigrants as well as numerous leisure activities for the workers in general. Since Henry Ford believed that dance could cure most social ills, workers were encouraged to take waltz or square-dance classes which Ford, himself, frequently attended. In addition, Ford's private police—the infamous Service Department under the leadership of Harry Bennett—employed almost 9,000 informers among the workers in the Rouge plant, controlling every aspect of workers' behavior at work and at home. Talking, whispering, humming, and smiling were strictly forbidden, and the grimace, which most workers developed, was referred to as "Fordization of the face."[26] As Samuel Levine put it: "Henry Ford paid men $2.34 an hour to do the work and the balance of $5.00 to live the way he wanted."[27]

Following the end of the First World War, numerous "personnel departments"—which functioned quite similarly to Ford's Sociological Department—sprang up in American factories. The war revealed the importance of the "human factor" in mass production. If workers were initially only appendices to the machines, wartime shortages of workers, massive outcry over the implementation of scientific management, and large labor turnover made it quite clear that "labor is both the source of demand for products and the source of supply of the same products. A nation of sick, ignorant, and rebellious workers produces enough products to keep them sick, ignorant, and unpatriotic."[28] In addition, the success of the U.S. Army in transforming civilians into soldiers in a very brief period of time appealed to the employers, and they were "eager to apply the War time personnel methods to peace time industry."[29] Having seen the effectiveness of "organized community singing, dances and athletic contests among the soldiers and war workers, employers adopted similar programs."[30] Welfare programs were extended and so were the instruments of control. The management found it necessary "to concern itself with such matters as what its workers do with their leisure time, what they eat, what kind of homes they live in, what they do with their savings, and occasionally how happy their family life is."[31] At their entry interviews, personnel officers submitted workers to a number of physical and mental tests, and the questions went all the way down to the kind of shrubberies they had planted in their gardens.

On the consumption side, the scope of fixed investments in new plants and large overheads forced manufacturers to find new means of disposing of their abundant product. If the extension of control from the workplace into the personal lives of workers aimed at producing reliable employees, the development of modern marketing techniques attempted to stabilize demand and produce reliable consumers for standardized goods. Increased quantities and the uninterrupted flow of generic products favored large wholesalers. As high-quantity buyers, they could lower the price of undifferentiated products and impose a higher markup when distributing them to local retailers. Therefore, as Susan Strasser has written in her wonderful study of early American marketing, manufacturers, burdened by enormous investments in their production facilities, could no longer "afford to be the passive factor of neoclassical economics or the relatively weak link in an old fashioned chain dominated by large wholesale merchants."[32] Fearing such dependency on the already powerful distributors, manufacturers "took their cue from a few industries, such as book publishing and patent medicines, where manufacturers courted customers directly," and where patents and copyrights endowed them with a quasi-monopoly position in the market.[33] The development of branded products such as Crisco shortening, Ivory soap, Kodak cameras and Campbell's soup enabled manufacturers to tilt the price elasticity in their favor: "the consumer who wanted no substitutes for Ivory soap or Steinway pianos would be unwilling to settle for another product just because it was cheaper."[34] By creating a customer who could come to the store with a clear idea of what he desired, manufacturers were hoping to develop a direct link with their customers and bypass whole-salers and retailers. Therefore, the establishment of manufacturers' dominance in the economy rested upon the construction of new, en-closed industrial sites which allowed the manufacturers to control the entire flow of production, of new enclosed institutions which enabled them to control both production and consumption of goods, and, most importantly, on a great deal of social engineering on both ends of the economic pipeline.

As we shall see in the rest of this chapter, both the problems and the solutions of mass production, which stemmed from the conflict be-tween manufacturers and merchants and the spatial reorganization of production, resonated quite strongly in the American motion picture industry. Placed between public and private, "organized production" and "organized consumption," work and leisure, the film industry oc-cupied a very special place in American society at that time. On the one hand, it was obviously an industry like any other industry. The re-quirements of mass production in film manufacturing were the same as the requirements of mass production in the automobile or the food processing industry: strict deadlines had to be met, workers had to be disciplined, quantity of output had to increase, continuity of produc-tion had to be maintained. The relationship between producers, dis-tributors, and theater exhibitors was every bit as turbulent as the re-lationship between manufacturers, wholesalers, and retailers in other segments of the economy. At the same time, however, the motion pic-ture industry was also an industry that directly intruded into that as-pect of workers' lives that other industrialists so clearly wanted to con-trol—their privacy. By the early 1920s, the impact of Hollywood on people's lives had become a serious concern for manufacturers like Henry Ford, politicians, and church organizations. Thanks to its broad economic, cultural and social significance, the motion picture indus-try in the mass production era acquired "the dubious distinction of being the most severely criticized of all industries."[35]

Faced with such dual constraints, Hollywood moguls found more exaggerated, more ingenious, and more conflicted solutions to the common problems than did their counterparts in other industrial sec-tors. The revolutionary aspect of the new industrial architecture was the placing of the entire production process on one floor and under one roof. Hollywood studios went a step further: they replicated the entire world in their own backlots. American manufacturers created welfare measures and branded products in order to micro-manage their workers and their consumers. Hollywood moguls combined the two innovations into a single one: the star system appropriated the privacy of Hollywood actors and transformed it into a consumer dream. Most American businesses pursued vertical integration in order to streamline their operations and ensure the manufacturers' control over commodity chains. Hollywood producers complemented vertical integration with much more subtle distribution strategies such as block-booking of films, theater zoning, and self-censorship in order to lessen, or altogether eliminate, the influence of independent producers and independent theater owners on the industry which they considered "theirs." Throughout Hollywood's studio era these elements, which we can metaphorically refer to as *occupation of space* and *occupation of privacy*, worked in concert to reinforce the power of Hollywood producers and minimize the impact of any extraneous forces, including the U.S. Government. To use Tino Balio's term, Hollywood moguls created a "controlled institution" to match the "controlled environments" of their studios.[36]

The *Occupation of Space:*
Controlling the Production Process

The establishment of manufacturers' dominance in the motion picture industry was, much as in other industrial sectors, directly related to the *occupation of space* and the *occupation of privacy*. In order to assert their role in the economy and achieve dominance in the commodity chain, film producers also had to reform the production process, the product itself, and the way in which the product was distributed and sold. The transition was neither simple nor uniformly successful: it involved an upward battle with workers over the *speed of production* and an equally difficult struggle with merchants and wholesalers over the *territories of consumption*. The concentration of film production in Southern California and, even more importantly, the construction of film studios—the motion picture equivalents of greenfield factories—enabled motion picture producers to increase the quantity of production and standardize their output. The sheer volume of production, however, could not guarantee either the stability of the production line or audience loyalty to the films of specific production companies. In order to regulate the behavior of their employees and capture the audiences, Hollywood producers employed a combination of formal and informal institutional arrangements, but the most important were probably the star system, a Hollywood version of branded products, and a series of more subtle mechanisms of labor and market control such as block-booking, zoning, and theater runs. The combination of these factors strengthened the position of producers and production in the entertainment industry. But it also, as this section will show, brought repeated calls for government regulation of the motion picture industry: by focusing their attention on the moral code of Hollywood film production, producers and merchants transposed their conflicts over the speed of production and territories of consumption onto the content of the movies. As historian Lary May put it, movies became "the most powerful national institution which offered private solutions to public issues."[37]

The shift from merchants' to manufacturers' capitalism in the American motion picture industry followed a path similar to the one blazed by other manufacturing sectors. In the first twenty years after its inception, merchants—wholesalers and retailers—dominated the industry. Production was not the key component of the movie business, and there was no clear spatial differentiation of either the production or the exhibition of the moving images. The attention of the companies engaged in the business focused on equipment—cameras and projectors—and the distribution of the generic film product. Cameramen were responsible for all aspects of production—they would select the topic, stage it or shoot on location, and eventually even show it to the public. Between 1895 and 1897, for instance, the French company Lumière dominated the American market because its lightweight camera simultaneously served as a projector.[38] Lumière's cameramen traveled around the country entertaining audiences with moving images of their own locale shot just a few hours before the show. The "instant" documentaries were so immensely popular that, when Lumière left the American market, Edison and his affiliates adopted some of its techniques. Pirating and copying were frequent at the time and films themselves had no identity of their own. Exhibition was mostly in the hands of traveling exhibitors who screened movies in amusement parks, circuses, or in small-town county buildings and opera houses. Even when the movies were shown in vaudevilles, which were more urban and stable exhibition venues, they were treated as just another transient form of entertainment, no better or worse than puppetry, *tableaux vivant,* freaks, or animal trainers. Vaudeville owners purchased films from catalogues, in bulk, and either screened them until they fell apart or put them aside after just a few shows.[39]

The demand for novelty films was increased by the formation of film exchanges in 1903, which enabled typical wholesalers with territorial rights to license movies to individual exhibitors for a limited period of time; and the development of nickelodeons, the first spaces devoted solely to the exhibition of motion pictures. The industry gradually phased out newsreels and documentaries, such as those about royal weddings, coronations, and wars, whose supply was unpredictable, and turned toward narrative films which could be more easily reproduced. Nonetheless, Edison's trust continued to focus on technology and distribution. The members of the trust tightened control over their patents and centralized the distribution system by acquiring fifty-eight out of fifty-nine film exchanges. Yet, throughout the period of Edison's monopoly, production remained scattered all around the country. Production companies which belonged to Edison's trust—Essaney, Kalem, Lubin, Biograph—had offices and facilities in New York, Chicago, Philadelphia, Ithaca, and Los Angeles. Movies were frequently shot in warm places, particularly during the long winter months when harsh weather shut down production in the northeast regions of the United States. Production companies, searching for sun, went to Jacksonville, Florida; San Diego, California; Tucson, Arizona; and to Cuba, the Bermudas, and Jamaica. French miracle maker Georges Mélies spent some time in Texas, working on *The Immortal Alamo,* (1911) and then continued his travels all the way to the Southern Seas. On the East Coast, one of the largest production centers long remained Fort Lee, New Jersey. Discovered in 1907 by Sidney Olcott from the Kalem Company, Fort Lee served as great and convenient stand-in scenery for the "Wild West." Between 1907 and 1919, film-makers—mostly from Edison's trust—made hundreds of "westerns" in the Palisades near Coyetsville and in Fort Lee. For a while, the area also hosted the largest and most modern glass studio in the world, Paragon, where Mary Pickford made *Poor Little Rich Girl* (1917), one of her greatest successes.[40] The increase in coal prices, the labor unrest of 1918, frequent fires, and the discovery of California closed down most of the eastern studios. In 1920, production at Fort Lee was just 5 percent of what was its peak in the period between 1914 and 1919, whereas California's share of output increased to more than 80 percent of all the motion pictures produced in the United States.[41]

There were two decisive factors in the shift of power from distributors to producers of films: the concentration of production in Southern California and the building of the first film studios. Southern California offered many advantages to independent producers running away from Edison's spies. Apart from distance, which proved attractive even to the more independent-minded members of Edison's trust, Southern California also had stable weather; cheap, non-unionized, and abundant labor; equally cheap and abundant land; and a great variety of landscapes. Los Angeles was known as the "citadel of the open shop in America," and labor costs were 25 to 50 percent below those in New York. Within an area of just a dozen square miles, producers could find mountains, deserts, and a coastline which could as easily stand in for the rugged parts of Scotland as for the French Riviera. As an industrial site, Hollywood combined the advantages of a company town and a greenfield factory; paternalism and scientific management; and a feudal manor and the modern urban environment.

But if the concentration of production in Southern California seemed logical, the construction of motion picture studios in Hollywood initially seemed like a contradiction in terms, particularly given the "open space" appeal of California. The prime reason for the building of the enclosed studios buildings in the East was weather. Eastern studios were either "roof-top" constructions which could be adjusted to both sunshine and rain conditions, glass edifices similar to garden houses, or—much less frequently—factory-like enclosed spaces with artificial lighting. Eileen Bowser writes that the Biograph Studio on

Fourteenth Street in New York, which was in operation from 1903 to 1913, was "unusual in being lit entirely by artificial light" and that "smaller and newer companies continued to do most of their filming out-doors."[42] The studios offered shelter from rain and snow, and—if lit with artificial lighting—allowed motion picture producers to be fairly independent from the daylight. More elaborate constructions—such as Lubinville in Philadelphia or Famous Players-Lasky Studio on Long Island—were in effect vast factory floors where, on stages subdivided by curtains, dozens of movies could be shot simultaneously.

In comparison with their eastern counterparts, Hollywood studios were a different breed, and they were built with a different purpose in mind: they were "controlled environments" of production intent on reducing the dependency of motion picture producers on the outside world. Years before coming to California, one of the Hollywood pioneers, William "Colonel" Selig, had already realized that working inside the studio did not just protect filmmakers from rain but allowed them to reproduce reality in any way they saw fit. In 1909, Selig Polyscope Company staged a "documentary" about President Roosevelt's safari in Mombasa, Africa, in its Chicago studio. Selig released the film without indicating that it had been staged, but *Colliers* magazine praised the "documentary" as an example of the "scientific nature-faking."[43] Appropriately, the main attraction of "Colonel" Selig's studio in Edendale, on the outskirts of Los Angeles, was a "Jungle Zoo" worth one–million dollars.

The studios in California occupied vast tracts of land and initially operated as self-sufficient communities with their own post offices as well as police and fire brigades. Inceville—the first "modern" studio in California—was, like Rome, "built upon seven hills" and covered "approximately eighteen thousand acres."[44] The backlot included a "Dutch village with a genuine canal and windmill, a Japanese village, an Irish village, Canadian stockades, Southern log cabins, East Indian streets, Sioux Indian camps and a real Scotch Street which was used in Billie Burke's first play."[45] Universal City had a hospital, several restaurants, garages, its own local government, and all the paraphernalia mentioned in the Introduction. Mack Sennett's Keystone Studios housed "all the industries to be found in the average city of several thousand population, including a five–story planing mill and restaurant."[46] The studios, as mentioned earlier, were cities within cities, industries within industries, worlds within a world. They materialized the tendency towards self-containment and self-regulation that was the key component of Hollywood producers' overall industrial strategy. Several decades later, in the mid 1930s, *The Motion Picture* magazine, the official publication of Hollywood's producers' association, still emphasized the self-sufficiency of studio production facilities and the elimination of privacy in the studios as their key advantages in pursuit of speed. "The completeness of studios," wrote an anonymous staff writer, "has this advantage: everybody can see everybody else and get whatever is needed within the least possible delay."[47]

The shift from decentralized and dispersed, mostly outdoor production to the combination of highly localized and in-house production enabled producers to increase and regulate the quantity of their output, which could then be used as a leverage in negotiations with exhibitors. Between 1912, when the independents started their feature production, and 1921, when nearly all feature production in the United States took place in Hollywood studios, the number of feature films produced jumped from two hundred to eight-hundred and fifty-four. The competition and exchange of ideas in a small, and still very rural, community stimulated creativity and the development of industrial standards. The physical isolation of Hollywood, writes Koszarski, quickly "inculcated a special 'Hollywood' way of looking at life that generations of audiences would instantly recognize."[48] "Hollywood" became a label that designated the product of certain quality and attracted newcomers into the area who hoped to benefit from the "brand name" of the place. The number of production companies and the employees in the motion picture industry grew at an amazing speed. Already in 1917, *The Moving Picture World* noted that the motion picture business was the largest single industry in Southern California.[49] The industry, according to conservative estimates, spent more than $30 billion a year in the Los Angeles area, and employed more than 20,000 people.[50] By the early 1920s, no other film center in the world could come even close to Hollywood, and competitors around the world recognized the studio—the physical plant—as the key to American superiority.

Occupation of Privacy: **Social Control of the Motion Picture Industry**

The occupation of Hollywood's open lands and the increase in production of feature films allowed independent producers to break the power of Edison's trust and establish themselves as the preeminent force in the motion-picture industry. But, in order to stabilize the production and consumption of motion pictures, Hollywood producers had to rely on other, subtle and imaginative, mechanisms of social control. The star system, as the motion-picture equivalent of a branded product and product differentiation, was the most important among them: it appropriated the privacy of motion-picture actors and transformed it into the essential commodity in show business. Initially, the stars were simply the brand names of particular studios and their identity remained restricted to the textuality of the pictures. Florence Lawrence, arguably the first motion-picture star, had been known as the "Biograph Girl" before she got "stolen" by Carl Laemmle who turned her into the "IMP Girl." Yet in the early teens the initial reliance on "picture personalities" as company "brands" was replaced by the more elaborate star system, and public attention shifted to the private life of actors. The actors became screen names, the centerpiece of film manufacturers' distribution strategy and "an economic necessity to the motion-picture industry (. . .) not only a 'production' value, but a 'trademark' value, and an 'insurance' value [both of] which are very real and very potent in guaranteeing the sale of this product to the cash customers at a profit."[51]

The transformation of actors into stars entailed the occupation of their privacy; according to Christine Gledhill, actors become stars only "when their off-screen lifestyles and personalities equal or surpass acting ability in importance."[52] The narratives that engulfed the stars of the silent era included forays into their homes, a complete inventory of their possessions, detailed accounts of their daily routines and a list of hobbies. Most stories emphasized the "normalcy" of stars with "healthy" family lives and stable homes, but they also, simultaneously, celebrated the stars as the "privileged sites" of consumption.[53] "The star system," writes Richard De Cordova, "worked to construct a particular kind of consumer around the star as commodity [. . .] in conspicuously displaying success through material possessions, the star vividly demonstrated the idea that satisfaction was not to be found in work but in one's activities away from work—in consumption and leisure."[54] The emphasis on gardening, parenthood, and the relationships of stars with their own parents went hand in hand with stories about the stars' enormous salaries, unlimited leisure time, and extravagant consumption habits. The tension easily lent itself to scandals—in the eyes of middle Americans the step between life-style extravaganzas and morphine addiction was fairly small—and it troubled the audiences, theater owners, and producers alike.

The dependency on stars and their intimacy also carried an internal contradiction that would eventually bring down the Hollywood studio system. While Hollywood producers eagerly exploited and generated the attention that surrounded the stars, they feared stars' autonomy, which came with their individualized publicity. Already in 1915, Carl Laemmle—the man whom historians generally regard as the "inventor" of the movie-star institution—attacked the star system as "the ruinous practice that has been responsible for high-priced but low-grade features."[55] The salaries of major stars, such as Mary Pickford and Charlie Chaplin, skyrocketed between 1912 and 1916 and so did their drawing power. Chaplin, for instance, joined the Keystone company in 1913 for $150 per week. In 1915, he was earning $10,000 per week, plus a bonus of $150,000.[56] The rentals for Mary Pickford's films trebled in 1916, and Famous Players-Lasky Corporation downloaded most of its other films thanks to the sales of Pickford's films. In the fall of 1919, fully conscious of their increasing market power, Mary Pickford, Charlie Chaplin, and Douglas Fairbanks, and director D. W. Griffith formed United Artists, the first company solely devoted to the distribution of independently produced pictures. In order to ensure the sales of their films, United Artists established a co-financing agreement with First National, an emerging theater chain. Although "notoriously difficult to organize," the exhibitors feared the increasing monopoly of Hollywood producers on the supply side and eagerly joined First National. The number of members in the first theater chain grew from twenty-six in 1917 to 639 in the beginning of 1920 to 3,500 in 1921.[57]

The alliance between exhibitors and stars threatened the essence of producers' power and forced them into vertical integration. In 1919, partly in response to those threats, Adolph Zukor, whose Famous Players-Lasky chain controlled approximately 75 percent of the stars and had already integrated with the distributor Paramount, started aggressively purchasing theaters. This phase of integration, wrote Mae Huettig, could best be described as a "Battle for Theaters," since most accounts of that period "sound like a journalist's account of a war."[58] Paramount's agents used all possible means to persuade theater owners to sell their property, and "were soon dubbed 'the wrecking crew' and the 'dynamite gang' by theater owners."[59] Most frequently, they "encircled" the theater owners, forcing them to either sell the theater at the price offered or be exposed to competition from a new theater located in their neighborhood. At the same time, by controlling the distribution system and the high-volume supply of films, Paramount made it almost impossible for independent producers to reach the theaters, threatening to withdraw its films if theater owners agreed to show the competitors' product. By 1923, Fox and Loew's were also expanding their theater holdings, relying on tactics similar to Paramount's. In the process, hundreds of exhibitors were forced out of the entertainment business, never to recover.[60]

In addition to vertical integration, Zukor refined the pricing and sales system for his motion pictures to allow for new temporal and spatial controls of the market. Theater zoning, theater-runs, and block-booking allowed producers to combine the drawing power of stars with their voluminous production and to maximize profits through an elaborate pricing mechanism. Having noted that the audiences were willing to pay a premium to see a film when it first came out, Hollywood producers divided theaters into first-run, second-run and subsequent-run theaters. Since the maximum revenues came from the first-run theaters, producers protected them through "zoning" and "clearance." Zoning protected first-run theaters from competitive screenings of the same film within a certain territory—sometimes as large as six-hundred square miles—while clearance determined the duration of "runs" for each particular theater. Finally, block-booking cornered the exhibitors into buying Paramount's entire output in order to get several A-pictures with stars. By mixing films with stars (films that exhibitors could not afford not to have) with "programmers" (generic features with no well-known actors) into "blocks," Adolph

Zukor and other major Hollywood producers could dictate the terms of sale to exhibitors. Simultaneously, block-booking limited the power of stars to demand higher wages since block-sales prevented the exact calculation of any particular star's contribution to the overall box-office gross.[61] The combined effect of these innovations in distribution strategy was to homogenize the U.S. market by creating national standards for film rentals, and to disempower independent theater owners by imposing fixed and pre-determined spatial and temporal criteria on diverse local markets.

Block-booking tilted the balance of power towards producers to such an extent that it became the most contentious issue in producer-exhibitor relations for decades to come. Thanks to the rise of First National, exhibitors succeeded in temporarily suspending block-booking in 1918. The practice, however, resumed as soon as the producers started buying the theaters and embarked upon vertical integration. Squeezed between Hollywood producers and emerging theater chains such as First National, Balaban and Katz, and Loew's (the motion-picture equivalent of department store revolution), independent theater owners resorted to legal action. But independent theater owners failed in all their national efforts against Hollywood majors until the late 1930s, due to their poor organization and fragmentation as well as to their association's suspectibility to the influence of the producer/distributors' organizations. In 1921, the Federal Trade Commission filed the first complaint against Paramount-Famous-Lasky Corporation. The main charges focused on Paramount's aggressive purchase of theaters in the late teens and its block-booking practices. The complaint, however, did not become a cease-and-desist order until 1927. Between 1921 and 1932, the Federal Trade Commission investigated the industry, filling some 17,000 pages of testimony and 15,000 pages of exhibits. The final report was, in the words of Harvard Business School professor Howard Thompson Lewis, "probably the most voluminous record compiled in any litigation involving trade practices."[62] Nonetheless, in 1932, the Second Circuit Court dismissed on appeal the charges of exhibitors against Hollywood majors, and the Federal Trade Commission decided to drop the case altogether.[63] During the same period, nearly every session of Congress introduced new bills against block-booking practices, but they all failed to pass either on the House or on the Senate floor. And despite numerous private law suits against Hollywood's oligopoly, both block-booking and theater acquisition continued until the 1948 Paramount decision, which divorced studios from their theater chains.

Theater owners were somewhat more successful, and definitely more ingenious, in their local efforts: they formed alliances with censorship boards and argued that block-booking was responsible for the decreasing moral value of Hollywood films.[64] The unlikely alliance between theater owners and local censors represented the most obvious attempt to re-introduce *economies of space* into the economy increasingly dominated by *economies of time*. Theater owners realized that their only leverage in negotiations with producers was their knowledge of their own communities. In urban centers, independent theater owners operated so-called neighborhood theaters, long bastions of ethnic culture in the United States. Theater managers knew most of their patrons by name, employed local kids as ushers, and catered to their communities by mixing standard, Hollywood, product with their own, home-grown entertainment: theater plays in Polish, Yiddish, or Croatian; local amateur contests; and ethnic orchestras as accompaniment to Hollywood silent movies.[65] In small towns, where theater owners exercised significant local monopoly power, theater was usually the only entertainment. The profitability of such operations depended mostly on a careful balancing of tastes in the community and a good relationship with churches, businesses, school teachers, and parents.

Theater owners, thus, had legitimate concerns about the content of the movies that they screened. But they also realized that local control of the content would significantly undermine the ability of producers to set the terms of exchange with an over-supply of product. In order to sustain their investments in studios and their increasing overheads, as well as their huge up-front investments in every single film, producers had to keep the production rolling and they needed a *homogenous* market. The prospect of being forced to tailor each movie to the requirements of each particular state or each particular community terrified them as much as the idea that theater owners could cut and paste movies as they saw fit. By focusing on the moral code of entertainment, manufacturers and merchants transposed their conflict over the *territories of consumption* and the *speed of production* onto the content of the movies.

Institutionalizing Social Control: Hays Office and Self-Regulation

Thanks to the studios and the star system, the motion-picture industry was, in the 1920s, one of the fastest growing sectors in the United States, but producers were paying dearly for their rapid success. Distant and isolated, Hollywood was the example of everything that was wrong with mass production for ordinary Americans. The stories of overnight wealth or fame insulted the fundamental values of frugal, hardworking Americans. Benjamin Hampton, the author of one of the first movie histories, wrote that "merchants and professional men, struggling to earn five or ten thousand dollars a year, began to curse the 'pretty boys' of the screen who received as much in a month or a week, and their wives grew caustic in commenting on the 'dough-faced girls who hadn't brains enough to act, but were lucky enough to get a fortune for being clothes-horses."[66] The city was inundated by thousands of young men and women whose hopes of instant stardom could not be satisfied. They often ended up on the streets of Los Angeles or mysteriously vanished into its underworld. Numerous scandals—from Mary Pickford's divorce to the rumors about widespread morphine addiction among members of the movie colony—created an image of Hollywood as the epitome of sin in a country still soaked in Victorian values. When the young actress Virginia Rappe was raped in San Francisco in 1921, and the crime attributed to one of the most popular comedians at the time, Roscoe "Fatty" Arbuckle, public outrage reached its climax. Pressures for censorship of both movies and Hollywood itself—which had haunted the industry for several years—were mounting across the country. In 1922, thirty-six states were discussing censorship bills in their legislatures, local censorship boards proliferated, and requests for the creation of a federal regulatory agency in charge of motion pictures were getting increasing support in the U.S. Senate.

The response of Hollywood producers to the combined pressures of the early 1920s—objective decline in Hollywood's morale, the increasingly restive behavior of stars, legal actions of the exhibitors, and the threat of local and state censorship—was the organization of the most peculiar trade association in pre-war America. The Motion Picture Producers and Distributors Association, formed in 1922, combined elements of Ford's Sociological Department and a religious organization to monitor the ideological, economic, and physical space of producers' operations. In order to quiet attacks on the industry, Hollywood moguls brought in Will Hays, former U.S. Postmaster General and an elder in the Presbyterian Church, to head the organization. Hays was endowed with such powers that he soon became known as the "Hollywood czar," and the organization that he chaired as the "Hays Office." The office, whose most famous product was the self-censorship code, attempted to systematize and standardize intra-industry relations as well as relations between the industry and its environment. By bringing some order into the relatively chaotic world of the 1920s, Hays tried to minimize the likelihood of the state's intervention in the industry and to divert "attention away from issues of trade practice into concerns about the film content."[67] Ironically, self-regulation, which served as the precondition for the expansion of the industry and conversion to sound, only aggravated intra-industry relations and brought the film industry much closer to the government than Hollywood moguls had ever aspired to do.

The quasi-official history of the Hays Office, written by Raymond Moley in 1945, praises Hays's efforts to win respect for the motion-picture industry, and focuses on his work in public relations and self-censorship. Starting in 1922, Hays conducted a broad public-relations campaign in an effort to improve the public image of the industry. He enlisted the cooperation of major newspapers and asked for removal of freelance writers whose "lurid" stories tainted the industry. His "Open Door Policy" established advisory boards and solicited opinions from numerous local associations and religious organizations— from Boy Scouts of America to the Daughters of the American Revolution—on the future course of the industry. Hays's public appearances and publications of the Hays Office stressed the important role of motion pictures in education and in the religious life of the country. In addition, Hays spearheaded the creation of the Central Casting Bureau that brought order to the casting of extras and—at least temporarily—reduced the number of hopefuls on the streets of Los Angeles trying to break into the industry. Finally, between 1922 and 1930, the Hays Office adopted a series of increasingly stringent self-censorship regulations, mostly driven by unabated pressures from local censors and independent theater owners.

Self-regulation in the industry extended from self-censorship to the standardization of producer-exhibitor and producer-labor relations in the motion-picture industry. The Hays Office engaged in all aspects of negotiations with independent exhibitors. At the time when Will Hays took office, between 500,000 and 750,000 producer-exhibitor contracts were written every year, each one representing a potentially lengthy and costly law suit.[68] Given the importance of producer-exhibitor relations in light of the pending FTC investigation and the continued pressure for government censorship, it is not surprising that Hays invested a lot of personal energy into the creation of the Standard Contract for exhibitors. Between 1923 and 1930, MPPDA supervised the creation of four contracts whose main clauses related to the establishment of Film Boards of Trade and arbitration boards in all key distribution centers. The Hays Office thought of arbitration as its greatest achievement. The exhibitors found it limiting and biased in favor of the producers/distributors. While the first three contracts (1923, 1925, and 1926) made arbitration mandatory—preventing the parties from resorting to court—the last contract from 1930 allowed for the voluntary arbitration of conflicts between distributors and exhibitors.

Similarly, the Hays Office attempted to standardize producer-talent relations. Shortly after his arrival in Hollywood, Hays helped producers "compile a list of 117 stars who were banned from the industry because of unfavorable publicity about their personal lives."[69] The scandals prompted producers to introduce a "morality clause" into their contracts with actors, and the first Standard Contract negotiated with Actors Equity under the auspices of the Hays Office included that clause. The clause allowed producers to dismiss any actor whose private life could cause a scandal and endanger studio profits. Implicitly, if not explicitly, it gave permission to the studio bosses and their publicity departments to impose standards of off-screen behavior on their most visible assets. In addition, fearing unionization, producers formed the Academy of Motion Picture Arts and Sciences in 1927.

The Academy, which in essence served as the company union for the industry, had five branches—producers, directors, writers, actors, and technicians—encompassing all industry-specific workers employed by the studios. At the same time, since membership in the Academy was by invitation, limited to individuals whose work had significantly contributed to the development of the industry, the Academy ensured that power remained in the hands of a select few. Skillfully guided by Cecil B. DeMille and greatly aided in its aims by internal dissent among actors, writers and directors, the Academy successfully forestalled unionization of Hollywood's talent groups for several years.

The Hays Office diffused protests within and outside the industry in time to allow for the introduction of sound and major expansion of Hollywood majors between 1927 and 1933. The appearance of industrial and labor harmony was critically important to the relationship between Hollywood moguls and the East Coast business establishment. The acquisition of theater chains and the new sound technology brought Hollywood majors much closer to Wall Street and to the producers of electrical equipment such as Western Electric, AT&T, and RCA. The profits accumulated by the first sound films encouraged the studios to purchase theater chains and complete the construction of their oligopolistic industrial structure: Warner Bros. bought the Philadelphia-based Stanley theater chain; Fox Corporation acquired the Poli chain in New England as well as a majority of shares in West Coast Theaters and attempted an integration with Loew's/MGM; Paramount sought a merger with Warner Bros.; RCA entered into the motion picture industry by establishing the Radio-Keith-Orpheum corporation, popularly known as RKO. And although the Justice Department blocked some of the planned mergers and acquisitions—a Paramount/Warner deal never took place and William Fox ended up in jail because of his merger with Loew's—the intense merger and acquisition activity gave nearly absolute control over the motion picture industry to the five major companies. By the end of this period, there were literally no theater chains left in the country, and independent theater owners were alone in their struggle against the Hollywood majors.

The costs of expansion were exorbitant. In 1928 alone, writes Michael Conant, the Hollywood majors "spent $161,930,000 on new theaters; the total number of theaters was about 20,500."[70] Estimated costs of conversion to sound varied from year to year and from source to source, but they seemed to have averaged $10,000 per theater.[71] Production costs also increased: the building of the sound stages was a short but expensive process. The studios spent $50,000,000 or almost as much as the total value of Hollywood studios at the time, to build sound stages on their backlots in 1929, while production cost per film—primarily due to the increased dependence on Broadway actors and writers—came to average between $200,000 and $400,000 at Warner Bros. and $500,000 at MGM during the Depression.[72] The money came mostly from Wall Street. Before the advent of sound and the acquisition of prestigious theater palaces, Wall Street financiers thought little of Hollywood; movies were a flimsy product, and the industry's profits too unpredictable. Theaters, however, represented durable assets, and bankers felt much more confident issuing loans and bonds against investments in real estate.

The accumulation of long-term debt between 1927 and 1933—in the midst of the Depression—exposed Hollywood to the scrutiny of financial markets and created the first cracks in its isolated and self-centered world. Starting in 1930, the Depression finally reached Hollywood: theater attendance declined rapidly and so did studio profits. Among the Big Five, only MGM was operating without loss, and in 1933—after the brief period in which it seemed that the motion picture industry was recession-proof—the future of Hollywood seemed grim if not outright hopeless.

Hollywood producers, not surprisingly, transferred the costs of expansion to theater exhibitors and talent. Independent exhibitors who could not afford an upgrade to sound went out of business; the wages of Hollywood employees were effectively frozen and their unionization was preempted by various means. By the end of the 1930s, the industry was once again flourishing at the expense of its labor and of intra-industry relations. Independent exhibitors, many of whom could not afford to pay for the installation of sound equipment, perceived the entire conversion to sound as a conspiracy of studio moguls against them and intensified their pressures for government regulation of the motion picture industry. The "talkies" provided a fertile ground for such attacks, and the studios—burdened by much higher production costs and sophisticated sound technology—were even

New York, ca. 1980 in one of the first science fiction films, *Just Imagine* (20th Century Fox, 1930). The film was visually inspired by Fritz Lang's *Metropolis* (UFA, 1927). Art directors were Stephen Goosson and Ralph Hammeras. Courtesy of the Museum of Modern Art, New York.

more vulnerable to the threats of either local or federal censorship than they had been during the silent era.

The attacks of exhibitors focused on the excessively permissive Broadway culture that permeated the first sound films—Mae West, who single-handedly saved Paramount from receivership, is the example often cited. Middle-class, mostly Protestant, groups felt particularly threatened by the intrusion of "alien," urban culture into small town America and joined in protest. The combination of the public's moral conservatism and theater owners' agitation, in the era of declining profits, seems to have frightened the Hays Office more than the producers themselves. As a result, the Hays Office exaggerated the crisis and went beyond its previous mandate in establishing moral guidelines for the industry: in 1934, it formed the Production Code Administration to police their implementation.

The Production Code Administration, in effect, strengthened the economic position of the producers while limiting the autonomy of studio personnel. The new office, led by Joseph Breen, requested that producers submit scripts for approval before shooting and made it mandatory for all MPPDA members to distribute only films which had the Production Code seal of approval. The economic effectiveness of the Code rested on the fact that the major production/distribution companies were also the operators of the five major theater circuits.[73] No film without the Production Code seal of approval could be screened in any of the first run theaters and, consequently, could not expect to make any substantial profits. By imposing restrictions on the exhibition side of the business and regulating the content, the Breen Office limited access to the production of motion pictures and ensured that control over the supply of films remained in the hands of Hollywood moguls. The success of the measure is evident from the fact that no film without the Production Code Administration seal of approval had been shown in the United States theaters before 1952.[74]

Apart from the Wall Street bankers, whose influence in the motion picture industry was debated throughout the 1930s, the introduction of sound brought to Hollywood hundreds of actors and writers from Broadway. The sudden exposure of the enclosed movie colony to the ways of the world led to cultural and economic clashes. Actors and writers of the talkies considered unions and the notion of authorship a fact of life. For the Hollywood moguls, who—like the legendary Louis B. Mayer—still treated all studio employees to their mothers' chicken broth, such ideas were not only radical but the equivalent of personal betrayal. In the 1930s, simultaneous with tightening of the content regulation, the studios stepped up their control over the stars and talent in general. Vertical integration allowed studio moguls to curb the power of the stars and maximize revenues based on their drawing power, while internal reorganization of production strengthened the role of producers vis-à-vis directors and writers.

It was during this period that stars mostly resembled contemporary Alexander dolls: delicate and expensive, they were sold to audiences around the world with new proper names, with enclosed, serialized "narratives" that emphasized some mythic element of their past, and with carefully guarded off-screen lives designed to match their on-screen personalities.[75] Publicity departments closely collaborated with journalists, particularly gossip writers such as Louella Parsons and Hedda Hopper, and controlled the flow of information by constantly supplying more news than necessary. The studio moguls arranged dates and marriages among their celebrated assets, covered up or exposed their mishaps when they found it appropriate, and kept them in check with a reinvigorated mix of paternalism and authoritarianism. The attention any particular star received was directly proportional to his or her drawing power, and the studios constantly re-evaluated their appeal by the amount of fan mail that they received, recent box office performance, and "independent" rankings in trade papers. Needless to say, the hope of stardom and the fear of losing it worked as the best possible barriers against broad-based solidarity among Hollywood actors.

The key legal instrument of studio control was the so-called option contract, usually signed for a period of seven years, which allowed the studio to fire its contract actors, stars included, at any point during those seven years.[76] The actor, on the other hand, could not leave the studio under any circumstances. The studios also retained the right to cast actors in any film they found appropriate, to suspend the actor or the actress if they refused a particular role, and to loan them to other studios for no additional pay. Since option contracts allowed studio moguls to groom stars and, presumably, to reap increasing returns on their investment in human capital as time went by, the studios created an entire stable of child actors in the 1930s whose careers were to continue for years to come. During the days of the National Recovery Administration (NRA), the producers attempted to introduce three other restrictions into the Motion Picture Code: (1) salary reductions with proposed fines for the studios which overpaid their talent; (2) an end to talent raids among the studios or, essentially, an end to the horizontal mobility of actors, writers, and directors; (3) severe limitations on activities of talent agents, the quintessential middlemen of the movie business. The proposed Code mobilized Hollywood's talent groups into opposition and initiated the long battle for the recognition of their unions.

Although grossly manipulated by the producers, the NRA did, however, make a dent in the powers of the Hays Office. Established as a parallel structure to the Hays Office and its arbitration boards, and as a substitute for the contracts negotiated by Hays, the Motion Picture Code made the Hays Office obsolete in the areas where it mattered the most: in intra-industry relations and labor relations. Thus, even after the official end of the NRA, the producers found it very difficult to bring the dormant institutions back to life. In 1938, when the Justice Department filed the anti-trust suit against the Hollywood majors, the industry found itself "without arbitration, without conciliation, without a uniform system of clearance, without a standard contract—in short, without any of the benefits, actual or potential, of self-regulation."[77] The only functioning areas of the once omnipotent Hays Office were the Production Code Administration and the increasingly important Office of Foreign Relations.

According to Moley, the Hays Office differed from any other trade association because it "sought to change the habits of its members and the tastes of its customers," and in the process had to "amend the law of supply and demand."[78] All activities of the Hays Office—from censorship to contract negotiation—aimed at the creation of a self-contained industrial structure which Moley—and presumably Hays himself—saw as the antidote to anarchy, state intervention and excessive competition within the industry.[79]

The stepped-up controls over the content of the movies and the lives of stars seemed a small price for the extended control over the oligopolistic industrial structure. But the politicization of everyday life had its costs. Throughout this entire period, despite the insistence of Hollywood producers that movies were nothing but sheer entertainment, their own self-censorship and surveillance betrayed their admission that movies had a much greater social role to play. The producers' strategy of self-regulation contributed to the creation of the motion-picture industry as a public institution par excellence. This status allowed producers to finally enlist the industry in the U.S. war effort, in hope that their service would sway the government's decision to intervene in the industry. Instead, it only created a fertile ground for a kind of government intervention very different from what they had bargained for.

The *Occupation of Space* and the *Occupation of Privacy:* When the Strategies Collide

As we have seen above, the precarious dominance of the Hollywood film producers in the studio era rested on two distinct strategies. While the *occupation of space* created the necessary conditions for the increase in speed and quantity of film production, the *occupation of privacy* regulated the much less tangible sphere of workers' and consumers' behavior outside the studios, stabilizing production and homogenizing demand. The producers solidified their position by creating the Hays Office, which institutionalized control over privacy by establishing strict self-censorship and surveillance codes of conduct for all industry participants. Despite continuous tensions between producers and merchants, these two processes seemed to work in concert in the interwar period, reinforcing the position of film manufacturers in the entertainment sector and enabling them to dominate the market with their continuous flow of product.

The inherently conflictual character of the *occupation of space* and the *occupation of privacy* came into the open only at the end of World War II. The problem was twofold. First, while the *occupation of space* clearly separated the spheres of public and private, politics and economics, work and leisure, the *occupation of privacy* inverted their relationship: the politicization of the sphere of everyday life turned privacy into a public matter and yet another "contested terrain" of the mass-production process. Secondly, and perhaps more importantly, the reliance on the *occupation of space* and the *occupation of privacy* also meant that self-regulation in the American film industry was directly proportional to the producers' territorial control over markets: the producers constantly and persistently purchased the expansion of the industry by extending self-regulation. Eventually, however, censorship and surveillance could not but collide with the proper functioning of the production process itself. Stifling creativity and censoring imagination, Hollywood was appropriately perceived as a quasi-totalitarian institution devoted to the transformation of the American dream, from the idea that all men are made equal to the idea that all men's dreams should be made equal.[80]

The catalyst which brought these tensions to the fore was the change in the relationship between the motion-picture industry and the U.S. government between 1938 and 1947. Not fully convinced that the state would take their side in the conflict with either labor or merchants, Hollywood producers preferred to keep the Federal government at bay for as long as they could. Any threat of government interference into the industry mobilized film manufacturers into pre-emptive acts of self-regulation, taking them at once a step forward and a step back from their ideally self-contained business community. But the Roosevelt administration's New Deal policies and the war strengthened the traditionally weak federal institutions and transformed the state into a relatively, if not completely, autonomous actor. The state ceased to act only and exclusively on behalf of special interests, and that made its acts much more difficult to predict or pre-empt. Hollywood producers experienced the change fairly quickly. In 1938, Arnold Thurman, head of the Anti-Trust Division at the U.S. Department of Justice, filed a suit against Hollywood major companies and asked for their divorce from the first-run theaters. Unlike before, independent theater owners figured only as witnesses, albeit very important ones, in this investigation. From the perspective of Hollywood producers this meant that the issues of monopoly and control in the motion-picture industry could no longer be avoided and that they had to enter into negotiations directly with the government.

Two other government decisions from the late 1930s had a profound effect on the habitual *modus operandi* of Hollywood studios. In 1937, the Supreme Court upheld the Wagner Act and the right of workers to organize. So in June of 1938, the producers had to recognize the Screen Writers Guild in addition to the already recognized Screen Actors and Screen Directors Guilds. In 1941, the Screen Writers Guild finally set up shop in Los Angeles. At about the same time, the Californian Assembly and the U.S. Treasury Department started an investigation into the relationship between organized crime and the Hollywood craft unions. In 1941, charges of extortion were finally pressed against William Browne and Willie Bioff, who ran the Hollywood craft workers, as well as against Joseph Schenk, head of Twentieth Century Fox, for giving a bribe to the mobsters as an insurance payment for industrial harmony. Although the infiltration of unions by the mob was no surprise to the Hollywood community, the actual charges still came as a shock. They also created the circumstances for the organization of the first truly independent crafts union—the Conference of Studio Unions—whose charismatic leader Herbert Sorrell soon turned into the nightmare of Hollywood moguls.

Finally, between 1938 and 1940, a newly formed congressional committee on un-American activities made several forays into Hollywood based on unsubstantiated claims that the industry was a "hotbed of communism." Initially, industry leaders gently pushed the investigators away. "Investigate Us—We're Clean," announced the major studios in *Variety*'s headline in August of 1940.[81] Somewhat more decidedly, the producers rejected the Senate attack on the overly pro-interventionist content of their films in 1941. In 1947, however, when the House Committee on Un-American Activities (HUAC) came back to Los Angeles, this time headed by J. Parnell Thomas, a Republican from New Jersey, the producers were far more accommodating. On November 24th and 25th of 1947, following the Committee's decision to cite with contempt the ten subpoenaed writers and producers who had refused to testify about their own and their friends' political activities, the producers met at the Waldorf-Astoria in New York. The statement produced at that meeting said that Hollywood moguls would not re-employ any of the Hollywood Ten until they purged themselves of contempt and declared under oath that they were not Communists. In addition, the producers guaranteed that they "will not knowingly employ a Communist or a member of any party or group which advocates the overthrow of the Government of the United States." The open-endedness of the last statement—of what exactly "knowingly" meant in the general climate of the "red scare"—laid the foundation for the Hollywood blacklisting period and significantly contributed to the decline of the Hollywood studio system.

The blacklist represented the ultimate limit of Hollywood's self-regulation and the trade-off between *occupation of space* and *occupation of privacy*. Once again, Hollywood producers tried to maintain their control over the industry by transposing their economic problems onto the issues of content and privacy. The studios negotiated with the state in the same way in which they had once negotiated with the theater owners—by expanding the spheres of self-censorship and surveillance. The Waldorf statement—while forthcoming—essentially promised that the studio leaders would extend their control over all of their employees—not just those who had a celebrity status—to include their political activities and that they would continue to police the content of their movies to include ideology and not just the morals of the country. By entering into a Faustian bargain with the state, Hollywood moguls were hoping that they would ensure the state's assistance in opening foreign markets while, at the same time, limiting the power of the independent unions and guilds in Hollywood itself.

The dual strategy had its roots in the wartime cooperation between Hollywood and the U.S. Government. Operating under the Damocles sword of anti-trust litigation and labor unrest, the studio moguls decided to endear themselves to the state and enlisted the industry in Roosevelt's war effort. Throughout the war, major Hollywood stars, writers, and directors—from Humphrey Bogart to Frank Capra—worked for Washington's Office of War Information. The Hays Office cooperated closely with the State Department, and Hays himself insisted upon the importance of the motion-picture industry in international relations. The growing importance of foreign markets—where the industry was hoping it would unload the glut of its product from the war years—became apparent in 1945, when Hollywood pro-

Stephen Goosson designed sets for Frank Capra's *Lost Horizon* (Columbia Pictures, 1937). The exterior set of Shangri-La, the Lamary where time stood still and Bauhaus-inspired designs encountered Tibet, was built on the Columbia ranch in Burbank, California. Courtesy of the Museum of Modern Art, New York.

ducers replaced William Hays with Eric Johnston, former U.S. Secretary of Commerce. Soon after taking office, Johnston formed the Motion Picture Producers and Distributors Export Association—or MPDEA—the key export arm of the industry with its main office in Washington.

Yet the effects of Hollywood patriotism were somewhat different than the moguls had expected, as the politicization of content as a way of securing control over the industry again brought pressures for increased government regulation. The Department of Justice proceeded with anti-trust investigation, and, in 1947, after a series of appeals and counter-appeals, the Supreme Court decision required the studios to divest from their first-run theaters. The end of the war also unleashed suppressed labor problems. Much like the rest of America, the studios found themselves in the midst of strikes, some of which—such as the protracted CSU strike at Warner Bros.—eased only when the Los Angeles police used tear gas and water guns against the strikers. Most important, the overt links between the film industry and Washington placed Hollywood in the midst of a conservative backlash against Roosevelt's New Deal policies and finally proved that show business was not just sheer entertainment, as Hollywood moguls had usually argued. Since the industry was and could be a very efficient tool of political propaganda, there was no reason why it could not be subject to communist infiltration.

The blacklisting era in Hollywood revealed all the ambiguities and limitations of the producers' strategy and their ideal of Hollywood as "controlled institution." The progressive *occupation of privacy* and an increasing control over content stifled creativity and separated Hollywood producers from their audiences. The blacklist did not—and that may have been its most peculiar aspect—truly prevent the Communist "infiltrators" from working in the industry and may not have even been designed to do so. Between 1947 and 1951, seven screenwriters from the "Hollywood Ten" still worked for the studios under pseudonyms. And although the situation became much harder after 1951, some of the most prominent names on the list continued to work on the "black market" throughout the entire period. The most notable case was Dalton Trumbo, whose scripts won Academy Awards under the pseudonym "Ronald Rich." But many other blacklisted artists wrote for television, using names of friends and friends of friends as aliases and hiring "fronts" who would do personal transactions such as contract signing and story conferencing on their behalf. And, on more than one occasion, studio bosses pleaded with their most valuable assets to "purge" themselves and cooperate with the Committee or to give the names of people who had already been named. There were speculations that in some cases the studios even "paid" for the clearances of their talented employees although no proofs of bribery had ever been established.

What the blacklist did accomplish was to destroy any hope of independent unionism in Hollywood for decades to come and to create an atmosphere of fear and mediocrity, which inevitably reflected itself on the quality of the Hollywood product. The number of openly anti-Communist films was relatively small, even if we include all the science-fiction films about alien invasion which were the most prominent new genre of the 1950s. But the number of social and psychological dramas dramatically decreased.

At the same time, imports soared. While Hollywood producers, still constrained by the overly zealous Breen Office, retreated into the safety of biblical dramas and Doris Day comedies, European and Japanese films appeared both politically and sexually liberating. Needless to say, despite all the efforts of the State Department to open markets for Hollywood, American movies lost ground to domestic product in most European countries. Forced to make a choice between the *occupation of space* and the *occupation of privacy*, Hollywood studios opted for control over privacy: they dispersed production, mostly to Europe, and turned toward technology and distribution as ways to keep them afloat. By the end of the 1950s, the industry was increasingly dominated by merchants and increasingly similar to the motion-picture industry at the turn of the century, before its revolutionary settlement in Hollywood.

THIS CHAPTER examined the rise and the fall of the studio system, the Hollywood equivalent of mass production, from a slightly different perspective than the one usually employed by either political economists or film historians. Although most analyses of the rise and fall of the studio system implicitly or explicitly focus on the temporal advantages and disadvantages inherent in mass production, the explanation offered in this chapter focused instead on the spatial, and hence, social aspects of the studio system.

In particular, I have argued that the studio system was a manufacturer/producer dominated system, and that their producers' power mostly depended on two strategies that I have metaphorically called the *occupation of space* and the *occupation of privacy*. In contrast to the merchant-dominated economy, which was prevalent in the United States until the turn of the century and which relied on dispersed production and centralized distribution, manufacturers concentrated production in the newly constructed greenfield factories. The new industrial architecture—the *occupation of space*—enabled producers to control the flow of production and maximize its speed. At the same time, however, it also created barriers between the private and public spheres, production and consumption, work and leisure. Therefore, in order to maintain their dominance in mass production, producers complemented the *occupation of space* with the *occupation of privacy*, creating more or less subtle mechanisms which helped them oversee the private lives of their workers and their consumers. Film manufacturers went a step further than their counterparts did in other industrial sectors in creating the institutions of social control. Their intricate and elaborate system of self-regulation combined an "industry of desire," the star system, with censorship and surveillance, giving them an unprecedented degree of control over the industry, their workers, and their audiences.

But producers, preoccupied with achieving and sustaining the economies of time, overlooked the inherent contradictions of the two strategies. The *occupation of space* and the *occupation of privacy* eventually collided in the aftermath of World War II. Throughout the studio era, Hollywood producers purchased the expansion of the industry by stepping up the elements of self-regulation. At the end of World War II, faced with labor unrest and unstable markets, Hollywood producers again tried to expand control over the industry by trading the private lives of their workers for the chance to expand their foreign markets, and, in order to do so, entered into a Faustian bargain with the state. The period of blacklisting, instigated by the congressional investigation into the anti-American, communist activities of Hollywood workers, represented the climax of the producers' reliance on censorship and surveillance. At the same time, because it resulted in a mediocre and sterile product, the blacklist also represented the beginning of the end of the producers' dominance. Finally forced to make a choice between the *occupation of space* and the *occupation of privacy*, producers abandoned their control over space. By export-ing production outside of the United States, producers created a chance for the merchants to regain their lost powers, thus starting a new cycle of tensions between manufacturers and merchants, time and space, public and private—all of which we shall investigate in more detail in the next chapter.

II. HOLLYWOOD ON LOCATION

We sell space, not fantasy.

Harry Friedman, President of the "runaway" studio,
The Studios in Las Colinas, Texas (Forbes, January 30, 1984, 60)

Ford Motor Co. meets Hollywood on location at Monument Valley, Utah. On the set of John Ford's *Stagecoach* (Walter Wanger Productions, 1939). Courtesy of the Museum of Modern Art, New York.

At the height of the blacklisting era, Hollywood producers started abandoning the safety of their studios, going places and taking film productions far away from Southern California. As production units scattered from Pinewood studios in London to Cinecittà in Rome, and from remote villages in Spain to the deserts of Morocco and Egypt, Hollywood itself became less and less important as the locus of film manufacturing. Instead, between the early 1960s and early 1980s, it became a place of lunch dates, handshakes, and deal-making, a site of cyclical TV production, fading stars, and tourist attractions.

Hollywood's declining geographical importance was a symptom of the inversion of power relations that had prevailed in Hollywood during the studio era. Increasing spatial distances—between Hollywood moguls and their crews on location around the world, between producers and their audiences, between labor, creative talent, and studio management—eroded the institutions of censorship and surveillance upon which the producers had relied throughout the studio era. At the same time, the re-introduction of *economies of space* into the entertainment economy created opportunities for merchants—distributors, financiers, and agents—to capitalize on producers' failures and assert their influence both within and outside the corporate hierarchies.

The ascent of movie merchants, which started off in the immediate postwar period but really peaked in the 1980s, reflected itself in the emergence of new, horizontally integrated corporate forms, in new transnational alliances between distributors and financial capital, and in new formulas for the appropriation of workers' and consumers' privacy. Most importantly, the rise of merchants resulted in a new social geography of entertainment production that further weakened the producers. The fragmentation and competition of places of production and their attempts at micro-regulation and spatial differentiation have, thus far, only succeeded in strengthening the merchants' position in the global economy.

This last aspect of the new media and entertainment industry—its very transparent spatialization—seems particularly important since it represents the key point of distinction between the manufacturers' economy of the Hollywood studio era and the contemporary merchant economy. The Hollywood studio system, as we have seen in the second chapter, was centered around time and economies of speed. The spatial dimensions of the studio system remained hidden by the very fact that production was localized and centralized within the studios themselves. Not surprisingly, it was the neglected contradictions produced by the spatial organization of production that eventually brought the studio system to its end.

The merchant economy, on the other hand, is both spatially expansive and highly conscious of its own spatiality; a glance through the current economic literature easily lends itself to the conclusion that time and speed no longer play any role in the economy, that the whirlwind of capital mobility has finally abolished the time barrier, and that regionalization, "localisms" and diversity represent both the only remaining limit to globalization and its greatest asset. Merchants, unlike manufacturers, are not necessarily trying to smooth out spatial differences and homogenize workers and consumers. Rather, they appropriate and commodify their distinctive characteristics and position themselves as the quintessential middlemen who thrive on the variance in their environment. But, just as space represented the ultimate barrier of the manufacturers' economy, the greatest obstacle for the further expansion of merchant domination may indeed be time and the diachronic aspects of the world which economies of space have attempted to exclude: the continued struggle over the pace of work, labor discipline, and historical aspects of places and identities which the merchants have commodified.

This chapter paints a picture of these changes with several broad strokes. The first part of the chapter will focus on the relocation of the U.S. film industry in the 1950s and 1960s and the devastating consequences that the creation of the global film factory had on the position of Hollywood moguls and producers in the entertainment industry. The second part examines the rise of merchants—distributors, financiers, and agents—and the establishment of formal and informal transnational links among them which have enabled them to dominate the industry. The third part of the chapter looks into the relationship between this grid of merchant power in the global entertainment industry and the competition among the new places and zones of production or, in other words, into the dynamics between space and place, global capital and decentralized production. Finally, the fourth part of the chapter discusses the often-mentioned fear of cultural homogenization in the age of global entertainment and presents an alternative danger—the increasing commodification of cultural products and personal lives as the key consequence of the reaffirmation of merchant power in the global economy.

EVERY YEAR SINCE 1985, Los Angeles has been the host of the most peculiar market of landscapes. Location Expo, as the market is known, is the annual showcase of states, cities, and counties that offer themselves to Hollywood as possible sites of film production. Between 1975 and 1999, membership in the International Association of Film Commissioners—and the number of exhibitors at Locations Expo—has risen from just a handful of film offices to more than three hundred film commissions in the United States and overseas. Most film commissions, public and private, are tied to state economic development offices or local chambers of commerce and offer similar services to attract film productions to their state—governors' airplanes, luxury hotel suits, free-of-charge location scouting services, and an amiable workforce. Some states also include tax subsidies and incentives for film productions, and some local film commissioners are willing to bend over backwards to satisfy the whims of filmmakers, offering to change river flows, grow crops on barren fields, or remove telephone poles so they don't distract camera moves and angles.

Yet the most interesting aspect of these marketing campaigns is the fact that film commissions do not necessarily stress the unique and authentic characteristics of the localities—the historical landmarks, climate, and beauty of their landscapes—but rather cite their ability to stand in for other places. Thus, the greater Cincinnati film commission offers "everything from an urban tenement area that has doubled for Harlem in the 1950s, Manhattan and Queens in the 1940s, Chicago in the late 1910s and the present-day New Jersey, to sprawling rural farmland and estates";[1] Vancouver is praised as "the biggest backlot in America with so many different looks that it can double for almost anywhere in the United States";[2] Toronto officials are happy that the city has withstood the test as Manhattan, Chicago, Pittsburgh, a fictional town in rural Pennsylvania called Dunston, and "any-city USA";[3] and the state of Israel offers American filmmakers a "unique opportunity to cast actors and extras from its population representing ethnic types of Europeans, Africans or Asians of all ages and backgrounds."[4]

Like most simple texts, these miscellaneous advertisements which film commissions use to lure Hollywood producers into their territories demand that we pause and carefully ponder their assumptions. What they unwittingly seem to reveal is an aspect of the new entertainment economy which is not frequently discussed in relation to Hollywood, its global dominance, and the alleged American cultural imperialism: a profoundly unstable—both politically and theoretically—relation between culture, power, and place in contemporary world economy.[5] By proudly presenting themselves as "any place, any time," film commissions openly contradict simultaneous efforts of their governments to protect local cultures from the onslaught of Hollywood products; indeed, if we were to judge by these advertisements, successful integration into the global entertainment economy would hardly depend on the protection of history, tradition, cultural heritage, or geography—all that we usually mean by "place." Instead, as the elements of self-creation and self-negation that transpire through these marketing campaigns seem to imply, the path towards participation in global cultural production depends precisely on the ability of places to successfully suppress their uniqueness and painlessly transform themselves into *whoever, whatever, whenever* sites. It is as if the new entertainment economy transforms our entire world not only into its studio, as a Time Warner annual report from a few years back proudly announced, but into an Epcot Center where it is possible to travel through time and space without ever moving away from Orlando.

Obviously then, much like most other industrial sectors, the world entertainment industry has been characterized by two divergent processes over the past two decades. On the one hand, the resurgence of Hollywood's dominance in world markets and the growing concern over the loss of national culture(s) outside the Unites States have placed the film industry in the midst of global trade debates and discussions about the relationship between (homogenizing) global and (endangered) local cultures. The renewal of the "American challenge" in the cultural sphere has thus far provoked a political struggle between Europe and the United States over trade in audio-visual products at the Uruguay round of GATT talks; mobilized filmmakers, politicians, and intellectuals from France to Canada against the Americanization of their culture(s); and led to the exclusion of culture industries from NAFTA. At the same time, the less-examined exodus of film production from the traditional U.S. film center—Los Angeles—to various right-to-work states in the American South, or to countries like Canada and Australia, has mobilized Hollywood directors, actors, and unions to seek, from their own state and federal governments, protection from further hemorrhaging of jobs and wages from Los Angeles. In the summer of 1999, provoked by devastating findings of a study commissioned by the Directors Guild of America and the Screen Actors Guild,[6] a newly organized labor committee has been conducting a full-fledged campaign to protect Hollywood jobs by organizing protests in Sacramento and Hollywood and by buying full-page ads in Hollywood trade papers which bluntly demand: *Bring Hollywood Home.*[7]

But when did American industry leave home? Those who know the history of American business know quite well that this is not a recent phenomenon. The relocation of U.S. manufacturing in the postwar

period—first to Europe and then to numerous Third World countries—
has been a subject of debate among political economists and the source
of serious political tensions both inside and outside the United States
for decades.[8] For some, the move was a simple and clear case of American imperialism, and they viewed the arrival of U.S. multinational
corporations in distant parts of the world as a prime example of renewed Western colonialism.[9] For others, the relocation of production
was a defensive strategy of U.S. manufacturers who could no longer
compete with lower labor costs abroad, particularly not in the sectors
which had already started sliding downwards on their product cycle.[10]
In both cases, however, the assumption was that the goal of relocation was to enhance the profits and the power of American manufacturers, and that the principle vehicles of that expansion were still
economies of time, quantity production, and the relentless search for
new, homogenous, markets.

The construction of greenfield global factories, once again best exemplified by the American auto-manufacturers, supported such views.
The spatial diffusion of automobile production started off in the 1920s
when Ford Motor Company set up its assembly line plants in Brazil,
Denmark, Japan, Venezuela, and a dozen other countries, as well as
complete manufacturing plants in the United Kingdom, France, Germany, Canada, and Australia.[11] In the aftermath of World War II, when
manufacturing plants were also set up in Argentina and Brazil, the
overall output of the foreign-based subsidiaries of U.S. automakers increased to such an extent that in 1957—for the first time in history—
the value of car imports exceeded the value of exports.[12] The main
characteristic of these operations was that each manufacturing plant—
much like Ford's plants in the United States—contained the entire
production line, manufacturing cars from A to Z. Although rarely put
into practice, the system—at least in theory—allowed for the production of entirely different cars in each country.

In the second phase, however, which evolved as a clear strategy only
after the oil shocks of the 1970s, the guiding principle of American
auto-makers became the so-called "world car" concept; the idea behind it being that production should be organized as a continuous flow
of interchangeable parts and products on a global scale. Sabel and Piore
have viewed this transnationalization of manufacturing as a micro-

economic substitute for the failure of macroeconomic efforts to re-
solve the problems of demand fluctuation in mass production.[13] In
their view, the dispersion of production was a way to secure
economies of scale, no longer attainable in the domestic market, by
producing goods that could be simultaneously sold in a number of national markets. Yet, as Erica Schoenberger has written, the basic premise behind this market expansion—or, more precisely, its precondition—was the mastery of time inherent in the mass-production
process.[14] The control over time, and the control over the continuous
flow of production, she notes, gave manufacturers an unusual degree
of spatial freedom: for as long as the same, or even interchangeable,
products or parts could be produced at two different sites at the same
time, manufacturers presumed that the distance between them had
little or no bearing on the functioning of the system as a whole. That
is why the dispersion of production could seem such an attractive solution to the problems of wage differentials and overproduction, which
had plagued mass production from its earliest days, and that is why
economies of time could seem to be the driving force behind the relocation of U.S. manufacturing overseas.

This very plausible argument, however, neglects to notice that both
place and space have actually played an extremely important role in
the postwar dispersion of production. Whether it was in response to
lower wages or to the closing of foreign markets, the relocation of U.S.
production overseas was also a response to the particulars of certain
places and was hostage to significant spatial distances. The introduction of protectionist measures, for instance, either at home or abroad,
has always represented a re-introduction of territoriality or, indeed,
of the primacy of territoriality into the economy. By carving a place
out of the time-space continuum created and required by mass production, postwar regulation in Europe, and later on in the Third World,
intended to protect local producers (and their own economies of time)
but gradually transformed the location site of the plant into an economic factor of equal, if not greater, importance than time.

At the same time, however, the newly created distances—between
headquarters and overseas subsidiaries and between managers, manufacturers, and their intended markets and customers—also led to numerous hidden costs. Sabel and Piore note some of them: unpredictable

threats and demands of host-country governments, difficulties in quality and inventory control, fluctuations in demand and exchange rates, and perennial labor unrest aggravated by cultural and linguistic differences.[15] The common denominator seems to be just one: the breakdown of the manufacturers' ability to monitor the continuous flow of production and/or govern the production process and, consequently, the substitution of economies of time for economies of space.

Hollywood Goes on Location

The dispersion of American film production in the postwar period followed a similar pattern and encountered similar problems to those encountered by other U.S. manufacturers. Although the origins of the motion-picture industry lay in dispersed production—newsreels and documentary accounts from "real" life collected on travels around the world—location shooting nearly vanished from Hollywood during the studio era. With few exceptions—John Ford, for instance, shot several Westerns in Monument Valley—major studios shot most of their films in the studios themselves or on ranches that they had purchased in the vicinity of Hollywood. Art directors replicated even the most exotic locations inside the studios, while Malibu beaches often stood in for the Docks of Dover and the French Riviera. Only when they felt particularly generous did Hollywood moguls send a second unit to the actual location. Such "original" shots made in Europe or Africa were then used in rear projection or freely interspersed with material filmed on studio backlots. In both cases, however, the studios recycled them over and over in numerous other productions.

The reasons for this spatial conservatism were clear. Shooting on location was prohibitively expensive and Hollywood moguls understood very well the risks inherent in "production away from home." Location wages were much higher than in Los Angeles. Labor unions frequently posed demands that could be ignored in Hollywood but had to be satisfied on location.[16] The pressure and intensity of the work often brought to the surface personal conflicts and attractions among the actors, making it difficult for producers and directors to supervise their interactions. Even the most trivial extraneous factors such as weather or noise could easily ruin numerous hours and sometimes days of shooting. Not surprisingly, throughout the studio era, Hollywood producers preferred to stay as close to home as possible. Location shooting, paradoxically, remained a privilege of small, low-budget, independent producers who found the costs of studio rentals even more prohibitive than the costs of filming in the deserts outside of Los Angeles.[17]

Thus, it took a powerful combination of push and pull factors in the aftermath of World War II to induce Hollywood producers to go on location. Some were related to the promise of greater creative— and financial—freedoms. Changes in the U.S. postwar tax structure made it more profitable for stars and directors to set up their own "shop," particularly abroad, and to act as "independent producers." Technological change (better sound recording, faster film, and more portable cameras) made location shooting easier, and a number of filmmakers—driven by a desire to explore the world and influenced by the "realism" of their European colleagues—ventured outside the confines of the studios in search of authenticity. With no special ties to the physical plants in Hollywood, they hoped that filming away from both the studios and their management would bring them limitless artistic freedom. Sometimes it worked. Films such as *Lady from Shanghai* (1948), *On the Waterfront* (1954), *Asphalt Jungle* (1950), and *Viva Zapata* (1952) still serve as prime examples of the increasing realism in American films and the highly creative utilization of "real life" backgrounds from the 1950s.[18]

But far more important than the power of creativity was the power of the purse. The transformation of Hollywood from a company town into a global factory, which started in the early 1950s, was directly related to increasing labor costs at home and the need to safeguard markets abroad. The attempts of craftsmen to establish independent unions failed in the 1940s but left an indelible trace on labor-management relations in Hollywood. Throughout the 1950s, Hollywood labor became increasingly restive and costly. Despite a significant decrease in employment, Hollywood craftsmen and extras could no longer compete with their overseas counterparts. Wages for the building trades increased on average 150 percent between 1945 and 1961. Even the evasive estimates of Hollywood unions stated that wages in Europe were approximately 50 percent lower than in the United States; and, in countries such as Egypt and Hong Kong, wages were less than one tenth of U.S. wages.[19] The unions' struggle for health and pension benefits resulted in the establishment of the Pension Fund in 1953 and the Motion Picture Health and Welfare Fund in 1959 and made prospective Hollywood productions even more costly. The request of talent guilds for royalties and fees from T.V. fees and overseas earnings led, in 1960, to one of the longest strikes in Hollywood's history. The guilds lost the rights to all pre-1948 films, but they successfully paralyzed the industry for more than six months and revealed the extent to which the industry was still susceptible and vulnerable to strikes. Finally, at the time of blacklisting in Hollywood, when biblical motifs and historical spectacles became increasingly popular among Hollywood producers as politically safe subjects, countries such as Italy, Spain, Egypt, and Yugoslavia provided locations and thousands of extras almost for free. Samuel Bronston filmed his historical extravaganzas in Spain employing as many as 7,000 extras on some of his productions; Italy hosted a whole series of spectacles—from *Quo Vadis* (1951) to *Ben Hur* (1959) and *Cleopatra* (1963); while Yugoslavia readily supplied its army for any historical war film that Hollywood could imagine.[20]

And while increasing labor costs and strikes in Hollywood threatened the continuous flow of production, Hollywood was also confronting a crisis in its export markets. At the end of World War II, Hollywood majors found themselves in a situation analogous to that of many other American industries—they had an oversupply of war-time products that they wanted to release in Europe and Asia, but they faced closed and impoverished foreign markets. In the general climate of post-war uncertainty and the dearth of foreign currency, films were an obvious luxury and most European—and not only European—governments instituted a combination of quotas, tariffs, and capital restrictions to prevent an excessive import of American films and to protect their local producers.[21] Yet successful lobbying on the part of the State Department and the fear of local theater owners that they would be left with no reliable supply of product transformed the import restrictions into a combination of blocks on American earnings, on the one hand, and government subsidies to stimulate local production, on the other.[22]

The extravagance of Hollywood on location was best exemplified by Samuel Bronston's productions in Spain. At the time, it was widely rumored that entire Spanish villages lived off Bronston's filmmaking largesse. Here, a sign for Bronston City during the location shooting of *El Cid* (Allied Artists, 1961). Courtesy of the Museum of Modern Art, New York.

Paradoxically, European governments treated local subsidiaries of foreign companies as "domestic" producers and allowed the Americans to benefit from their funding programs. The most prominent example of this peculiar subsidy scheme was the so-called Eady Levy in Great Britain which transferred a certain percentage of box-office receipts back into the joint Producers Fund. Since all Hollywood studios had distribution offices in London, they could easily qualify for the Fund's subsidies. Thus, although the exact impact of subsidies may be difficult to estimate, Britain became the favorite location of

Hollywood producers, accounting for more than 30 percent of total U.S. overseas production between 1949 and 1961.[23] During the 1950s and 1960s, between 80 percent and 90 percent of British films were produced with American backing, and British studios such as Elstree and Pinewood served as home ground for numerous U.S. productions.[24] The extent of American involvement in the British film industry in the 1960s was such that the Government-operated National Film Finance Corporation declared in 1967 that the financial involvement of U.S. companies was not only welcome, but that "Without it, indeed, there would scarcely be a film industry here."[25]

Therefore, by the early 1960s, the exodus of U.S. manufacturing production abroad, and particularly to Europe, had reached such proportions that it raised serious concerns on both sides of the Atlantic. In 1961, the House Committee on Education and Labor held special hearings on the impact of imports and exports on American employment, the first official debate on the phenomenon which would later become known as the "hollowing-out" of the national economy.

The hearings also brought to Washington representatives of the Motion Picture Producers Association and Hollywood unions. The debate mostly centered around the definition of the term "runaway production." The unions expressed their reasonable concern over the outflow of production from Hollywood, claiming that the number of U.S. productions abroad had tripled between 1949 and 1960 and had severe consequences on employment levels in the motion-picture industry.[26] Eric Johnston, MPAA president, argued, on the other hand, that the loss of film jobs was more than compensated for by an increase in TV production in Hollywood. According to Johnston, the term "runaway" was inaccurate as it implied that "production pulled out and left the workers stranded." Instead, said Johnston, overseas production was "supplemental international production" which "provided additional income and jobs in the United States."[27] Among the reasons for the increase in overseas productions, Johnston listed the search for authentic locales, good relations with foreign countries, frozen funds and foreign subsidies. Unions, on the other hand, sought reasons for "runaway productions" in foreign subsidies and U.S. tax exemptions, and they requested domestic subsidies and tax reform to remedy ailing local production. Interestingly enough, both sides seemed reluctant to mention the rising cost of labor and contentious nature of the labor-management relations in Hollywood as possible stimuli for "runaway" production.

Thus, at least on the surface, the dispersion of American film production around the world seemed to benefit Hollywood moguls and producers immensely. By relocating production abroad, Hollywood producers were hoping to gain access to their blocked earnings, docile and cheap labor, and substantial foreign subsidies, while avoiding all the accumulated problems at home. Nonetheless, profits in the American film industry continued to decline throughout the 1950s. The spatial expansion of production reduced the ability of Hollywood producers to both monitor the flow of production and control expenditures incurred on location. Hence, despite obvious cost-advantages of filming abroad, the average cost of films produced outside of the United States turned out to be higher than the cost of films produced in Hollywood.[28]

This discrepancy stemmed from two factors. Location shooting generally reduced the so called "below the line" costs—extras, craftsmen, and skilled workers such as musicians—but "above the line costs," the costs related to creative talent—story, director, stars, and character actors—were supposed to be the same as in Los Angeles. In actuality, however, the latter costs were much higher on location since producers had to pay travel expenses, accommodation, and often excessive per diems for their "above the line" workers. The second reason was related to a combination of frozen funds and local subsidies. Since their earnings were not otherwise available to them, Hollywood producers tried to spend as much on location as they could, indulging in largesse unimaginable even by the standards of the Hollywood Golden Age. Consequently, films produced on location frequently went over budget and resulted in serious losses for their production companies. Although an underestimated phenomenon, particularly nowadays when most films are produced outside of Hollywood, it may be interesting to note in this context that all the major Hollywood financial disasters—from *Ben Hur* (1925) to the most recent *Waterworld* (1995)—were shot on location.

One such production—the ill-fated Twentieth Century Fox production of *Cleopatra* which co-starred Elizabeth Taylor and Richard

Burton—exemplified all the problems inherent in location shooting and the extent to which Hollywood producers had depended on the appropriation of the privacy of their major stars in the studio era. The production of *Cleopatra*—mostly conducted in the Cinecittà studios in Rome—lasted four years and resulted in ninety-six hours of footage which cost between $60 million and $90 million. The inflated cost reflected a series of unpredicted and unpredictable disasters in production which ranged from the invasion of stray Roman cats on Cinecittà's studio lot to the illicit love affair between the film's main protagonists, Elizabeth Taylor and Richard Burton. The latter generated enormous, if undesired, publicity and allowed Twentieth Century Fox to exert exorbitant guarantees from theater owners, close to $15 million; request 70 percent of the box-office gross instead of the usual 50 percent; and increase the price of theater tickets three times to an unprecedented $5.50. However, despite all the media hype and nine Academy nominations, *Cleopatra* could not recuperate its costs: even as *the* box office hit of 1963 it grossed *only* $26 million, remaining to this day the most expensive film ever made.[29]

The *Cleopatra* debacle caused a management reshuffle at Fox and forced the owners to temporarily close down the studio, fire most of its personnel and sell the studio backlot in order to remain solvent. The debacle also produced a series of lengthy lawsuits. While Taylor and Burton sued the studio for withholding their share of profits and interfering in their personal affairs, the studio sued its stars for disruption of production and moral misconduct. Most importantly, *Cleopatra* usurped the principal convention of the studio era: it allowed for the intrusion of "real" life into the production process to such an extent that "reality" eventually overshadowed the film itself. As discussed in the previous chapter, one of the key aspects of the producers' power in the studio system was the quasi-monopoly on information about the industry personnel which they had enjoyed. In Hollywood proper, producers could control the flow of information about actors and directors in the press, hush up potential scandals or use them against those who were involved in them, and closely monitor the behavior of their employees off the set. Shooting on location, particularly abroad, made such control almost impossible. The arrival of Hollywood production companies in other parts of the world mobilized the local press and served as a continuous source of news, gossip, and trivia for their publications. The emergence of the paparazzi phenomenon—locust-like photographers for the tabloid press—was directly related to the relocation of Hollywood production to Europe in the 1950s. The scandals related to Hollywood stars such as those that occurred during the production of *Cleopatra*—illicit love affairs, illegitimate children, drug abuse, and alcoholism—easily found their way back into the United States, shaking Hollywood's presumed grip on public morality and the status of producers themselves.

Thus, ironically, at the same time when cooperation between Hollywood moguls and HUAC created a pretext for unprecedented intrusion into the private lives of Hollywood employees, and when location shooting served as the vehicle for biblical and historical epics with politically correct content, the relationship between public and private in the American film industry was completely inverted. In contrast to the fabricated and controlled narratives produced by the studios, the industry was increasingly dependent on the whimsical character of its talent. Unable to control either the off-screen affairs of their employees or the press coverage of their lives, producers often attempted to appropriate negative publicity and scandals in order to generate interest in their films. Yet although the financial remuneration and effectiveness of such campaigns were often just as successful as those of the tightly controlled studio press machine, the need to rely on actual events surrounding the shooting significantly reduced the ability of producers to manipulate reality. Instead, by the end of the 1950s and the beginning of the 1960s, Hollywood seemed to be a captive of reality itself in much the same way as the motion-picture pioneers had once relied on wars, coronations, royal weddings, and local scenery as sources of inspiration and to attract audiences to their screenings.

The diffusion of production and the opening of the post-war economy in general also undermined the more subtle instruments of the producers' power—the institutions of censorship and surveillance. Excursions from the former controlled environments of Hollywood studios into the messy and unpredictable world outside their gates could not leave the Breen's Office—the former Hays Office—unchanged. Just as the increased spatial distances decreased the ability of Hollywood

Production of *Cleopatra* (20th Century Fox, 1963) at Cinecittà Studios in Rome was mired with problems. The Italian Communist Party organized a boycott of the production because of alleged racial discrimination against "slave girls" on the set, while the "slave girls" themselves protested constant pinching by Italian technicians. Courtesy of the Museum of Modern Art, New York.

producers to control the interactions and the behavior of their employees, they also limited their power to censor and control the content of their films and to influence the formation of preferences of their audiences. By the mid-1960s, the industry leaders were quite aware that the old self-censorship code was curtailing their profit opportunities. The audiences were increasingly flocking to see European and Asian films which exhibited a far greater degree of sexual and political freedom and which Hollywood majors could neither produce nor distribute. Consequently, in 1968, the Production Code Administration was dismantled, and the rigid moral code was replaced with a much more flexible rating system. The latter divided audiences by age, and categorized films by the extent of sex, violence, and nudity in them and, as such, became the driving force behind new marketing techniques based on audience segmentation. Thus, with the abandonment of the Production Code Administration, producers also abandoned their ambitions to homogenize the markets and dominate the industry with a high volume of a relatively standard product.

Finally, both directly and indirectly, the dispersion of Hollywood production abroad helped the development of other national film industries and the creation, as U.S. economists would generally argue, of its own competition. Although the situation was somewhat more complex—the variety of inexpensive foreign films actually worked to the advantage of U.S. distributors—it is certain that Hollywood companies played an extremely important role in the transfer of industrial know-how from the United States to the rest of the world. The U.S. producers employed thousands of people—it is alleged that entire villages in Spain depended on Samuel Bronston's productions—but even more importantly, they frequently hired and trained locals to work as production aides and craftsmen. An entire generation of Italian, Spanish, and Yugoslavian film directors started their careers as gaffers, drivers, set designers, and sometimes even assistant directors on Hollywood productions and co-productions. To Europeans, whose own film industries never really got the chance to develop into mass production empires like Hollywood, Americans brought organization, systematization of tasks, specialization, and technical expertise which could only be acquired through a learning-by-doing process. As a result, by the beginning of the 1960s, America was importing more films than it was producing, and the once near-monopoly which Hollywood had over the supply of motion pictures for the world audience was gone.

Thus, the spatial expansion of Hollywood production in the 1950s and the early 1960s—originally designed to enhance the power of Hollywood producers—actually challenged their dominant position both in Hollywood and in the motion picture industry in general. Relocation of production in search of cheap labor and open markets eroded the very basis of the producers' power. Distance undermined the ability of producers to control the production process and, perhaps even more importantly, their workers and their audiences. The relocation of production abroad ended decades and decades of subtle *occupation of privacy* by Hollywood majors through their intricate and elaborate institutions of censorship and surveillance. By the end of the 1960s both America and the world were beaming with diverse and daring products, but Hollywood producers no longer dominated the industry.

The Rise of Hollywood Merchants

The dispersion of American film production abroad and the emergence of new film centers outside the United States initiated a period of industrial restructuring in the global entertainment complex whose consequences are still being felt. Decreasing profits of Hollywood majors, accumulated losses in production, and an increased reliance on *economies of space* rather than *economies of time* in the 1950s and 1960s undermined the power of producers in the motion-picture industry but greatly aided Hollywood's long neglected merchants—distributors, financiers, and agents. While ascending to a position of dominance in the entertainment industry, the merchants have completed a process of vertical disintegration which started with the divestment of the Hollywood majors from their theaters in 1949.[30] In the decades that followed, they have completely externalized production from the Hollywood majors, shed most of their old studio facilities, and engaged in relentless merger activity with other media companies. At the same time, the merchants have also created an informal network of power, which now entwines domestic and international distribution companies, financial capital, and the most powerful Hollywood agents. This new international orbit of merchant capital successfully excludes producers and those engaged in production from fair participation in profits and leads to an ever-increasing commodification of films and other cultural products.

The relationship between the establishment of these formal and informal networks of merchant power and the spatial reorganization of the economy may be best understood by the distinction which David Harvey makes between "appropriation" and "domination" of space.

According to Harvey, "appropriation" refers to the way in which space is occupied by objects such as houses or factories or by social and economic activities such as land use. Although Harvey does not mention Hollywood studios, their relation to space—with all the accompanying activities of spatial enclosure, reconstruction, and decomposition of the world within the confines of backlots and sound stages—would be an excellent example of such "appropriation." "Domination" of space, on the other hand, reflects the way in which groups or individuals influence "organization and production of space through legal or extra-legal means so as to exercise a greater degree of control either over the friction of distance or over the manner in which space is appropriated by themselves or others."[31] In other words, we could think of the domination of space as a grid, or a map, or a set of links superimposed over a space whose main task is to minimize the impact of distances and influence the way in which particular places are regulated, yet without—and this is very important—ever necessarily having to either control them overtly or literally appropriate them.

As mentioned, the creation of commercial networks in Hollywood and in the motion picture industry in general has taken two distinct paths since the late 1950s but both have aimed at spatial domination in Harvey's sense—that is, in both cases the merchants have tried to close the gaps between organizationally or physically distant and disparate places of production while simultaneously retaining the distance between themselves and the process of production. The first path was the path of corporate reorganization. Between the mid-1960s and mid-1980s, an alliance of Hollywood distributors and Wall Street traders completely reorganized the structure of Hollywood majors, turning them, as Rosabeth Moss Kanter would say, inside-out.[32] Accumulated losses in production and the divestment of Hollywood studios from the theaters undermined the credibility of Hollywood moguls, strengthened the role of distributors within corporate hierarchies, and aggravated relations between Wall Street and Hollywood. Thus, when declining corporate profits forced Hollywood moguls to leave the studios, they were replaced by the quintessential "office boys"—the men who understood well the intricacies of financing and sales but knew little and cared little about film production or about the films themselves. Not surprisingly, most of them had risen through corporate ranks from the distribution side of the industry, seizing on opportunities available in their environment as much as on the fact that their performance was completely untainted by failures in production. The interests of distributors coincided with the interests of the Wall Street community. Both held that the value of the Hollywood majors was eroding due to losses in production and that their assets—old movies whose "exchange" value had increased thanks to television and real estate in Hollywood and New York— made the studios far more valuable than they seemed on paper. In the early 1960s, new Hollywood managers turned to Wall Street in search of "white knights" who would be willing to buy and save the studios. They came back with an eclectic group of Wall Street traders whose diversified investments included funeral parlors, zinc production companies, parking lots, and significant parts of the Caribbean.[33] By the end of the 1960s all of the largest studios were parts of conglomerates and all fell under the controlling influence of Wall Street investors.[34]

Financiers and distributors transformed the studios from film production companies into global wholesalers of a wide range of media products—from films and TV series to comics, magazines, books, and themed entertainment. As soon as they took office, the new corporate owners stripped the studios of their production facilities, sold their backlots to Los Angeles real estate developers, or transformed them into parking lots, shopping malls, and theme parks. Sales of studio property and film libraries kept the studios afloat through the 1970s and early 1980s and essentially financed purchases in other distribution and related media companies.[35] The studios eliminated links with firms and businesses which had little in common with films and entertainment, ceased most of their in-house production, and supplanted them with links to cable and T.V. companies, publishers, theme park owners, and record companies. The mergers culminated over the past decade in the formation of Time/Warner, Viacom/Paramount, Sony/Columbia, Disney/ABC and MCA/Matsushita (later Seagram and then Vivendi) corporations; all were greatly aided first by somewhat dubious financial transactions on Wall Street and then by a significant infusion of international capital. Although many of the decisions made by the owners and the management of the Hollywood majors along the path of corporate restructuring may have been made in haste or haphazardly, they have all aimed at attaining the same goals—the centralization of distribution and the multiplication of distribution channels as well as an arm's-length separation from any direct involvement in the production process itself.

In addition to corporate restructuring and the development of marketing techniques, merchants have developed a second path toward the "domination of space." It involves the construction of a less formal, although by no means less binding, set of relations between the U.S. and overseas distributors and financiers. Corporate restructuring has aimed at overcoming organizational distances between different segments of the entertainment industry in order to both centralize control over the rights to a product and externalize production. The creation of a commercial network of international financiers and distributors is intended to simultaneously overcome and exploit the territorial barriers between different foci of production and fragmented overseas markets. Once again, the merchants have developed several schemes which all complement each other. The first scheme—limited partnerships—has strengthened the role of Hollywood majors as distributors/financiers. A major innovation from the 1970s and early 1980s, limited partnerships initially gave an opportunity to smaller individual investors to participate in the movie business. Between 1980 and 1990, almost all Hollywood studios established their own limited partnerships and some—such as Disney's Silver Screen I and II—attracted as many as 130,000 people by 1988.[36] However, while limited partnerships—in the financial world—usually work in such a way that individual investors provide a percentage of total production cost and, in return, expect to share in profits or losses on a proportional basis equal to their individual investment, Hollywood's limited partnerships became a source of interest-free credit financing for the studios. By relying on limited partnerships instead of short-term debt, it was estimated that Disney alone saved approximately $27 million through Silver Screen I and II between 1985 and 1990.[37] In addition, the studios, which held distribution rights for all the movies they financed, transferred the risk of financing to the investors and independent producers. While the producers were accountable for the losses, investors could expect only a share of "net" profits, which, in the movie business, were either non-existent or negligible.[38]

By 1988, investment magazines were rating motion-picture partnerships as a poor choice since they paid only a quarter of what regular money market accounts would pay.[39] In the early 1990s, Hollywood studios transferred their experience in domestic limited partnerships into foreign investment. Disney formed Touchwood Pacific Partners—a $600 million partnership—and lured Japanese to invest an additional $1 billion into it. In the "new deal," Disney's terms were even more favorable to the company itself: Touchwood promised to return to investors only 6 percent instead of 13 percent like Silver Screen, and investors were told in advance that they would not see much of their money until most of Disney's distribution costs were reimbursed. Other Japanese investments, in smaller Hollywood production companies, were structured in a similar way. Not surprisingly, Jeffrey Katzenberg, the head of Disney production until 1994, could offer the following evaluation of limited partnerships in general, and Touchwood in particular, in 1990: "The Silver Screen stands as the best financial investment vehicle ever created for movies. We wanted to make Silver Screen V. But when somebody comes and offers better terms, I have an obligation to the investors to take them. And if our movies are successful, the Japanese will get a good return."[40] Even less surprisingly, in mid-90s, the Japanese withdrew most of their funds from Hollywood and started shifting them to Europe. For even when the movies were successful—which they often were—the Japanese investors got little of their money back.

The other two schemes were relatively more complex. The second scheme engaged overseas distributors as financiers of international coproductions with a mix of foreign and U.S. creative talent (although actors usually tended to be American) and/or pre-sale agreements with major U.S. distributors/studios. Private TV stations and media companies—such as Canal Plus in France, Channel 4 in Britain, Kadokawa Publishing Company in Japan, Penta in Italy—would act as principal buyers of films so that their sales agreements could serve as collateral for the banks which actually lent the money. Such investments were further stimulated with fiscal incentives which, treating films as physical plants, allowed for generous tax write-offs in Europe and in Japan.[41] Consequently they brought into the movie business banks and corporations which previously had little connection with the film business—from Barclays in London to C. Itoh in Japan. This kind of financial arrangement—with local distributors as guarantors of investment—served a dual purpose. On the one hand, it nominally satisfied "local content" regulations which a number of foreign governments introduced in the 1970s to stimulate local production, protect the market, and ensure the transfer of "know-how." On the other hand, it allowed smaller, national distributors and TV stations to enter into the U.S. and world markets by using Hollywood studios as majority partners. As one of the first Japanese investors in Hollywood, Terry Ogisu, head of Sanrio, put it succinctly in 1977: "When you consider the fact that the American exhibition industry, even in what it considers a difficult and threatening time, represents more than half of the returns of the normal film, you confront the fact that Hollywood is the only portal to a truly world market."[42]

Finally, the third scheme reversed the relationship between distribution and finance by placing international financiers into the position of overseas distributors. The so-called pre-sale agreements allowed bankers, institutional investors, and a number of shady international financiers to invest in individual film productions by preselling films to local distributors around the world on a territory-by-territory basis. Allegedly, the strategy was an invention of Samuel Bronston who, in the late 1950s, financed a number of his nonexistent films by selling their rights to local distributors around the world.[43] It was perfected in the 1970s, when an abundance of petro-dollars on world markets made lending in general extremely profitable, and when flexible exchange rates gave international financiers yet another variable of territorial differentiation that they could exploit. Unlike the Hollywood majors, which usually used the cross-collateralization clause when selling their films overseas—i.e., the right to offset the losses in one territory with profits from another—and tended to standardize their overseas contracts, financiers engaged in pre-sale agreements negotiated their deals separately and tailored them to each particular country and each particular market in order to maximize their profits.[44] Particularly successful in such deals was the Netherlands branch of the French state-owned bank Credit Lyonnais. Starting in the early 1970s, Frans J. Afman, head of entertainment lending at the Rotterdam branch of Credit Lyonnais, began extending loans to independent filmmakers based on his familiarity with foreign distributors in Japan, the United Kingdom, Italy, Spain and Germany. By 1987, Afman had financed about 350 pictures and lent more than $2.5 billion to the industry since his first investments in the movie business for Slavenburg Bank—the movie-business predecessor of Credit Lyonnais—in the late 1970s.[45] Since Afman covered his loans in advance, he was able to be fairly indiscriminate in the choice of his clients. The latter included the largest independent companies of the 1980s—Canon, Carolco, Orion, and the Dino De Laurentis Group; a full range of producers and directors—from Oliver Stone and Merchant and Ivory to the producers of Bs such as *Assault of the Killer Bimbos* (1987) and *Sorority Babes in the Slimeball Bowl-O-Rama* (1988); and problematic characters such as Giancarlo Paretti, a temporary owner of MGM/Pathé corporation.[46] While stimulating production, Afman's deals left his clients empty-handed. Despite promises to the contrary, the majority of Afman's clients—having forfeited the distribution and ancillary rights to their films in exchange for production loans—made no profit even when the films were blockbusters such as *Terminator 2: Judgment Day* (1991). Hence, by the early 1990s almost all of them—particularly the production companies completely dependent on Afman's financing—had filed for bankruptcy.

The pivotal, even if less visible, role in most of these transactions was played by Hollywood agents. Despised in the studio era as "ten-percenters," and literally banned from the studio lots by Hollywood moguls in the NRA period, the agents' position improved tremendously with the advent of television and the breakdown of the studio system. The relationship between agents, stars and producers is probably the most obvious example of the inversion of power relations, which characterized the Hollywood studio era. As the studios abandoned long term contracts and the number of possible venues for their talent went up, the agents' opportunities for deal-making also increased. The control over directors, screenwriters and stars—key ingredients of the most lucrative pre-sale agreements in the film industry—gave agents a strategic advantage over other economic actors in the film industry. The establishment of so-called "package" deals in the 1960s, which allowed agents to become de facto producers of films, further enhanced their advantage. Through "packaging," agents assembled all the critical "above-the-line" talent for a film from a pool of their clients, and then offered them to producers on a take-it or leave-it basis. In an industry such as entertainment, where the success of production presumably depends on the right chemistry, packaging minimized the risk of putting together conflicting personalities. At the same time, it strengthened the role of agents in a way similar to the way in which block-booking practices strengthened the role of producers vis-à-vis independent theater owners in the studio era. By mixing bigger and lesser stars, the agents could easily force producers into accepting a much higher price for the entire package than they could ever obtain by negotiating each contract individually. Thus, by combining their knowledge of personalities and relationships with their concentrated ownership of critically important talent, talent agencies turned into "mini-studios" without ever owning even a bit of any production facility.

In the 1980s, agents extended their powers far beyond the pool of talent offered by their own agencies and diversified their activities. Positioning themselves as the quintessential Hollywood insiders, they offered their services to both international and domestic financiers who were willing to invest in Hollywood. By the late 1980s, the Creative Artists Agency (CAA) and its CEO, Michael Ovitz, had control over most of Hollywood's major stars, had brokered the Sony and Matsushita takeovers of Columbia and Universal respectively, and were acting as consultants to the largest American corporations with merchandising, licensing, and tie-in deals with Hollywood. Meanwhile, CAA's main competitor, International Creative Management (ICM), started offering financial advice and services to independent producers. Taking advantage of its greater pool of international clients and a better-developed network of overseas offices, ICM specialized in presale arrangements with overseas distributors.[47] Not surprisingly, according to most industry observers, no films in the 1980s and early 1990s could be made in Hollywood without substantial involvement of at least one of the two agencies.

In many respects, the interlocking of distributors', financiers', and agents' interests and powers has turned producers into the captives of merchant capital. In order to obtain financing and distribution for their films, independent producers have to surrender in advance their distribution and merchandising rights—either to the Hollywood studios or to local distributors overseas. In addition, if they are really interested in getting a distribution agreement before they start with production, the independent producers are more or less forced to get a talent "package" from one of the Hollywood agencies. Finally, even the directors and actors are frequently asked to forego their own rights—to foreign residuals, ancillary sales, and, sometimes, even to their own image—in order to secure a part in the production. Not surprisingly, the producers of some of the most profitable films ever—such as *The Terminator* (1984) and *Forrest Gump* (1994)—have actually registered losses after their films have become box-office hits. Similarly, attempts of some Hollywood studios to break out of the pattern and resume their old leadership role as film producers have failed spectacularly over the past decade. In the 1980s, both Columbia and Disney tried to bring production in-house, increase the number of films produced, cut budgets, and avoid stars. Although their strategy showed signs of success—in particular at Disney where formerly moribund film and animation departments became generators of growth under the leadership of Jeffrey Katzenberg—it was fairly short-lived. The increase in lower-budget production clashed with the interests of agents, distributors, and financiers to such an extent that it quickly resulted in management reshuffling and corporate reorientation towards distribution and merchandising as in most other Hollywood studios.

The attempts of producers to avoid "packaging" and limit the power of agents met with considerable resistance in Hollywood proper. In the mid 1980s, David Puttnam, a distinguished British producer whose credits included critically acclaimed films such as *Midnight Express* (1978) and *Chariots of Fire* (1981) came to the helm of Columbia Pictures, subsidiary of Coca Cola. Several weeks into his reign at Columbia, Puttnam gave a speech at the Los Angeles screening of *The Mission* (1986) in which he accused Hollywood agents and their well-established "packaging" practices of being responsible for the deteriorating quality of Hollywood's product and its escalating cost. "In Hollywood now," said Puttnam, "you are no longer shooting movies, you are shooting deals." Puttnam promised that he would try to reengineer Columbia back into its old fame and make it, once again, into the "production" site where most films would be generated in-house. Within months, Puttnam had the entire Hollywood establishment against him—Michael Ovitz, head of CAA; stars such as Dan Akroyd, Bill Murray, and Sigourney Weaver who had just finished *Ghostbusters* (1984) for Columbia; Dustin Hoffman and Warren Beatty who made *Ishtar* (1987); producer Ray Stark, *eminence grise* of many Hollywood studios; and Bill Cosby, *the* advertising star of Coca Cola. Fifteen months after he took over, David Puttnam was forced to leave Columbia. He subsequently turned to the Japanese to obtain financing for his new films, most of which have flopped in the United States.[48]

Similarly, through the 1980s, Jeffrey Katzenberg, then head of production at Disney, tried to reestablish the rules of Hollywood's Poverty Row at Walt Disney in hope that quantity production with no major stars would revitalize the company's fledgling film division. Katzenberg succeeded—and lost his job. Under Katzenberg, Disney established a pool of excellent yet "out of favor" actors such as Bette Midler, Richard Dreyfuss, and Nick Nolte and placed writers on long-term contracts. The company produced a number of forgettable mid-range films, which brought a steady flow of revenue, and a number of box office hits. Disney became known as the only studio in Hollywood not affected by "packaging." Despite frequent complaints about Katzenberg's rigidity and frugality, his experiment transformed the formerly moribund film and animation units into the generators of the company's growth. The success encouraged Katzenberg to write a twenty-eight-page internal memo about the "status of the industry" in January of 1991. In the memo, Katzenberg reaffirmed Disney's commitment to medium-cost films with no major stars; clearly stated that it was in Disney's interest to produce films which leave the studio as the sole proprietor of copyrights, licensing rights, and the rights to sequels; and urged the Disney employees to bring passion back into their work.[49] The memo, once leaked, created a scandal similar to Puttnam's speech. The company town interpreted the memo the way that it was supposed to—as an attack on agents' "packaging" and the star system. Katzenberg's loudly voiced opposition alienated him from Disney's CEO Michael Eisner who perceived Ovitz as a useful ally in dealing with Disney's Japanese investors, the refinancing of EuroDisney, and his own future plans for corporate expansion into new technologies. The memo precipitated Katzenberg's departure from Disney in 1994, while the appointment of Michael Ovitz as the president of the newly formed Disney/ABC media conglomerate sealed the power of Hollywood's traders.

New Geography of the Entertainment Industry

Obviously, the phenomenon of dispersed production is not unique to Hollywood. As the U.S. trade deficit continues to soar, and as the U.S. economy continues to grow, workers from the Rustbelt to the Sunbelt continue to fear that their jobs would soon be exported to Mexico, Canada, or to places such as Indonesia or Romania where labor is even cheaper. Business historians view this divergence as the symptom of "footloose" corporations, of an era in which an unprecedented mobility of capital and production has enabled corporations to constantly seek—and find—friendlier and friendlier business environments. Political scientists warn that the end result of this incessant corporate mobility and insatiable desire of places to attract businesses to their locations may be the "competitive state" and the ultimate "race to the bottom" in terms of wages, jobs security, taxes, and weakening union power. Many of these discussions—in Hollywood as well as in other industrial sectors—can be subsumed under another highly contested debate among political economists and cultural theorists: the debate about globalization and its impact on smaller units of social organization. In fact, the changes in the film and media industries in the 1970s and 1980s may be the best place to unravel the discussion about the effects of globalization on states, regions, and localities. The hope that globalization, and globalization of the media industries in particular, could bring about a borderless world and create citizens of the world seems perfectly matched only by the fear that global markets will, at worst, eradicate the particulars of local cultures and undermine the sovereign powers of nation states or, at best, recreate some combination of medieval city-states and Christendom on a new global level.[50]

Many analytic approaches, however, shy away from both of these extremes and focus instead on the mechanisms of interaction between global and local, usually arguing that space and place, global and local, represent two sides of the same coin. Thus, liberal economists are paying increasing attention to the relationship between international trade and regional industrial specialization and, in the process, rediscovering the links between economy and geography.[51] From their perspective, regional agglomeration of industries, external economies of scale, and a mix between path dependency and micro-regulation of economy, which could create more conducive business environments, are frequently offered as the optimal economic solutions for a world of constant capital flux and mobility.

Critical political economists—although approaching the problem from a different perspective—are also inclined to see the global-local nexus as the central problem of a new economic order. According to David Harvey, the main characteristic of the capitalist economy—the increasing time-space compression—reduces the importance of physical distances but increases the importance of place as an institutional and regulatory environment.[52] Similarly, Roland Robertson writes that local and global are always reflected in each other: while national economies, urban architecture, and local governments seem to succumb to the pressures of international capital mobility, global developers and communication technology, the aspects of local and "ethnic" are simultaneously appearing in postmodern architecture, heightened sensitivity towards "community," and even in the individualized yuppie culture.[53] Going a step beyond the world of images, Lash and Urry argue that local is often a precondition for global: the development of global financial flows, they say, has presupposed a thousand years of history of the City of London and the "specificity of place, of its workforce, the character of its entrepreneurialism, its administration, its buildings, its history, and especially its physical environment, become more important as temporal and spatial barriers collapse."[54] Therefore, they note, the emerging global-local nexus is far more likely to pose a threat to the intermediary national cultures than to their local counterparts.

The establishment of the transnational commercial network of distributors, financiers, and agents in the film industry, described in the previous section, confirms most of the above observations about a heightened salience of place in the new global economy but also brings to light some of the complexities of this process which have thus far been largely ignored in the economic literature. As we have seen, the formation of the global-local nexus in the film industry has reinforced the trend towards dispersion of film production and inspired numerous places, which previously had no link to the film industry whatsoever, to enter into the competition for production dollars. Much like all other places in competition for direct investment, these wanna-be film centers are trying to attract film production companies by stressing their unique features and offering incentives, which presumably cannot be found anywhere else. Yet their efforts often end up being frustrated. The touch of imitation which pervades such competition leads to increasing institutional convergence among the new zones of film production and transforms, paradoxically, all the elements of spatial differentiation between them into the common factors characteristic for *economies of time*—low labor costs, unrestricted work hours, expediency and efficiency of production, micro-regulation, and infrastructural investments favorable to the continuous flow of production. The process, therefore, resembles more closely Lefebvre's duality of global/fragmented space—space pulverized and fractured according to some common denominator such as property rights—than it resembles the above-mentioned romantic notions of resurgent localism as the accompaniment of globalization.[55] Perhaps, just as importantly, it shows the extent to which the theoretical focus on the *economies of space* and the neglect of the *economies of time* can inadvertently serve as legitimizing factors for the continued "domination of space" by commercial interests.

This abstract discussion will become more concrete if we look into the details of changes in the geography of film production during the past two decades. The main impetus for continued interest in location shooting among filmmakers has been the rising average costs of film production and distribution. Between 1980 and 1994, the average negative—that is, production—costs of feature films have increased from $9.4 million to $34.3 million, while the average marketing and distribution costs went up from $4.3 million to $16.1 million.[56] The increase in marketing costs was mainly attributed to the dependence on extremely expensive TV advertising and the so-called "saturation releases"—the simultaneous opening of films in several thousand theaters. Negative costs, on the other hand, which are divided between "below-the-line" costs (craftsmen and unskilled labor) and "above-the-line" costs (actors, directors, screenwriters) have risen, most analysts agree, due to escalating stars' salaries. It has become commonplace for directors and stars to earn several million dollars on a single project. Recently frequent auctions of "spec" scripts (ready-to-produce scripts) in an "open market" have also led to above-the-million-dollar range for Hollywood's top screenwriters. The increased earnings of Hollywood's top talent have, in turn, been interpreted as a reflection of the increased power of agents—whose only source of income, after all, is a percentage of their clients' salaries—and of their close relationship with distributors and financiers.[57]

Therefore, merchants' control over the industry has split the labor market in Hollywood and turned "below-the-line" costs into the only variable costs which studios and producers could manipulate. And since the unions were controlling the wage scale in Los Angeles, the bifurcation of costs eventually forced producers to take production to the southern "right-to-work" states, Canada, and, less frequently, Australia, where labor costs were much lower and the environment was relatively familiar and congenial.

"Below-the-line" labor cost differentials were truly impressive and, in the case of Canada, greatly helped by the strength of the U.S. dollar in the 1980s. According to Department of Labor statistics from 1987, residents of right-to-work states employed in film and TV productions were earning—on average—83 percent less then their counterparts in non "right-to-work" states.[58] The industry representatives were also cited as saying that the general level of fringe benefits was about 3 percent of the payroll in "right-to-work" states compared with 32 percent in southern California.[59] Even with the plummeting of the dollar at the end of 1980s, the costs of production in Canada—where production was unionized—remained 20–30 percent lower than in the United States. With this in mind it is not surprising that Los Angeles lost its supremacy as the center of production in the United States and that new places such as Wilmington, North Carolina; Florida; Vancouver; and Toronto became increasingly attractive destinations for Hollywood producers. Thus, in 1982, only 30 percent of the U.S. film production was taking place in California.[60] In 1988, an influential study by KPMG Pete Marwick commissioned by the California Film Office estimated that California was losing $2.9 billion worth of production to other states each year.[61] In 1993, L.A.'s Economic Development Office estimated that approximately 60 percent of feature films, 50 percent of made-for-TV movies and commercials, and 87 percent of TV series—the only remnant of mass production in Hollywood—were still being made in California.[62] In 1999, the already-mentioned study commissioned by the Directors Guild of America and the Screen Actors Guild, the U.S. was losing at least $7.4 billion and 24,000 jobs to runaway productions, the majority of which were going to Canada (81 percent) and to Australia and the U.K. (10 percent).[63]

Producers frequently accused U.S. union workers of being "inflexible" in addition to being expensive. "They are still running, they don't walk," said producer Norman Jewison comparing Canadian crews with their L.A. counterparts.[64] "You don't hear anyone saying 'I don't pull cables, I only move cameras,'" said Scott Siegler, head of Columbia Pictures T.V. group, about Australians.[65] Responding to such criticism, Hollywood crafts unions tried to defend their jobs with a combination of reconciliation and threats, but to no avail. In contract negotiations, union representatives offered to introduce more flexibility in the scheduling of production, to abolish some of the most contested issues such as the "lunch-break" clause, and even to temper the wage scale.[66] When the offers were not met with much enthusiasm, the unions resorted to threats. In the late 1980s, more hardened leadership of IATSE and the teamsters literally chased production companies around the country, forcing them to sign contracts with unions. Their targets were primarily quasi-independent productions which had significant backing from Hollywood studios and pre-arranged distribution deals but which—due to their "independent" status—were not signatories of the unions' contracts.[67] In several instances, the unions were accused of destroying film with infra-red lights and slashing tires on mobile homes and vehicles that belonged to production companies.[68] The combination of flexibility and threats occasionally brought unions some small victories—they succeeded in forcing smaller production companies such as Cannon to become signatories of unions' contracts by offering a scale adjusted to the film's budget—but the situation, in general, remained the same.[69] The relative weakness of unions in Hollywood and the availability of cheap labor elsewhere made it easy for producers to sign contracts and leave California nonetheless.

The exodus of production from Los Angeles caused concern among L.A. officials because the city's revenue greatly depends on the entertainment industry. According to the already-mentioned study by KPMG Pete Marwick, motion-picture production has significant trickle-down effects: an average film production company spends $32,450 per day when filming in Los Angeles on items such as dry cleaning, catering, donuts, equipment rentals, props, and so on.[70] Given the high level of interaction between the film industry and other industrial sectors, tourism in particular, Los Angeles officials have been arguing that the multiplier effect of each dollar spent in production outside of California is equivalent to four in terms of revenue and six in terms of employment. In other words, each dollar spent in production outside of California actually costs the state four dollars in revenue, and each job passed on to other locations means six lost jobs in the state of California.[71] Such high stakes forced both the California and Los Angeles government into action. In 1985, Governor George Deukmejian formed the California Film Commission, and Los Angeles city and county officials soon followed. The offices have since tried to create a "business-friendly" environment—reducing the wait periods for film permits, creating a one-stop permit office which issues permits for all of L.A. county, and reducing fees for services such as police escorts and security. In 1988, the county even began to float municipal bonds in order to underwrite low-bargain interest-rate loans for independent productions. Yet jurisdictional disputes between localities within the County, and competition among California's numerous film offices—close to fifty—hindered most of these efforts and only succeeded in stabilizing the outflow of production from Los Angeles.

The situation is equally precarious even in the places which have seemingly benefited from Los Angeles' loss of production. Thus, in Wilmington, North Carolina, which had long served as a miracle example of a community resurrected by film production, the continued existence of the film industry has been seriously questioned more than once in just over a decade. The city—a dormant port on the North Carolina shore mired in racial tensions—was accidentally discovered in 1983 by Italian producer Dino De Laurentiis who shot Stephen King's *Firestarter* (1984) at Orton Plantation between Wilmington and Southport. Following the successful production of *Firestarter*, which was extremely well received by the then-governor of North Carolina, James B. Hunt, De Laurentiis decided to build a film studio on a thirty-two-acre plot near the airport in Wilmington. Since June of 1984, when the studio was officially opened, several dozen feature films have been shot in Wilmington, from David Lynch's *Blue Velvet* (1986) and the Coen brothers' *The Hudsucker Proxy* (1994) to several *Ninja Turtles* and *Super Mario Brothers* movies. Local economists now estimate that the film industry accounts for at least 12–15 percent (without the multiplier) of all economic activity.

The growth of Wilmington into the second-largest film-production center on the East Coast in less than a decade reflects both the successes and failures of North Carolina's overall developmental strategy in the postwar period. The latter has mostly focused on the creation of conditions which attract investment, relying on the state's right-to-work status, on its abundant and impoverished agricultural labor force, and on a package of incentives which includes free industrial training and the creation of industrial parks for high-tech sectors such as micro-electronics.[72] The combination of these factors has transformed North Carolina into one of the most attractive low-cost production areas in the United States as well as the state most acclaimed for its "friendly business climate." However, the constant influx of capital has never really changed the socioeconomic map of North Carolina or helped develop indigenous industries. The state still ranks thirty-fifth in per capita income, most higher paying jobs are reserved for out-of-state scientists and engineers, and the growth of wages and salaries remains concentrated in a few metropolitan areas. Similarly, the North Carolina film industry now has twenty-nine sound stages, (more than any other state other than California), a state-sponsored film school in Winston-Salem tailored to the needs of visiting film production companies, and one of the largest and best trained pools of technicians and crew members in the country. Yet, local production is almost non-existent, and enormous investments in the human and physical infrastructure remain a poor guarantee both of continued film production in North Carolina and of a relatively constant employment in the state's film industry.

So, although the city has grown, in just ten years, into the second-largest film production center east of Los Angeles, Wilmington can hardly rest on its laurels. Events in Hollywood have shaken film production in Wilmington twice already, and they will probably do so again. The studio and its sound stages have changed hands three times since 1984 because the Hollywood production companies, which owned the studio, have gone bankrupt. In 1987, Dino De Laurentiis, the founder of the studio, had to fold his business property due to accumulated production losses. In 1989, after two years of precarious existence as no one's property and a considerable slowdown in production, the studio was sold to Carolco, the film production company responsible for such box office hits as the *Rambo* movies, *Terminator*, and *Total Recall* (1990). However, in 1995, Carolco also had to file for Chapter 11 bankruptcy. In the summer of 1996, the studio was purchased by Frank Capra Jr.—the son of the famous director and producer of *Firestarter*, the first film made in Wilmington. The most interesting aspect of these transfers of ownership is that both Dino De Laurentiis and Carolco went out of business because they were completely dependent on pre-sale arrangements with overseas distributors and financiers. Despite buffers to protect their earnings, and despite their box office hits, neither of the production companies could make sufficient profit to maintain their most valuable asset—the studio in Wilmington. Capra's company, the current owner of the studio, remains susceptible to similar financial problems in the future. Thus, the vulnerability of the studio, and by default of Wilmington's economy, stems from the fact that it occupies the tail end of the commodity chain in the entertainment industry. So even if we dismiss for a moment other dubious aspects of the film industry's growth in North Carolina—its dependence on non-unionized labor in particular—it is troubling to conclude that even a best-case scenario—such as Wilmington's—may not necessarily lead towards the stable and sustainable development of a local economy.

The situation in Florida, the other southern state that has benefited the most from Los Angeles' travails, is somewhat different. Since

1974, when Florida set up its Film Bureau in Tallahassee as part of the Department of Commerce, both the film industry in the state and the Film Bureau itself have experienced tremendous growth. With a budget twice the size of that of the North Carolina Film Office, four times as many employees, and the blissful presence of Disney World, the Florida Film Bureau was able to lobby Hollywood majors and become the site of two "Super Studios" in the late 1980s—Universal Studios and the Disney/MGM Studio, both located next to Disney World and Epcot Center in Orlando. However, while the Super Studios centralized production and postproduction facilities in one geographic area— and predictably so since the studios would mostly be used for mass-produced TV series—location shooting remained dispersed throughout the state. Thus, by 1991, Florida had a network of thirty-three private and public film offices jealously guarding their own territories and competing over the incoming Hollywood productions. The effects of their fratricidal struggle were such that the state started lagging behind North Carolina both in the number of films produced and in the revenue generated by film productions.[73] In order to reverse the trend, Florida's Department of Commerce formed a new entity in 1993— Direct Support Organization—as the principal marketing organization for the Florida film and television industry.[74] Yet, even though cooperation among film offices has somewhat improved, North Carolina still attracts more feature productions than Florida. Paradoxically, however, the number of film offices in North Carolina now seems to be on the rise: since 1990 new offices have been formed in Wilmington, Asheville, Durham and Winston-Salem, and the effects of their jurisdictional fragmentation are still difficult to estimate.

This last phenomenon—the stiff competition among numerous state and film offices for film production—accentuates the paradoxes of the global-local nexus in the film industry and reveals some of the most perverse effects of decentralized production. The crucial paradox of the intense competition between states and localities for investment dollars is that their attempts to differentiate themselves from each other are ultimately making them more similar. For as long as the basis of their offerings continues to consist of relatively low labor costs and the willingness to adapt to the needs of businesses that they are trying to attract, there will be little real difference between disparate and dif-

While looking for locations for *The Truman Show* (Paramount, 1998), director Peter Weir was struck by the visuals of Seaside, Florida, a planned community built in 1980 by developer and "new urbanism" guru Robert Davis and his wife, Darryl. "It looked like [the town] had been built for our show," said Weir. Photo by Alex S. MacLean. Courtesy of Seaside Public Relations Office.

fused places of production. Mimicry, after all, has always been a by-product of competition. In turn, such produced—rather than inherited—similarities make these new sites of production far more susceptible and vulnerable to the whims of mobile businesses than they had originally set out to be. Even the most successful zones of film production, such as Florida or North Carolina, still depend on events in the corporate headquarters of media companies in Los Angeles and New York—despite their enormous investment in infrastructure, creation of a skilled labor force, and attempt to integrate film production into the fabric of their communities and other industrial sectors.

Therefore, it is probably not an exaggeration to conclude that the merchants' domination of space has made place more important, but that the simultaneous process of homogenization and differentiation, or convergence and divergence, is actually more complex than the literature generally recognizes. The contemporary reestablishment of the merchant economy has brought back forgotten concerns with space and place, which had more or less vanished from the economic literature at the end of the nineteenth century. Ironically, the attempts of places to differentiate themselves from other similar places through micro-regulation—by establishing various forms of business subsidies or, more frequently, by disciplining their own labor force—have only reinforced the power of merchants in the world economy. The relocation of production to right-to-work states, of animation work to Japan and Hong Kong, and of mass production work on motion picture paraphernalia to the sweat shops of Mexico, South East Asia, or New York has not abolished the need for labor discipline or reduced tensions over the pace of work. Large trading companies and less formal networks of local and global merchants seem uniquely capable of navigating among distinct places of production and exploiting their differences. The end result is similar to the process of decentralized-centralization first noticed in relations between localities and their federal governments: a fragmented and highly competitive world of local producers confronts a coordinated network of global merchants empowered with cognitive, legal, and economic instruments of coercion.[75] Thus, the new geography of the entertainment industry shows that Lefebvre's notion of fragmented and pulverized space is a logical counterpart to Harvey's concept of domination of space and that competition, ultimately, reverts back to the now concealed economies of time: local is not being threatened by global but by the very affirmation of locality, by the very insistence that it is the site of economic transformation and the appropriate site of economic regulation, and by its very attempts to enhance the business environment and make it more difficult for footloose companies to leave.

Whither Cultural Production?

But what, if any, is the future of cultural production in the merchant economy? The gravest concern of most observers of the American film industry and the global entertainment complex is the fear that film and cultural production will either wither away or that their meaning and symbolic value will be radically transformed due to the changing economics of entertainment. "The time has come," wrote one of the legendary French producers, Anatole Dauman, whose credits include Alain Resnais's *Hiroshima Mon Amour* (1959), Volker Schlöndorff's *The Tin Drum* (1979), and Wim Wenders's *Wings of Desire* (1987), "for a 'declaration of independence' signed by all the great names of world cinema. A declaration of solidarity which would affirm the need for cultural pluralism as the defense of all the national film industries against American domination [. . .] as the defense against the drowning of an art in the ocean of standardised and one-dimensional images."[76]

There are, definitely, reasons for concern. With the exception of straight-to-video productions, the number of films produced in the United States and overseas has been declining for years and so has the proportion of films responsible for most of the global box-office revenue. In Japan, which was the world's largest producer of films through the 1960s, the level of production has dropped from close to 600 films per year in the early 1960s to some 200 to 250 in the early 1990s. Meanwhile, the largest Japanese film companies have become a lesser imitation of Hollywood conglomerates mostly focused on the distribution of imported films. The situation is similar in France where, despite state subsidies and determined national efforts to protect French producers, the industry continues to lose ground to U.S. imports, in part because its own film and TV companies prefer to finance international coproductions and American films capable of reaching the global market. Even in India, where the practice of mass production once seemed bound to survive thanks to the weakness of the local theater owners and a relatively closed and impenetrable market, domestic distributors are quickly learning that they can earn as much or more by importing successful foreign films as by investing in much riskier local productions. The shift from production into distribution, thus, questions the entire notion of "national" film industries and "national" cultures. As the Japanese film director Nagisa Oshima wrote several years ago, once the Japanese studios had ceased producing films, they "lost their ethics as film companies. As long as they were called film companies, the unifying factor of each company centered on film making, and what they made was 'Japanese film.' When they stopped production, the film companies lost their ethics, their unity and identity and the 'Japanese film,' ceased to exist."[77]

In all fairness, however, most of this pessimism is based on the assumption that cultural production is a spatially defined process—in other words, that culture itself is first and foremost defined by the place where it is produced—and that it is currently threatened mostly because production and distribution are no longer bound by any territorial limits. Such is definitely the assumption of many, primarily European, governments that are currently attempting to protect their local producers by establishing quotas, tariffs, and subsidies to both enhance local production and minimize the impact of American distributors and Hollywood films in their markets. The measures can easily become counterproductive: territorial protection will, most likely, further aggravate relations between local producers and globally-minded distributors by encouraging the former to speak only to their own audiences and the latter to seek links with transnational capital and international coproductions in order to access the U.S. and worldwide markets.

From the perspective of the movie audience, the situation is far less tragic. The new entertainment economy ensures a greater variety of product than did Hollywood's Golden Age. The global outsourcing of production, even if still heavily biased towards English-speaking countries, has opened the doors of world markets to films from Australia, New Zealand, Ireland, England, and Canada. The presence of sizable immigrant communities in the United States—Latin American and Asian in particular—encourages U.S. distributors to import films from China, Taiwan, Spain, and Latin America. Much like ethnic food and clothing, which have been readily accepted by Western urbanites, movies and culture are now becoming a necessary ingredient of multicultural life styles. Thus, it seems rather unlikely that local and national film industries will be devoured by global entertainment companies or that all American cinema will turn overnight into *Jurassic Park* (1993) or *Basic Instinct* (1992).

The danger, as I see it, comes from another direction—from the increased marginalization of cultural products and cultural production in the new entertainment economy and from an equally important tendency towards explicit commodification of the privacy of both producers and consumers. The dispersion of production that took place in the postwar period has changed the way in which power, space, and privacy interact in the global economy. As the old institutions of censorship and surveillance, which had once supported the Hollywood studio system, started to collapse under the pressure of newly created distances, new mechanisms of social control and appropriation of intimacy have emerged to take their place. The shift in the boundaries of public and private has reflected itself both in the activities of the former Hays Office and in the production and marketing strategies of Hollywood studios. Just as importantly, it has created new zones of contestation between producers and merchants—over brand names and intellectual property rights—and, consequently, as we shall see in the next chapter, ushered Hollywood into the Information Age.

The two most obvious manifestations of this shift in boundaries have been the growth of marketing research on the one hand, and the return to news stories as a form of entertainment, on the other. The multiplicity of distribution and licensing channels has increased the importance of marketing and distribution departments within film companies and in their new corporate headquarters. Both producers and distribution departments now openly acknowledge that the power to green-light movies now resides with marketing and distribution personnel. The fate of the movie is decided on the basis of its merchandising potential, and market research—which became a major factor in the industry only in late 1970s—serves as "scientific" justification for the decision-making process. Justin Wyatt is probably correct when he notes that the adoption of market research has been closely related to the conglomeration of the industry.[78] Studio executives who had previously relied on intuition and hunches in their decisions could no longer discuss multi-million dollar investments with their corporate directors in such "irrational terms." A 1976 article about marketing research in *Variety* started with a question "You must be wondering 'What can marketing research do to me?'" and ended with the statement that "market research is vital as a basis for accurate marketing judgment."[79] Reluctantly at first, studio executives embraced market research mostly as a way to justify their own decisions. Soon, however, market research became a growing industry in its own right.

Building on the rating system and its inherent audience segmentation, market researchers have helped develop new and valuable audiences among teenagers and minorities. The development of sophisticated marketing research methods and target marketing over the past two decades has created a consumer-centered world in which the tastes and preferences of the consumers appear to be driving the economy. Even the linguistic rediscovery of the word "customer" tries to evoke the world of close personal relations between merchants and consumers, which died out at the turn of the century. Yet, the formalization of "intimacy" at a distance creates new patterns of surveillance and appropriation of privacy. From hotel chains such as Sheraton to large distributors/retailers such as Wal-Mart, successful businesses base their operations on data banks about their "customers," which register the details of their shopping and consumption habits. The accumulated facts allow them to predict customer desires, reduce inventories, and plan in advance their flexible production lines. The most amazing example of the new form of intrusion is the "Smart Agent" software developed by the MIT Media Lab and recently purchased by Barry Diller, former head of production at Paramount studio and now the owner of the QVC, the television shopping network. "Smart Agent" guides a "customer" through a series of questions unrelated to his or her consumption dreams to construct a solution—the product which the customer really wants even though he or she does not even know it—which QVC can immediately provide. Thus, it is difficult to resist the impression that such strategies of "mass customization" do not actually rest on desire to please the customer but rather on a skillful exploitation of the viewer's privacy and identity that often act as self-fulfilling prophecy. Hidden behind a deceptive variety of choices offered by a handful of companies, consumer sovereignty seems as much of a myth as it did during the studio era.

The end result of the establishment of these formal and informal commercial networks has been a loose contractual entity focused on acquisition, maintenance, and sales of intellectual property rights with a completely different time horizon than that of the vertically integrated corporation. Since profits are mostly made through pre-sales of rights to films, images, and characters, the creation of brand names and the struggle over copyrights and royalties have become the main sources of tension in Hollywood. As the 1995 Time Warner annual report openly acknowledged, the motto of the industry is that "brands build libraries, libraries build networks, networks build distribution, distribution builds brands."[80] Thus, the proliferation of actors and directors who regard themselves as "their own industries," as Elizabeth Taylor once remarked about herself, and who eagerly translate themselves into clothing lines, bottles of perfumes, and mail-order catalogues finds its logical counterpart in the merchant's tightening of the legal, economic, and organizational framework intent on protecting their exclusive copyrights.[81]

Not surprisingly, the association of Hollywood studios, which once exercised its control over the industry by controlling the moral behavior of its employees and its audiences, now focuses only and exclusively on the protection of intellectual property rights. For the past two decades, the Motion Pictures Producers' Association (MPAA) has been making a claim that its members—major Hollywood companies—have the right to colorize movies and alter their format for reproduction on TV and video without consulting the original authors. The purpose of this somewhat banal and mostly impractical request is not the desire of the studios to improve the quality of their libraries but to prevent filmmakers and producers from making any future claims on their own products. On the other hand, ever since the advent of the VCR in the 1970s, the MPAA has made the struggle against piracy into its first and foremost priority, establishing hot lines, toll-free numbers, and even rewards for anyone who could offer information on potential copyright infringements. Once again, and quite predictably, the real aim of this effort is not to punish the average consumer who is copying videos, but to protect merchants' exclusive rights to translate products from one medium into another, collect royalties, and have absolute control over global distribution. By forming an alliance with publishers, software makers, and the record industry, the MPAA has successfully lobbied the U.S. government to protect the studios' interests both at home and abroad. The complaints were particularly successful in countries such as Japan, where distribution was also the dominant side in the entertainment industry. But the allegations of piracy have encountered opposition in places such as China or India, where distribution was either monopolized by the state or fragmented and weak, and in countries such as France, where intellectual property rights stand firmly on the side of the producers.[82]

The focus on pre-sale agreements also means that the quality, quantity, and expediency of production are no longer vital to the industry. The simultaneous release of a film on two- or three-thousand screens, combined with the sale of rights for video release, merchandising, and licensing—regardless of the film's actual quality—is just as profitable as the production of several hundred smaller films but involves much less risk. The monitoring of the production process is left to producers and directors themselves, who are in turn solely responsible for the losses incurred by production, whereas the merchants mostly concentrate on the distribution, marketing, and promotion of films. Similarly, the monitoring of production and often sales of various film paraphernalia such as toys or film-related apparel are left to individual licensees, often located in Southeast Asia or Mexico where the costs of mass production are much lower than in the United States. The commercial network in the entertainment industry functions much like a transnational franchise, and the embedded power asymmetry between the franchisers—the holders of the intellectual property rights—and the franchisees—the lessors of the rights—ensures a continued and uneven distribution of profits and risks between the two groups. Thus, the horizontal integration of media companies, the pre-sale agreements between bankers and distributors, and the simultaneous multiplication and conversion of distribution venues are all buffers created to protect middlemen and their earnings. Such factors distance producers from their own works to such an extent that they ultimately have no control over the sale of their own movies; and they inject layers and layers of merchandising products between consumers and the original so that consumers have little or no choice but to purchase the films in one form or another.

The effects of these numerous "degrees of separation" on the product itself are different than they were in the "age of mechanical reproduction" denounced by Walter Benjamin in the mid 1930s.[83] When Benjamin wrote about film as the quintessential art of modernity—

where "the sight of immediate reality has become an orchid in the land of technology"[84]—he was primarily concerned with the fact that film blurred the distinction between reality and the imaginary, between the original and its copy. Since mechanical reproduction was inherent to film, the penetration of technology into the reality was, according to Benjamin, so deep that technology itself was no longer visible. What remained as art was the semblance of a reality more real than reality itself. The reproduction took the place of the original—depriving the original of its "presence," of its existence in time and space, of its tradition—and embarked upon a life of its own. The "age of mechanical reproduction," feared Benjamin, was the age of "mass participation," and film—whose audiences were critical but in an absent-minded way—was particularly conducive to the "reproduction of masses." In the "age of mechanical reproduction," the separation of art from reality was such that art absorbed reality and became a purpose in itself. As such, as a sheer *l'art pour l'art*, it perfectly corresponded to the world in which war—the ultimate form of the world's own self-alienation—had become an aesthetic phenomenon par excellence.

Benjamin was writing under the assumption that originals still existed. And, indeed, contrary to many of his darkest visions, the "age of mechanical reproduction" actually increased the value of the original since it was precisely the original that made mass reproduction possible. By contrast, the current reorganization of the entertainment industry transforms the original into the epiphenomenon of its alternate identities: it is not film as the "mechanical reproduction" of reality which is relevant but film's permutation into consumer goods, travel options, and software programs. Film has become a by-product of financial transactions, distribution deals, and technological advancement; and the distancing from production, artistry, and "reality" is so great that cultural products are ephemeral. One does not have to search too far for examples: Jane Austin's novels are sold with the label "now a major motion picture," just as consumer goods are advertised in magazines with the label "as seen on TV." The copies of the copy—for that is what ancillary products are in their essence—no longer increase the value of the original; they guarantee its authenticity and its continued existence.

There is, therefore, little point in discussing either a decline or a resurgence of "national" culture in a world in which "identity" itself is a derivative of consumption. The entertainment world dominated by merchants is not concerned about the "nationality" of the cultural product, just as it is not necessarily concerned with the film itself. The French company Ciby 2000 has financed films of Charles Burnett and Jane Campion; Disney is distributing French classics partly to appease the French for its failed EuroDisney and partly because it has nothing to lose; formerly Dutch Polygram is the largest distributor of Japanese adult animation; and Jack Valenti, the head of the American Motion Picture Export Association—the presumed bastion of American cultural imperialism—is proposing to help Europeans establish a competitive distribution and marketing network. The good salesmen are always in demand. Yet whether or not nation-less also means culture-less is difficult to say. It is, however, obvious that even the most prestigious art films these days cannot avoid the process of commodification: to repeat it once again, as Sam Grogg, a former Dean of the North Carolina School of the Arts, would say, "all the movies nowadays lead to the Gift Shop."

THROUGHOUT the studio era, Hollywood producers did their best to keep distributors, financiers, and agents at bay. The strategic importance of distribution was structurally predetermined—through the oligopolistic structure of the industry—but distributors themselves lingered on the margins of the studio hierarchies and of the studio system as a whole. Financiers and agents shared their fate, albeit each for different reasons: although the studio moguls would have appreciated closer relations with the American financial establishment, they had little but disdain for Hollywood agents.

The situation changed dramatically in the 1950s when the spatial dispersion of production undermined the very basis of producers' power and created numerous opportunities for merchants to affirm their role in the industry. The reassertion of merchant power, as we have seen, reflected itself in a complete corporate restructuring of the Hollywood studios, in the creation of formal and informal global alliances between distributors, financiers, and agents, and in new formulas for the appropriation of workers' and consumers' privacy. In addition, the ascent of the merchants has brought renewed interest in the politics and *economics of space,* particularly in the idea that space and place represent both limits to globalization and its greatest asset, both an object of possible cultural homogenization and a source of diversity and plurality.

Yet, just as the focus on temporal advantages and disadvantages of mass production once served as the basis of producers' dominance and concealed the spatial contradictions of the studio system, so does the current reassertion of space in social sciences now serve as the cognitive foundation of merchant power, concealing the tensions and contradictions still related to *economies of time.* In particular, affirmation of space tends to obscure the competition among the numerous places of production, the ever-more-drastic measures of controlling and disciplining labor, the endless process of commodifying cultural products and personal lives as the only real possibilities for producers to capture some segment of the rising entertainment profits. The merchants' firm grip on power has marginalized producers and all those involved in the production process to such an extent that their chances of striking any sort of balance in the buyer-driven commodity chain have been reduced to a minimum. Not surprisingly, and as we shall see in more detail in the next chapter, the producers have resorted to the only remaining alternative path—technologically invented spaces—thereby starting both a new spiral of struggles with the merchants and a new spiral of investments in the motion-picture industry, the generator of growth in the American economy of the late 1990s.

III. HOLLYWOOD IN CYBERSPACE

Reality is a tough thing to deal with.

George Lucas, author of *Star Wars*

I have a sneaking suspicion that if there were a way to make movies without actors, George [Lucas] would do it.

Mark Hamill a.k.a. Luke Skywalker

The orientalist contours of Theed, capital of the planet Naboo and the heart of democracy in a world threatened by the evil Trade Federation. This is, of course, George Lucas's *Star Wars, Episode I: The Phantom Menace* (LucasFilm, 1999). Photo reprinted by permission of LucasFilm, Ltd.

Throughout Hollywood history, there has always been an alternative, if not appreciated, path that producers could turn to in order to establish temporal and spatial control over the production process: the world of special effects. Almost since the inception of the film industry, the evolution of special effects has been closely related to producers' desire to achieve full control over the production process by replacing labor, actors in particular, and locations with tricks and technology. In the studio era, smaller and lesser studios often relied on special effects as a substitute for much more expensive and capricious stars or as a supplement to their hastily written scripts and thin narrative plots. Hollywood majors, on the other hand, had little respect for self-conscious effects but used their less visible counterparts as substitutes for location shooting. The establishment of merchants' dominance in the entertainment sector, the intensification of struggle between producers and merchants over brand names, and difficulties and problems inherent in labor disciplining and location shooting have forced Hollywood producers to turn, once again, to special effects as means to increase the volume of production and reestablish their control over the industry.

Yet Hollywood's technological renaissance is ridden with paradoxes. For producers, special effects and digital technology signify the possibilities of regaining lost *economies of time* and increasing the vol-

ume of production without any of the perennial problems of the production process: dependence on the fickle human character, interference of "reality" into the manufacturing of make-believe, and the
costly monitoring of time and place. But the world with no spatial and
temporal barriers appeals equally to Hollywood merchants. Digital
technology facilitates both the simultaneous transmission of sounds
and images across the globe as well as their unlimited replication and
permutation through various media outlets. Hence, the control over
digital distribution channels, much like the control over distribution
and finance over the past two or three decades, will most likely simply consolidate the power of Hollywood merchants. Thus, the introduction of digital technology into the entertainment sector is not necessarily bringing about a revolution in power relations or industrial
peace. Rather, it is intensifying old conflicts between manufacturers
and merchants, distribution and content, *economies of time* and
economies of space.

However, this time it is likely that neither Hollywood producers
nor merchants will be the main beneficiaries of the entertainment industry's lavish investments in technology. Instead, entertainment is
rapidly turning into the key financier of the U.S. high-technology sectors and the former military-industrial complex, whose development
was once entirely dependent on defense budget. In addition, the expansion of the distribution network and large investments in delivery systems have other disturbing consequences, reminiscent of the
period of rapid vertical integration of the film industry in the 1920s.[1]
On the one hand, the capitalization has increased the level of indebtedness in all major companies—their common long-term debt now
equal to the debt of the Russian Federation—leaving the majors highly
susceptible to the whims of the financial community. On the other
hand, the expansion has created tensions between local and national
cable and broadcast providers, Hollywood and the telecommunications industry, software and hardware manufacturers and, once again,
put the issues of censorship and content control on the table. By increasing their holdings in cable TV and getting closer to the telecommunications industry, both of which are regulated by the government,
the infotainment industry has exposed itself to possible attacks on its
content. And, as we shall see later in this chapter, the end result of

the renewed censorship debates and Hollywood's intimacy with the military-industrial complex is not just an increased regulation of the utterly malleable fantasy worlds and the continued expansion of the commercial worlds but also an inscription of war and violence into the very economy of the entertainment industry.

The true relevance of Hollywood's venture into cyberspace cannot be grasped without looking at the broader context of the resurgent American hegemony, "privatization of authority" in domestic politics and international affairs, and consolidation of merchants' power in the world economy.[2] The chapter, therefore, starts by looking at forces within the film industry which have encouraged the development of new media and technologies and proceeds by analyzing the interests outside of Hollywood—military, and the state, in particular— which have come to endorse it as the new generator of growth in the American economy. The second half of the chapter examines the consequences of this rapprochement between entertainment and warfare, play and politics with respect to issues of censorship and surveillance, the reconstruction of American dominance in world affairs, and our understanding of politics. Combined, these two aspects of the same phenomenon—production of cyberspace but also of hegemony—can provide some insight into Hollywood's future, into the shifting boundaries of public and private fostered by the current political and economic transformations, and into the perplexing and still-evolving relationship between fantastic, utopian, digital space and the world that its masons intend to leave behind.

Given the power that merchants have amassed over the past few decades, it should probably come as no surprise that George Lucas' prequel to the original *Star Wars* trilogy, *Star Wars: Episode I—The Phantom Menace*, revolves around trade wars and protection of merchant routes. Whereas the original *Star Wars*, as a thinly veiled Cold War fantasy, focused on the perennial struggle between good and evil in the form of political empires, the just as improbable plot of *Phantom Menace* evokes more recent fears of the alleged Japanese and Chinese protectionism, the UN incapacity to act decisively in face of aggression and human rights abuses, and the inherent frailty of democracy. In the masterful, if disturbing, display of corporate multiculturalism, the prequel trilogy also, not surprisingly, hosts an array of ethnic characters suitable for merchandising and commodification, some more offensive than others. But Lucas's real ambitions these days lie elsewhere. After having been caught for decades in his own version of the struggle between manufacturers and merchants, Lucas is now developing a new distribution platform that would enable digital transmission of films directly onto theater screens and, thus, by bypassing distributors, loosen their grip over film producers. The second prequel in the series, *Star Wars: Episode II* has been shot, in its entirety, with digital cameras. Within a few years, Lucas hopes, digital projectors will replace old film projectors, and images will be beamed via satellite into theaters across the country. Using the same language of inevitability that Universal Pictures used to explain the building of Universal Studio, Lucas recently said: "This is all going to happen because it has to happen. I love film, but it's a 19th-century invention. The century of film has passed. We are in the digital age now, and trying to hold on to an old-fashioned technology that's cumbersome and expensive—you just can't do it."[3]

Lucas's attempts to undermine the power of Hollywood merchants started with the production of the first Star Wars in 1976. His strategy since then has been twofold: lowering the cost of production by resurrecting the cottage industry of special effects and in-studio filmmaking and controlling future revenues by retaining the rights to the Star Wars story line and its characters. Digital effects, introduced into the industry by Lucas, are not only blurring the line between fantasy and reality, they are also making some of the most expensive aspects of production—sets, costumes, stars, stunts, locations—unnecessary. Control over franchising and merchandising rights over *Star Wars: Episode I—The Phantom Menace* (1999) sequels and prequels, which Lucas requested in lieu of an additional $500,000 director's fee for the original *Star Wars* (1977), has already brought him billions of dollars. Ironically, though, both strategies have been successfully appropriated by distributors, leaving Lucas and his friend Steven Spielberg as the sole contemporary Hollywood filmmakers with absolute, to use Marx's and Lucas's own words, "control over the means of production."[4]

But the *Star Wars* films have had another inadvertent consequence: the seeming naïveté of this political fable has paved the way to a rapprochement between Hollywood and the U.S. military-industrial complex that nobody could have predicted just a decade ago. Lucas's preoccupation with speed, technologies of warfare, and cyborgs, displaced in a childlike fantasy, has done more to naturalize digital combat, so lavishly displayed in the Gulf War and the recent NATO intervention in Kosovo, than any Pentagon-orchestrated propaganda could have achieved on its own. Consequently, the growth of the special-effects industry and of the new infotainment sector, which Lucas has helped inaugurate, create a baffling confluence of economic and technological interests between the U.S. defense industry and Hollywood mythmaking and, thus, as we shall see later in this chapter, play a crucial role in the resurrection of American hegemony at the end of this very *American century.*

Hollywood, the Military-Industrial Complex, and Digital Technology

As we have learned from previous chapters, the way in which space, architecture, and landscapes speak about power is frequently more revealing than any analysis of the far more transient and ethereal economic indicators. Thus, it is quite indicative that old hangars of the former Hughes Aircraft factory in Playa del Ray, just a few miles away from downtown L.A., have lately been used as makeshift movie studios. Portions of *Titanic, Men in Black* (1997), and *Independence Day* (1996) have all been shot there. For a while, it seemed certain that Steven Spielberg's DreamWorks SKG would also place its eight-billion-dollar studio—the first motion picture studio to be built in the Los Angeles basin in seven decades—on the grounds of this old airplane plant. Despite SKG's pullout from Playa Vista in the summer of 1999, Los Angeles city officials are still prepared to offer considerable subsidies to transform this last tract of undeveloped land in greater L.A. into a multi-media industrial park. The project's developers— Morgan Stanley Dean Witter & Company and Goldman, Sachs & Company—say that they will proceed with the construction and rental of their own sound stages. The continued transformation of the former defense contractor into a movie studio reveals the extent to which Hollywood is gradually merging with (or becoming a replacement for)

A 1985 artist's depiction of the real Star Wars: the interception and destruction of nuclear-armed re-entry vehicles by a space electromagnetic railgun. Courtesy Defense Visual Information Center, U.S. Department of Defense.

the American military-industrial complex. For even as SKG abandons the project, Mr. Spielberg's enterprise continues to search for solace in the reconstructed relationship with the U.S. military past. *Saving Private Ryan* (1998)—the "ultimate anti-war movie" about "the last great war"—has already saved DreamWorks SKG from economic troubles by transforming a movie-going experience into the "realistic" experience of warfare. The film, a logical culmination of Mr. Spielberg's career as a filmmaker as much as of the Pentagon's research in simulation technologies, has brought its author a Defense Department's Medal for Distinguished Public Service. According to the citation accompanying the medal, given in recognition of the impact that *Saving Private Ryan* has had on American people, "Mr. Spielberg helped to reconnect the American public with its military men and women, while rekindling a deep sense of gratitude for the daily sacrifices they make on the front lines of our Nation's defense."[5]

Hollywood's ties to the U.S. military-industrial complex are rapidly transforming California's economic landscape. Over the past few years, the entertainment industry has become the single largest employer in Southern California, surpassing the air-and-space industry and absorbing many of the former defense contractors in its own ranks.[6] Throughout California, old bases are being transformed into studio lots and entertainment playgrounds, and the Pentagon has recently simplified, as much as possible, the rules for issuance of film permits on its former or current property.[7] Computer companies, such as Silicon Graphics, whose income and research and development once largely depended on the Department of Defense, are increasingly turning to Hollywood in search of projects, ideas and funding. Even the moribund artificial intelligence projects, brainchildren of the Cold War, are being revived by demand from the entertainment sector. The diminishing influence of the Gunbelt economy and the rise of Siliwood—the mix of Silicon Valley and Hollywood—will quite likely change not just the balance of power within Hollywood but the position of Hollywood in both the American and global economy in general. For all these reasons, and in light of the immense attention now bestowed upon the "infotainment" sector as the pillar of America's "soft power,"[8] it is now possible to argue that, for better or for worse, "the new media order is set to become a global order."[9]

The current embrace of digital technology by both producers and distributors in Hollywood and the emergence of the entertainment sector as the alleged successor to the military-industrial complex represent, at least on the surface, a breach with history and a challenge to the prevailing theories of technological development. There have never been any indications, in either the history of Hollywood or America, that the entertainment industry would or could become a proxy for the U.S. military-industrial complex.[10] Although cinema was first and foremost a technological novelty at the turn of the century, the relationship between the motion-picture industry and technology has since been very ambivalent. The producers resorted to technological innovation whenever the industry faced an internal or external crisis but mostly perceived it as a cheap substitute for the lack of talent or a gripping film narrative. Distributors, on the other hand, distrusted any technology that they themselves did not control and relied, often unsuccessfully, on "gimmicks" such as Technicolor or 3D to improve their position in the industry. Both were so reluctant to invest in research and development that technology within the film industry hardly changed between the introduction of sound in the late 1920s and the first digital applications of the 1980s.

The U.S. military, on the other hand, long monopolized research in basic sciences and information technology and few, if any, of its products trickled down into the consumer market. The commercialization of the information technology in the U.S. started only in the early 1970s when a confluence of factors—the formation of dissident, market-oriented semiconductor companies in Silicon Valley, the introduction of the microprocessor, and the emergence of the Japanese consumer electronics industry-showed that it could have some applications outside the scope of national security.[11] Even then, however, Hollywood seemed like an unlikely candidate for research, development or even the application of digital technology. Given the prevailing perceptions of the two sectors—the former as the paradigmatic industry of leisure and make-believe, the latter as the symbol of the scientific state and the bastion of American postwar Realpolitik— Hollywood and the Pentagon stood on the opposite sides of the political, economic and social spectrums, and only a tectonic political or economic change, or so it seemed, could bring them together.

Theories of technological change do not take us much further in understanding the rapprochement between the film industry and the military-industrial complex and its connotations, or even the technological convergence between sectors such as telecommunications and software design, which previously had little in common. Traditionally, economists have viewed technological change as exogenous to both market and the state. Decline of the American economic power and the ascent of the Japanese manufacturers in a number of

A precursor of *Jurassic Park*, which Leonard Maltin calls the "granddaddy of all prehistoric monster movies," was *Lost World* (First National, 1925). Special effects, the achievement of the animator Willis O'Brien, are still remarkable. Courtesy of the Museum of Modern Art, New York.

high-tech sectors revealed the extent to which product and process innovation could be dependent on their organizational environment. The realization that innovations did not take place on their own, independently of economic institutions and actors, encouraged American political economists to search for alternative, endogenous explanations of technological development.[12] However, they continued to posit technology and innovation as beneficial to the economy and failed to investigate in detail either the social consequences of new technologies or the elements of social choice present in the process of their adoption.

By contrast, critical political economists concerned themselves with exactly those aspects of technological development. Questioning, in particular, the optimistic accounts of the postindustrial era, they stressed the labor-replacing and de-skilling elements of new technologies, threats of further bifurcation of the labor force in the information age, and the potential for surveillance and control embedded in the military origins of information technology.[13] But their views of technological change remained limited by their skepticism in much the same way as their optimism restrained the analysis of their less critical colleagues. In both cases, the predetermined outcomes overshadowed the complexities and uncertainties of political and economic processes that surround the introduction of any new technology. Perhaps just as importantly, the presumed objectivity of their analysis allowed them to neglect their own role—and the role of academe in general—in the continued American obsession with technology and in the major shift in the sponsorship of technological research and development, which they had implicitly or explicitly proposed.

Thus, if there is any common denominator in what is mostly a tale of multiple causalities and unintended consequences, it may be the thought that dramatic technological change is more likely to take place at moments of social, political or economic impasse than at times of complacency. It is in such moments, when all other roads appear more difficult, that the adoption of new technology may seem appealing to a number of diverse actors who are willing to invest it with their own desires, frustrations, and expectations. Thus, the broad-based support for particular technology does not have to mean that all the differences among various economic agents have disappeared or that new coalitions of unseemly actors will truly bring about social justice and industrial peace. On the contrary, every new technology, just like any other form of social change, is bound to mobilize adversaries, create conflicts, exacerbate tensions, break old coalitions, encourage new pacts, and generally increase the level of uncertainty in the economy. Yet what creates the semblance of an orderly rather than chaotic process is the fact that technology, as the exclusive focus of all social debates, absorbs all hopes and fears of its environment: in other words, it becomes fetishized. Therefore, it is not the technology itself, or any of its inherent characteristics, that is critical in its acceptance and diffusion but the willingness of actors to suspend their disbelief and to see in technology the possibility of their own continued existence.

The support for digital technology in Hollywood was born out of an industrial impasse and into a national and political impasse. Perhaps the key factor in Hollywood's technological conversion has been the intensification of intra-industrial conflict between producers, on the one hand, and distributors, financiers, and agents, on the other. As we have seen in the previous chapter, following the collapse of the studio system—Hollywood's version of a Fordist factory—in the 1960s, distributors, financiers, and agents have become the dominant force in the film industry. Hollywood shifted from being a "producer-driven" into a "buyer-driven" commodity chain. The establishment of merchants as the most important group in Hollywood and the global entertainment industry, since the 1970s, has led to the creation of franchise-like media organizations which derive most of their profits from royalties and licensing fees and, therefore, place enormous emphasis on the purchase, development, and maintenance of rights to brand names and characters. At the same time, the salaries of the agent controlled above-the-line talent—stars, directors, and, more recently, screenwriters—have skyrocketed, making it nearly impossible for independent producers, without studio backing, to include any well-known players in their projects. In addition, the rising above-the-line costs have forced producers to search for inexpensive locations, to avoid unions, and to do their best to manipulate below-the line-costs, the only flexible part of the budget that they controlled. The combination of these factors has led to the near exclusion of producers from fair participation in profits and has put them in a very precarious position vis-à-vis distributors, agents, and financiers.

In order to re-establish their stature in the industry, a group of young, maverick Hollywood directors and producers resorted in the 1970s to the tradition of low-budget science fiction film production, filled with explosions and special effects, and relatively neglected by all major studios at the time.[14] The new era of special effects—and of consistent efforts on the part of the producers to assert their rights—started, as was mentioned in the introduction to this chapter, with *Star Wars* and *E.T.: The Extra-Terrestrial* (1982) by filmmakers George Lucas and Steven Spielberg.[15] It has since become the dominant trend in Hollywood production, the filmmakers' equivalent of the myth of an automated factory which came to life in a number of industrial sectors in the 1970s. The principal elements of Lucas's and Spielberg's strategy have been lower production costs, the replacement of stars with technology and special effects, and control over merchandising and licensing rights. George Lucas has been consciously working on the reduction of production costs for years, mostly through the development of new technologies. His special effects firm, Industrial Light and Magic (ILM), has played a critical role in the innovation and adoption of digital technology in the entertainment world.[16] As a result, the firm and its owner have successfully developed brand name recognition with audiences and have brought to a new high the mass appeal of "technology" as the star of the system. Similarly, Spielberg's new digital studio DreamWorks SKG, founded with music agent David Geffen and the former head of production at Disney, Jeffrey Katzenberg, revolves around the hope that technology, which is now prohibitively expensive, will soon become so accessible that it will allow for the resurgence of high-quantity production, akin to the mass-production era, and of the renewed dominance of content—and producers—in the entertainment industry. Spielberg's attempts to reaffirm the role of producers and production are even more assertive and openly political than Lucas's efforts. Having lured to DreamWorks SKG a number of Disney's best animators, Spielberg has announced that his firm would acknowledge authors' rights to any future release of their works, require the authors' permission prior to any alteration of their work, and begin percentage payments out of gross profit to animators.[17] In addition, SKG sided with Hollywood guilds and unions in the negotiations over HDTV and the digital broadcast standard. A relatively broad coalition of actors from the production side of the industry lobbied the FCC trying to ensure that technological non-alteration of filmed material becomes a part of the digital standard rather than an issue in subsequent contract negotiations, as requested by the studio/distributors' organization, MPAA.[18] Given the fundamental interest on the part of distributors and financiers in maintaining their firm grip on intellectual property, Spielberg's announcements have represented a serious breach with the official MPAA policy and have caused concern within major media companies. If SKG and its numerous director/producer followers were to become truly employee-friendly, production oriented, film factories, they could set a dangerous precedent for the rest of the industry.

Apart from Sony's Imagework studio, the major entertainment companies have not as yet responded to the possible strengthening of producers' power by trying to bring digital production in-house or by showing any interest in the production side of digital technology. The attempts of Hollywood studios to forge creative links with web designers and software producers and to develop new Internet content have failed.[19] Thus, instead of investing into production, and in an obvious effort to solidify their control over communication channels, Hollywood majors have adopted Lucas's merchandising strategy and have invested heavily in new distribution technologies based on their preexistent strengths. Some, such as Rupert Murdoch's News Corporation, have focused primarily on the construction of satellite systems. Murdoch's Star TV is the largest provider of programming in Asia; Zee TV covers India; and Sky TV supplies most of Europe with satellite programs. Viacom has joined with IBM in developing a digital delivery system and customer selection systems for its Blockbuster stores and is closely collaborating with AT&T and Nynex on interactive TV. Disney has acquired an amazing distribution network, particularly abroad, through its partnership with ABC, but its exploration of interactive media still focuses on the translation of Disney's old titles into new media formats. By far the greatest investments into distribution technology have been made by Time Warner: its cable operations are now greater than John Malone's TCI; it is working on new laser-disk format with Toshiba, developing a telephone network and an on-line service in upstate New York, and has a series of partnerships working on a range of products from digital mini-dish satellites to the distribution systems for video games on demand via cable TV. The ultimate recognition of this strategy, though not necessarily its payoff, was the acquisition of Time Warner by America Online, once a north Virginian e-mail provider and now the largest distributor of Internet content in the United States.

Hollywood's and the Pentagon's Technological Rapprochement

The focus on technology as the instrument of battle between producers and merchants has created a vicious or a virtuous cycle of investment in research and development whose economic impact on the entertainment sector is still very difficult to assess. From the strictly economic point of view, digital technology remains excessively expensive, and improvements in the efficiency of either production or delivery cannot be noticed. Profit margins in special-effects productions are very low, mostly due to the high number of manpower hours required to do computer design, the high costs of capital, and the increasing number of digital production firms. But if the impact of digital technology on the entertainment industry itself is still a mixed blessing, the fervor of investment has already affected a number of actors and sectors outside the industry. As mentioned, numerous new actors—from the software giant Microsoft to Baby Bells and the world's largest electronics companies—have now entered show business. At the same time, thanks to its spending spree, the entertainment industry has become the main source of financing for firms whose existence was once completely dependent on the defense budget.

The links between former defense contractors and Hollywood are based on fundamental similarities between simulation technologies intended for military use and technologies used in computer design, interactive entertainment, and special effects.[20] Some links date as far back as the late 1970s when scientists, hackers, and computer nerds first started traveling between NASA and the Warner Bros.' Atari lab, MIT and Silicon Valley, Lucas's ILM, Air Base in Dayton, Ohio, and the Universities of Utah and North Carolina, the places where most pioneer work on virtual reality was being done at the time.[21] Most links blur the distinction between the worlds of warfare, surveillance,

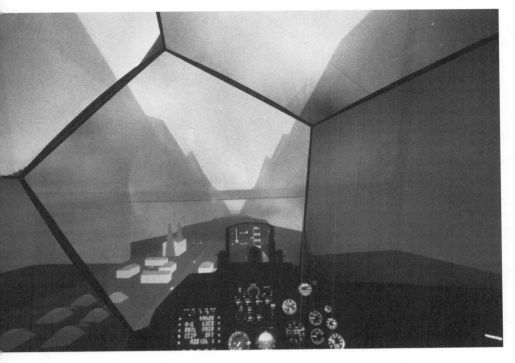

Pilot's-eye view of an aircraft simulator. Exact date of the shot unknown. Courtesy Defense Visual Information Center, U.S. Department of Defense.

and sheer entertainment: systems for monitoring Ozone data are used in digital imaging for special effects, flight simulators are placed in theme parks, submarine sound detection technology is used in music recording, image generation technology, which served in missile rehearsal, has been transformed into a part of computer-game software. The convergence is actively supported by the U.S. government. Defense budget cuts have put simulation technology at risk, and the government has created a series of incentives for the conversion of military technology to civilian use. The most prominent among them are the promotion of dual-use technologies (products which can have both military and commercial use) through the Clinton Administration's Technology Reinvestment Project (TRP), and the strengthening of the government-industry partnerships through the Commerce Department's Advanced Technology Program (ATP).[22] In California, federal programs are complemented by state and local programs that encourage the shift from the military-industrial complex in other sectors, entertainment in particular.[23]

Thus, whereas previous government interventions in the entertainment sector have attempted both to limit the industry's economic power and to regulate its content, the latest wave considers Hollywood an economic and strategic asset, enhancing its distribution technologies through the removal of government regulations and its labor replacement technologies through the support of dual-use technology. The purpose of these initiatives is "not only to strengthen civilian industry but also to promote the cost-effective development of new technologies for national defense and to stimulate the creation of an integrated civilian-military industrial base."[24]

Therefore, the true relevance of Hollywood's obsession with technology becomes more obvious if we look beyond *Star Wars* and *Star Trek* to the broader context of political and economic change in the United States and the global economy. In that context technology is both the means and the ends to U.S. economic power and global hegemony: information technology is inextricably linked with U.S. military dominance and with the development and daily functioning of the global financial system; and technology is an absolutely necessary ingredient in the coordination of geographically dispersed activities in global commodity chains. But information technology is also a product itself, and the sectors which most directly engulf its development—the telecommunications, computer and entertainment industries—are among the fastest growing in the United States. The sustained development of high technology industries, regardless of their social impact, is readily perceived as the sine qua non of American military and economic survival.

Not surprisingly, the decline of American economic power and the success of the Japanese in high-technology sectors—semiconductors, consumer electronics, and computer manufacturing—inspired a diverse body of economic literature in defense of high technology. Despite ideological differences, most interpretations of the state of the American high-tech industry focused on military over-extension as the principal cause of its decline, either because military spending exerted enormous pressure on the U.S. budget or because the military, as the ultimate user of information technology, did not successfully promote the development of consumer friendly high-tech products.[25] Hence, the debate about the role of the U.S. government in U.S. postwar technological development had a dual and somewhat paradoxical subtext. On the one hand, it supported arguments for reduced military spending and a de-politicization of the American economy as the way to increase American international competitiveness in high-tech industries and reestablish America's dominance in the world economy. On the other hand, it served as the justification for continued state intervention in the economy in an era dominated by the rhetoric of the marketplace. Ironically, the insistence on military conversion and the creation of the strong state has resulted in the consolidation of the merchant economy and the fostering of "private authority" networks not only in the United States but also globally. The state-initiated conversion has done little to increase the transparency of military financing or to open it to public debate; rather, it has created a novel form of commercial-military alliance in which even the state's monopoly over violence now depends on global consumption of entertainment, communication, and transportation.

Navigable Space: Morality Plays and Reality Violence

The intimacy between Hollywood, the U.S. military-industrial complex, and the U.S. government has not completely removed the threats of government control over the content of entertainment. But the wave of debates about family values, rap music, public support for the arts, and violent content on TV, which continue to polarize the U.S. public, have had peculiar and perverse effects on the entertainment industry and its relation to the world at large. Instead of regulating the content of commercial entertainment, they have limited the space for public expression; instead of limiting the amount of violence on TV, they have limited the space of fictional, fantasy violence and created space for reality programs, including coverage of wars and crimes; and, finally, instead of restraining the power of entertainment companies, the censorship debates have contributed to the removal of the last anti-trust obstacles to mergers between telecommunications, broadcasting, media, software, and movie companies. The ensuing reconfiguration of the American moral and economic landscape now reshapes not just our perceptions of world order but, perhaps, the order itself.

It may be good, therefore, to start this brief analysis with yet another interpretation of Hollywood's malleable space and its new digital frontiers. One of the major characteristics of visual digital technology, writes art historian Lev Manovich, is the production of "navigable space."[26] Basing his analysis on fascinating and complex comparisons of video games and cinema, paintings and computer-generated images, Manovich provocatively contends that "there is no space in cyberspace."[27] Indeed, Manovich writes, although new media have a tendency to spatialize "all representations and experiences (the library is replaced by cyberspace; narrative is equated with traveling through space; all kinds of data are rendered in three dimensions through computer visualization),"[28] virtual spaces are not really spaces but collections of separate objects without any unifying point of view. Thus, the key attribute of computer space, as opposed to other forms of visual representation, including cinema, is that it is navigable. Much as the usual metaphor of the "information super-highway" would imply, and just as any fan of video-games would attest, computer space is the subjective space of fast-transit, high-speed connections between distinct, functionally significant, places, which leave the rest to abandonment and ruin. In its lack of attention to any zone not functionally used, argues Manovich:

> [T]he spatialized Web, envisioned by VRML (itself a product of California) reflects the treatment of space in American culture generally [...]. The marginal areas that exist between privately owned houses, businesses and parks are left to decay. The VRML universe, as defined by software standards and the default settings of software tools, pushes this tendency to the limit: it does not contain space as such but only objects that belong to different individuals.[29]

Not surprisingly, the moral order which corresponds to the mapping of these subjectively defined and privately owned places and non-places is itself highly dependent on spatialization, on successful zoning of the places of decency and obscenity, morality and immorality, and, increasingly, violence and security. The spatialization of moral order is a novel phenomenon, quite different from the ways in which morality was organized in the studio system or at the height of Hollywood's exodus into worldwide locations. Namely, as we have seen in the first chapter, the moral code of the studio era was highly dependent on two entwined yet divergent processes: *occupation of space* and *occupation of privacy*. The centralization of motion picture production within the studios found its equivalent in the centralization of moral authority within the Production Code Administration—the Hays Office—and its set of common rules for on-screen and off-screen behavior. With its codification of both fantasy and reality worlds, the Hays Office actually attempted to put an end to the fragmentation of moral space in pre-Fordist America, where localities, individual churches, and state censorship boards used to regulate behavior of their immediate community members.

The dispersion of Hollywood production and the resulting power shift from manufacturers to merchants unraveled the institutions of censorship and surveillance associated with the studio era. As mentioned in the previous chapter, in 1968, the Production Code Administration was replaced with the voluntary rating system, once again paid for and administered by the Motion Picture Association of America, the exclusive club of Hollywood majors. The ratings encouraged audience segmentation and niche marketing of Hollywood films, fortuitously aiding the merchants, distributors in particular, in their conquest of the entertainment business. In an essay focused on the historical trajectory of X-rated film, Justin Wyatt notes that the infamous X label (the only one available to independent producers without going through the costly rating process controlled by MPAA) has helped Hollywood distributors marginalize independent producers and theater owners in the post-studio era. By co-opting the soft-core aspects of the sexually explicit material and expelling the rest into the realm of pornography, Hollywood majors have neutralized the threat of art house films and theaters and, once again, solidified their control over the vast and dissonant moral and economic spaces of the post-Vietnam United States.[30] Consequently, the X rating has become the thing of the past (indeed, so much so that it could be the focus of

Hollywood's nostalgic look into the 1970s—witness the 1997 film *Boogie Nights*) and of the shrinking red-light districts in U.S. urban areas.[31] Meanwhile, sex and obscenity—and moral outrage about them—have moved into the virtual reality of chat rooms and Internet websites where they are now spatially policed with warnings, parental advisories, firewalls, and pay-per-minute services.

However, this does not mean that the specter of censorship has left Hollywood for good. On the one hand, it is quite fascinating how long and how successfully the voluntary rating system has inoculated Hollywood majors from moral criticism amidst the U.S. culture wars of the past two decades. While Hollywood as an imaginary creature continues to be blamed for the deterioration of family values in the U.S., specific instances of censorship battles in recent years have mostly taken place in different media spaces—museums, broadcast television, independent documentary film, the music industry, or the Internet. Only occasionally have Hollywood films stirred controversy, and then it was usually provoked by its stereotypical representation of women, ethnic minorities, or gays and lesbians.[32] On the other hand, the sheer scope of the battle over family values in the United States, and the increased convergence between Hollywood and other media and entertainment sectors, could not but leave trace on Hollywood itself. Much like in the studio era, different actors within the entertainment and media industries have begun to translate conflicts over values into economic benefits and, vice versa, to camouflage their material desires with quests for the regulation of fantasy. Consequently, the new censorship wars have reshaped, and continue to reshape, both commercial and moral dimensions of Hollywood's entry into cyberspace.

The most indicative and, perhaps, the most significant issue in the restructuring of the entertainment industry over the past two decades has been the question of media violence and its effects on children. Since 1982, when the National Institute of Mental Health issued a new and alarming report on the effects of media violence, there have been at least a dozen congressional hearings and special White House meetings devoted to this issue. Two aspects of these debates—the trade-off between anti-trust legislation and moral self-regulation, and the problematic separation of reality and fantasy violence—deserve special attention because of their political and economic implications within and outside of Hollywood. Namely, a careful examination of congressional hearings and White House meetings devoted to media violence reveals profound divisions between various segments of the entertainment business in response to possible government oversight. Since motion picture companies were relatively protected from government interference by their voluntary rating program, initial targets of government investigation into the effects of media violence were broadcasting networks, already subject to government control because of their dependence on public spectrum. Development of new technologies and distribution platforms in the 1970s, such as cable and satellite TV, promised an end to the spectrum scarcity and increased competitive pressures on the networks. Cable companies such as CNN quickly realized that they could easily trade economic favors with the government. In exchange for compliance with regulations of fictional violence on TV, they were given favorable treatment in the era of government economic deregulation. Thus, in 1983, Daniel Schor, CNN anchorman, led the attack on TV violence in Congressional hearings; in the early 1990s, Ted Turner, CNN founder, demanded stricter regulation of violent programming "Congress will have to 'keep a gun to the heads' of network executives to get them to curb violence in television programs," Turner allegedly said.[33] And, in 1994, cable representatives announced their endorsement of V-chip despite broadcasters' opposition. In each instance, cable companies acted as the greatest cheerleaders of government interference and control over violent programs. Consequently, as cable's position vis-à-vis the networks considerably improved with its support for anti-violence measures, the position of broadcasters also began to soften. By the mid 1990s, both broadcasters and cable providers came to see as their major concerns the "elimination of cross-ownership restrictions, protections for video markets in and against the telephone industries, and securing access to the 'information superhighway.'"[34] For the relaxation of anti-trust regulations in these areas, they "were willing to make concessions in what, in the larger scheme of things, appeared to be relatively minor program matters."[35] The end result of these ritual debates and strategic bargaining was the Telecommunications Act of 1996, which was simultaneously perceived as the greatest victory of anti-violence forces and as the greatest defeat of the First Amendment and anti-trust legislation in the history of the U.S. telecommunications industry.

The consequences of this trade-off between economic and moral spaces were twofold. The Telecommunications Act of 1996 and the ensuing merger activity have both reinforced the trend toward the integration of various segments of the entertainment business and further empowered the distributors. The multiplication of distribution channels, threats of strikes in Hollywood, and rising costs of brand-names, a.k.a. actors and stars, have pushed for further development of Reality-based television and made-for-TV movie productions. Reality-based TV has gradually grown into the most popular form of entertainment in America: from 1980s hits such as *America's Most Wanted* and mid-1990s serialized lives, such as programs depicting Hollywood's Madam Heidi Fleiss and the O.J. Simpson saga, to the new millennium hits such as MTV's *Real World*, CBS's *Survivor*, or Fox's *Temptation Island*. The popularity of Reality TV signals an important shift in media programming. The emphasis has moved from fictional stories, which, as we have seen via the example of fake documentaries in the pre-Studio era, were once assumed to be more controllable and easier to produce, to real-life stories whose erratic occurrences can now be managed thanks to the low cost of satellite connections, a number of globally dispersed freelancers willing to risk their lives in order to record a story, and a public eager to supply its private life to the media. Meanwhile, the insistence of the legislators that the only problematic violence in entertainment programs is fictional violence makes the reality violence—such as continuous news coverage and direct transmissions of wars—into an easy substitute for fiction. The live transmission of the Gulf War brought about a 28 percent increase in advertising revenue for CNN and led many to believe that coverage of wars and humanitarian disasters could be both morally right and profitable as well. Coverage of violence in Somalia, Haiti, Bosnia, and Kosovo followed. Not surprisingly, sheltered by its presumption of reality, CNN—and its parent-company Time Warner—agreed quite willingly to exchange censorship for anti-trust legislation.

So what exactly is the purpose of these debates on media violence which appear with ritualistic regularity in American politics? What is the purpose of blaming fictional characters—such as Murphy Brown—or stylized and stylish science-fiction worlds—such as *A Clockwork Orange* (1971) and *The Matrix* (1999)—for the incongruities, falsities, and violence of our own world? A simple and, perhaps, for that reason, overlooked answer is that the principal task of political debates about violence is to affirm the boundary between the fantastic and the real, the kernel of any ideology. It is indicative, for instance, that all government-sponsored studies and all congressional hearings insist that "reality violence" in the media is not a problem; the problem is only "gratuitous violence," "unnecessary violence," "inconsequential violence," in short "fantasy violence." The insistence on regulating fantasies rather than reality, mediated or not, accomplishes two things at the same time. First, just as regulation of sexual fantasies transforms sex into pornography, regulation (or attempts at regulation) of violent fantasies transforms violence into a pathological, abnormal, perverse act, an aberration from the normal. As such, regulation of fantasy violence obfuscates the degree to which violence—real or fantastic—is a systemic, integral, part of our everyday life. Second, by shrinking the media space available for fantasy violence, regulation enlarges the space for reality violence—wars, crime, disasters—transforming it, paradoxically, into entertainment, fiction, fantasy itself. This duality then spatializes the symbolic order by structuring the way in which violence is experienced and perceived, by perpetuating the illusion that world without violence is always within reach, and, most importantly, by separating the zones where violence is permissible from those where it is not.

Debates about violence in the media and attempts at the regulation of fantasy violence affect the political and economic world much more profoundly than is usually assumed. The expansion of the economic space, which Hollywood entertainment companies have acquired through the haggling over fantasy violence with the government, has come at the expense of space available for public expression. It is not a coincidence that the relaxation of anti-trust regulations has coincided with attacks on publicly sponsored art. The most famous cases of politically provocative art that have caused public outrage in the late 1980s and early 1990s—from Marlon Riggs's documentary *Tongues Untied* (1991) to Robert Mapplethorpe's photographs—have inadvertently enlarged the space for commercial programming. Ever since Congress reduced the funding for the NEA, the NEH, and PBS, HBO has been the largest sponsor of independently produced political documentaries.[36] The vastness and malleability of digital, "navigable," space have thus been purchased through the regulation of moral space, the division and ordering of reality and fantasy violence (with an implicit preference for the former), and an ever-increased commercialization of our political life. And as the entertainment industry comes to rely—technologically and economically—on the production of crime and warfare as a substitute for fantasy violence, it may be safe to say that it is reinventing the character of American hegemony.

Private Authority, Public Intimacy

The role of Hollywood in the resurgence and restructuring of American hegemony at the end of this very *American century* affirms Peter Taylor's portrayal of world-system hegemons as inventors of "ordinary modernity" deeply rooted in civil society, cultural practices, and everyday life.[37] As mentioned in the first chapter, in his interesting insertion of Gramsci into the world-systems theory, Taylor rightly insists that economic or military preponderance are neither sufficient nor critical for the maintenance of hegemonic power; rather is the particular separation of public and private spheres, focused on the creation and extension of "comfort zones" for ordinary consumers, that has been critical in the sustenance of the three modern hegemons: the Dutch, the British, and the Americans. However, Taylor's view that Americanization, defined first and foremost by Hollywood movies and suburbia, would inevitably lead both to an extraordinary political and economic impasse and to the end of the modern world-system seems to have underestimated the ability of cultural and military Americana to reinvent itself. By blurring the boundaries of public and private, allowing for the emergence of new hegemonic blocks, and constructing new spatial "comfort zones," Hollywood movies and suburbia have seemingly found a new way to take us into the new millennium.

The unseemly and unexpected success of the rapprochement between Hollywood and the U.S. defense industry questions the prem-

ises of both neo-realist and neo-Gramscian interpretations of hegemony. Neo-realists' interpretations of "hegemonic stability" focused
almost exclusively on the well-known institutions of Pax Americana
and defined hegemony as the "the ability of the dominant state to determine the conditions in which interstate relations are conducted
and to determine the outcomes of these relations."[38] Neo-Gramscian
critiques of such interpretations, on the other hand, have stressed that
a hegemon is defined not by its powers of coercion but by its powers
of persuasion: namely by the ability to present its own interests as
universal and objective and thereby to create willing followers of its
own vision.[39] In addition, as Mark Rupert perceptively writes, whereas
neo-realists assume "the long run harmony" between wealth and politics, neo-Gramscians view the separation of private and public, economics and politics, as both the premise and the product of capitalist
hegemony. In other words, according to Rupert, the production of
hegemony should be viewed as a continuous process of abstraction,
objectification, and estrangement of politics from economics and of
public from private interests.[40]

The emergence of Siliwood, however, complicates both of these perspectives and indicates that construction and re-construction of successful hegemonic blocks is neither a simple issue of state power nor
of the public/private distinction per se. Rather, hegemony appears to
depend, first and foremost, on the ability to draw (or blur) the boundaries themselves, that is on the ability to create obscure power lines—
cognitive, normative, or economic—and to keep them independent
both from political structures and from visible and well-known instruments and institutions of domination. The insertion of Hollywood
into discussions of hegemony (even among neo-realists) clearly shifts
debates about U.S. economic and military power to debates about culture, play, and entertainment; at the same time, it obfuscates—both
discursively and spatially—the distinctions between public and private, politics and economics, work and leisure that have long been regarded as the foundation of modern capitalism.

The blurring of the boundaries between public and private materi-
alizes the fear which Hannah Arendt once expressed with respect to
mass society: "both the public and private spheres of life are gone, the
public because it has become a function of the private and the private

because it has become the only common concern left."[41] The re-construction of American hegemony and the principal component of the new global order may no longer be the politics of "estrangement" and "objectification" but the exact opposite: the shift from military to commercial interests, from political to economic power, from universal to particular politics, and from public to private authority. The truth, as Slavoj Žižek and *The X-Files* would say, is *out there*. These political trends are apparent on the macro as well as on the micro level. Globally, they reflect themselves through the creation of transnational "buyer-driven" commodity chains and corporations which act as coordinators of dispersed production activities; the insistence on privatization and liberalization of national economies, mostly in sectors indispensable to commerce such as telecommunications, finance, and transport; the emergence of formal and informal transnational merchant networks; and the rise of diasporic communities and politics, particularly within the U.S. On a national level, they are evident in the transformation of intimacy into the principal public concern: the issues of body politics (health care, euthanasia, abortion), identity (gender, ethnicity, and sexual orientation), and family (family leave, family values, single parenthood) dominate the domestic political agenda to such a degree that it seems that the political continues to exist only if and when it can be transposed into the personal. Therefore, the fundamental principles of contemporary political order do seem like a puzzle to both neo-realists and neo-Gramscians. The former, oblivious to the private/public distinction, continue to reify the state and view international politics only thorough the lens of the rise and fall of great powers; the latter, convinced that the separation of public and private is the foundation of bourgeois hegemony, have difficulties conceptualizing politics and a hegemonic project which purposefully blurs the boundaries between public and private and appears to bring capitalist relations out into the open.

Digital Coalition(s)

Going back to the discussion about entertainment and warfare, reality and fantasy violence, it may now be more clear why fetishization of technology, privatization of research and development, and, particularly, the odd relation between Hollywood and the military-industrial complex may be such a potent tool in the construction and re-construction of American hegemony at the end of the twentieth century. Apart from being the principal new financier of digital revolution, Hollywood—or, more precisely, the American-dominated global entertainment sector—has played multiple other roles in this process. Once defined as "the most powerful national institution that offered private solutions to public problems,"[42] Hollywood was exceptionally well qualified to become an important player in the era of personalized high-tech politics. The industry has always thrived on the appropriated privacy of its employees or of its consumers, carefully crafting and publicizing the lives of its stars to match the desires of its audiences, or playing upon the most intimate characteristics and fantasies of its audiences to sell its relatively generic products. This play on the sensitive issues of morality and intimacy has also exposed Hollywood to public scrutiny far more than other industrial sectors, so the industry developed elaborate self-regulatory institutions combining censorship, self-censorship, and economic control. The phenomenon of "private interest government," which Streeck and Schmitter identify as the (possible and positive) cooperative trend in advanced industrial countries in response to the devolution of state responsibilities,[43] has been the main characteristic of Hollywood almost since its inception. Both as an industry and as a cultural or normative institution, Hollywood learned a long time ago how to carry the burden of presumed public interest while never losing sight of its own goals or, vice versa, how to present its own private interests as the interests of society at large.

As Nye and Owens have put it quite bluntly, in this day and age, "knowledge, more than ever before, is power."[44] Hence, it is really not so important whether governments should continue to monitor traffic on the Internet, whether military origins of information technology create an inherent bias for its future use, or even whether *Toy Story* (1995) and its merchandising could possibly finance production of missiles. What seems far more pertinent is the creation of a discursive sphere that allows for the consolidation of merchant power and the continued existence of the military-industrial complex beyond the reach of public scrutiny and possible contestation. Aside from Hollywood, critical in this process has been the creation of the new historical bloc which, despite its internal discord and heterogeneous composition, continues to garner public support for further expansion and privatization of high-technology sectors.

"Digital coalition," as this alliance of political and economic actors within the United States may be called, embraces academic institutions (particularly those located near high-tech zones such as Silicon Valley, Boston's Route 128, and North Carolina's Research Triangle), information technology sectors, entertainers, financiers, former hippies and college drop-outs, and a bipartisan group of political representatives in Washington, D.C. Much like the technology which it espouses and which appears to transcend the limits of time and space, the digital coalition derives its power from its strategic location on the nexus of the previously fixed political and economic coordinates: national and international, global and local, private and public, past and future, state and commerce, business and academia. The paradigmatic example is probably the MIT Media Lab which started out over ten years ago as an off-shoot of the MIT Artificial Intelligence Lab, a cold war–sponsored institution. Ever since, the Lab has persistently worked on the transformation of digital technology from an indispensable, abstract and dull ingredient of military and industrial products into an indispensable, entertaining, and hip attribute of the yuppie lifestyle.[45] In the process, it has enlisted the support of transnational corporate sponsors that can directly benefit from such popularization of digital technology—from Sony, Philips, Sega, Lego, and Nintendo to Intel, Disney, Nike, Microsoft, Viacom, and dozens of others.[46] Similar functions—suspension of disbelief and creation of hype—have been filled by the MIT-Lab-endorsed magazine *Wired*; annual *Technology, Entertainment, and Design* conferences in Monterey, California; *Whole Earth Review*, once an environmental magazine with its own subculture turned techno-global through its electronic link WELL; Ester Dyson's Electronic Frontier Foundation and her varied corporate holdings in transitional economies through EdVenture Holdings; and by millions of children who have, over the years, become ardent supporters of digital technology thanks to their parents' consumption of video games and play-software. But the most important popularizer has obviously been the mass customized World

Wide Web itself and the numerous "personal" services that it offers, including the opportunity given to any individual with access to the net to create his or her own storefront—a web page—thereby finalizing the process of commodification of the "self" and publicization of intimacy characteristic of postmodernity.

But there is also another, more particular, level of affinity between Hollywood and high technology: the idea that simulated environments allow us to control within them all that would otherwise be impossible to control outside of them. The special effects industry has become the common, and quite telling, denominator between Hollywood and high technology. As Michael Stern notes in an interesting essay on the problems of conceptualization in the film industry, it is much more difficult to define what special effects are—what constitutes their "specialness" as opposed to all other methods of falsification of reality in the movies—than most viewers generally assume. In contrast to the usual distinction between effects that emphasize their status as artifacts and those that try to hide it, Stern suggests that, at least in science fiction films, special effects that the audience most easily recognizes as such are those which "enact the possibilities, delights and terrors of glamorous new technologies: space flights, death rays, matter transmitters, cloning, living on the moon or at the bottom of the Pacific, socializing or fighting with aliens, being raped by a computer and so on."[47] Such effects, he notes, perform double effacement: on the one hand, they efface technology which has gone into the creation of these special effects; on the other hand, they transform all other effects which have gone into the creation of the film from cultural artifacts into natural objects. Thus, concludes Stern, by simultaneously naturalizing technology and displaying it as a special effect, the special-effects industry has helped to "construct and legitimize a world in which technology is an abstract category of effects without any specific social and political context, rather than a critical part of a whole way of life."[48]

The transposition of the principal economic activities into the computer-generated world leaves its imprint on the world of common men. Simulation technology, which stands at the heart of Hollywood's transformation, does not limit itself to special effects, computer games, and digital environments. It spills over into urban areas, leisure

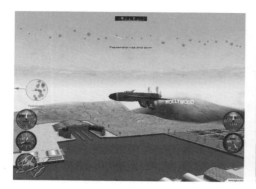

Microsoft's airplane destroys the Hollywood sign in *Crimson Skies,* a video game released in 2000. In this alternate history, the year is 1937, and the United States has fractured into a myriad of squabbling nation-states as a consequence of Prohibition, the Great Depression, and rising isolationism. Screen shot reprinted by permission of Microsoft Corporation.

parks, and the well-protected zones of consumption. Special effects designers, computer animators, and software engineers are constructing theme park rides, imaginary submarines, and virtual reality war games and placing them in theme parks and shopping malls around the world, from Los Angeles to Nagoya, Japan. Their purpose is to put potential consumers into familiar narratives and childlike situations, encouraging them to spend money along the way. As Michael Sorkin perceptively wrote several years ago, "one of the main effects of Disneyfication is the substitution of recreation for work, the production of leisure according to the routines of the industry."[49] But many of these new entertainment cities also aspire to be something more than just hybrids of malls and theme parks. As we have clearly seen in the "thick description" of the Universal CityWalk, their ambition is to be more public than any public place precisely because they are private and more real than any real place precisely because they are "controlled environments." Similarly, although not as enthusiastically, the architects and designers working on the revival of Times Square in New York, *42nd Street Now!*, view the project as an attempt to introduce "prescribed, nostalgic, staged chaos" into a crime-ridden urban area.[50] Disney's Celebration combines a 1940s town atmosphere with 1990s amenities, including a Disney-sponsored state-of-the-art public school.[51] Thanks to the changes in local merchant laws over the past decade, many of these places now operate like mini-states with rights to charge extra taxes in order to hire extra security. As a consequence, the number of private police troops in the United States has come to exceed the number of regular policemen: privatization of space apparently leads to privatization of violence.

The emergence of privately owned public space has its parallel in the disappearance of the clearly delineated private space. Technological convergence brings to a logical conclusion the process that started earlier in this century with Sears, Roebuck mail-order catalogues: the construction of the household as the privileged site of consumption. Inch by inch, Hollywood, like all other industries in the United States, has been conquering this terrain. What started off with occasional co-productions of radio shows as a way of movie merchandising will soon turn Epcot Center into a monument of the past. From telecommuting to video-on-demand, Internet, and shopping channels, the public—work and commerce—is colonizing the sphere of private life disguised as entertainment, play-work, flirtation, and convenience. The future, we are told, will be interactive: we will be able to enter into our favorite movies the way we can now pretend to be animated objects in pixels on the Internet; we will be able to fly around the world with a virtual-reality helmet on our head; soon we may no longer even need computer screens—the images will be transmitted directly to the retina of our eyes. Not surprisingly, observers of the information age now argue that the body, not the home, is the ultimate frontier of capitalist expansion. Jean Baudrillard perceives the new boundary as a loss, as the vanishing of subjects, agency, and politics in the world of simulations; the late Timothy Leary thought that simulation places us—mortal individuals—in the position of absolute control over our political and personal destiny. Either way, in the world of science fiction, and increasingly in our everyday life, it is the body—with its genetic codes, implants, and transplants—that acts as a computer terminal plugged into the universe of wireless communication.[52]

The success of hegemonic projects depends, therefore, on their ability to reveal what is beyond dispute and to hide what ought to be discussed. The re-constitution of American hegemony over the past decade has been closely related to the commercialization of its high technology sectors, a result of bringing them, quite literally, close to home; at the same time, it was also a reaffirmation of traditional business and military interests at home and abroad. Through the privatization of the discourse, not just of the industry itself, the sectors which had once been tied to public expenditure have acquired a second lease on life. Commercialization has placed technology into the seemingly apolitical zone of entertainment where even warfare takes place only on TV and where private violence turns into a norm. Not surprisingly, the shift took place exactly at the time when the last ideological barriers to public discussion of cold war spending were being lifted. In that context, Hollywood's ability to bring technology into everyday life and straight into our fantasies through special effects, Busch Gardens, Disney Worlds, and the invasion of the household was critical; it has created an impression that technological development and the particularistic interests behind it were nothing but a fulfillment of our own desires. Thanks to its work, technology has come to represent another "parallel realm," another sphere of "private authority," quite similar to the law merchant described by Cutler.[53] The naturalizing and legitimizing of digital technology has pushed into the background the undercurrents of contemporary economic transformation—the centralization of distribution capacities in the hands of a few telecom and entertainment companies, the monopolization of the public sphere by the media, the level of indebtedness of multimedia corporations, the increasing gaps between technological haves and have-nots, the shifting burden of communication costs from businesses to the average consumers, the continued military expenditures for information technology, the inscription of violence into the very structure of the entertainment industry. The creation of the global communication infrastructure, the laying down of cables rightly compared to the laying down of railroad tracks in the last century, is a process laden with inequalities and power asymmetries which cannot be resolved through the democratization of access and protection of privacy. Commercialization of digital technology has brought us *Terminator 2*, cellular telephones, QVC, and the Internet; it has also transformed us into the willing followers of an unexplored path towards a dystopian future.

THE DEVELOPMENT of digital technology and the production of cyberspace have brought new hopes and old fears to Hollywood. The intensification of the struggle between producers and merchants has turned Hollywood into one of the main financiers of high-technology sectors in the United States and a possible successor to the military-industrial complex as a generator of growth in the American economy. Thanks to both the high level of investment in research and development and the expansion of the entertainment sector, Hollywood is now receiving accolades not just as the export success story in the U.S. economy but as one of the most important strategic sectors in its future development.

Yet the main beneficiary of all this activity and attention has not been Hollywood itself. Producers, led by the Spielberg-Lucas team and their numerous off-springs, support the development of digital technology with the hope that it will someday, in a still-uncertain future, allow them to reestablish their control over the production process. Hollywood merchants, the large multimedia companies in particular, are mostly focusing their investments on new distribution technologies. By creating additional distribution venues, they are trying to consolidate their own position in the entertainment sector. However, the frantic investment activity has, thus far, only increased the level of indebtedness in the entertainment industry and placed Hollywood in the precarious position of dependence on Wall Street financiers and foreign investors. In addition, the rapprochement between the Hollywood majors and the government-regulated telecommunications sector has revived dormant concerns about Hollywood's morality and has renewed pressures and quests for government censorship of the industry.

Most importantly, however, Hollywood has become a building block in the construction of what some political scientists have termed "private authority": a set of relatively obscure legal, cognitive, and economic threads of power that runs through global economy and shields its governance structures from broader popular participation or even public discussion. The "retreat of the state," as Susan Strange warns, has not created a power vacuum. Rather, it has created new formal and informal links of power that run bellow and beyond the nation-state level, often assuming the state's role but without any responsibilities of public office.[54] Hollywood has played a dual role in such reconstitution of authority in the United States. First, as mentioned, it has assumed the duties of a financier of high technology sectors that constitute the core of U.S. military and commercial power. And, second, it has shifted the boundaries between reality and fantasy violence, public and private space, contributing, this time quite literally, to the creation of gated communities both in cyberspace and in our urban or quasi-urban areas.

The production of cyberspace reveals, therefore, the extent to which the production of space is always directly related to the production of power. But it also reveals the ultimate paradox of this relationship: as the technological world becomes bigger and bigger and as the entertainment and leisure sector continues to overtake the old manufacturing sectors, both pose limitations on the livable world that we inhabit. The expansion of make-believe puts restrictions on our imagination; and an already realized utopian or, even, dystopian future cancels the need for the here and now. Coming full circle to our point of origin, to the world delineated by Universal Studio and Universal CityWalk, it becomes completely obvious that the growth of Hollywood at the end of the twentieth century seems as divorced from sheer entertainment as it was in its beginning.

Space may be the final frontier
But it's made in a Hollywood basement.

Red Hot Chili Peppers, *Californication*

S uccessful laboratories of postmodernity, writes Hans Magnus Enzensberger, include elements of cannibalism and flourish thanks to their pre-modern vestiges.[1] The abandonment of production in contemporary Hollywood, the "hollowing out" of Hollywood's studios, and the creation of the global merchant empire on the debris of the old production world are not without their historical precedents. As economic and business historians often remind us, production has not always been the key activity in capitalist economy. As Charles Tilly notes, "Capitalists have often existed in the absence of capitalism, the system in which wage-workers produce goods by means of materials owned by capitalists. Through most of history, indeed, capitalists have worked chiefly as merchants, entrepreneurs, and financiers rather than as direct organizers of production."[2] The dispersion of production, the power of merchants, the control over distribution and marketing—all greatly resemble the traits of the "putting-out" system that served as the backbone of the European proto-industrialization in that long, Braudelian, sixteenth century. Namely, in the period between the fourteenth and the seventeenth century, when European economies first became truly global, a succession of Portuguese, Dutch, and British merchants dominated the world economy. The goods traveled on regular basis from China to the New World to European ports and back. At home, and in remote parts of the world, European merchants supplied artisans with funds and, sometimes, even with raw materials necessary for production. They gave orders, designs, and detailed descriptions of goods to producers. They traded unique products and different peoples between continents and faraway lands. Their power derived less from their ability to control the flow and quantity of production and much more from their near-monopoly over transportation; their knowledge of consumers' desires and ability to match them with producers' skills; and their talent to tickle consumers' fantasies with stories about unseen regions, exotic countries, and their mysterious fruits. The world surrounding the merchants was a mess, torn apart by warfare between impotent localities, communities linked by trade and little else, and emergent absolutist states. Dutch historian Jan de Vries describes the last century of this period as "an age of crisis" that deeply affected the most intimate aspects of peoples' lives: contagious diseases proliferated due both to the increased mobility of goods and people and to the breakdown of closed communities; birth rates significantly declined and marriage age increased due to uncertainties of the economy; romantic love, paradoxically, became more and more common since the value of assets—once the basis for the strategic alliance called marriage—was no longer stable.[3] Still, despite its inherent uncertainty, merchants' capitalism, for as long as it could, thrived on the world's disorder and generated enough capital to jump-start the industrial revolution.

These days, a ride across the United States, or a trip around the shrinking planet on CNN Headline News—the stroll from one Kmart (the movie-merchandising paradise) to another, from one satellite dish to another, or from one McDonald's (also a movie-merchandising paradise) to another—could easily make us believe that our homogenous world has nothing in common with the richness, diversity, and plurality of the sixteenth and seventeenth centuries world economy. Nothing, not even the deserts of Arizona or Zuni reservations in New Mexico, appears to be untouched by the brave-new-worldism of our era. But appearances are deceptive. For we have gone beyond McDonald's, beyond Kmarts and Wal-Marts, beyond Hollywood zones, and stepped into the cold. Abandoned continents, countries, former colonies and company towns, deserted mills, and roach-infested inner cities stand in sharp contrast with the society of all-encompassing plenitude and uniform serenity depicted by Huxley in the 1930s. Even Prozac, unlike Huxley's tranquilizer, soma, with all of its 1.2 billion dollars of worldwide sales, is not available to everyone. The old "controlled environments" of production and induced, involuntary inclusion are being pushed to the margins and replaced by exclusive "controlled environments" of consumption, organized leisure, and entertainment. But these oases of falsified happiness and make-believe wealth are also few and far between. In this new Brave New World, Huxley's dystopia has become many a man's utopia. The places of savagery proliferate around the world and compete in their tragic abandonment for attention of those lucky enough to be still visibly controlled.

And if the parallels between this pre-industrial world of merchants and contemporary global economy occasionally seem striking, it is not simply because De Vries's descriptions of the European capitalism in "an age of crisis" often read like the most recent copy of the *New York Times*. Wholesalers and large retailers have learned by now that they occupy the key strategic position in commodity chains linking manufacturers and consumers. Hence, the role of merchants as the coordinators of both the U.S. and world economy is becoming increasingly transparent in a number of sectors. In a survey conducted by the magazine *Industrial Distribution* several years ago, hundreds of U.S. manufacturers conceded that they had followed distributors' recommendations when purchasing parts and products ranging from rubber and adhesives to power hand tools.[4] Pharmaceutical conglomerates, global in scope just like the large entertainment companies, now act primarily as coordinators for a number of quasi-independent research institutions and as distributors of products to hospitals, pharmacies and drugstores. Automobile dealers have lost a huge share of their sales and service operations due to the distribution expediency of franchises like Midas, NAPA, and Goodyear.[5] In addition, giant new national dealerships—one of which was, not surprisingly, founded by the former owner of theater chains and Blockbuster Video—are now threatening to completely disempower both smaller dealerships and the Big Three car manufacturers. Business literature is replete with examples of "brand loyalty" due to the successes of wholesalers/

retailers such as Ikea, Wal-Mart, Kroger, or Toys-R-Us in global markets. Thus, rather than being a system whose essence lies in quantity production or product innovation, the emerging "buyer-driven" commodity chain is the system governed and ruled by merchants and/or providers of financial services in both exporting and importing countries. The merchants/financiers on both sides of the trade link provide manufacturers, located anywhere in the world, with necessary funds and product specifications, based on presales and their intimate knowledge and observation of local markets and trends. The process of industrial reorganization which started off with the breakdown of mass production has created not just new, *hybrid*, forms of industrial organization or inflated trade volumes, but transnational links among the merchants and a dividing line between them and manufacturers. The consequences of this rift may very well indicate the emergence of a new and quite different, social order than in the era of mass production.

But in order to understand the functioning of this system we have to dispense both with the belief that value is created first and foremost in production as well as with the notion that markets are free and ungoverned. The history of pre-industrial capitalism does not fully support either of these views. The market is never an impersonal force, it is run and organized by traders and wholesalers who thrive on inequality, not equality, of exchanges. Hence, societies and economies organized by merchants are entirely different than those organized by manufacturers. Merchants are not interested in the continuity of production, they are only interested in the continuity of supply. They are not interested in expansion of production, they do best with products which are scarce. They are not even particularly interested in how production is organized, for their only concern is the standard quality of a finished product. They do not need full employment, a few craftsmen can do. They care little about social order as long as their routes of communication and trade are left untouched. They regulate and control the economy by providing a link between production and consumption but they do not need all-encompassing "controlled environments" of mass production, a few "safely chaotic" areas of consumption are enough.

Hence, although historical analogies have obvious limitations, the parallels between the pre-modern and postmodern capitalism may be a good reminder that economic prosperity and social disorder are not mutually exclusive categories but often reinforce each other. The contemporary merchant economy, much like De Vries's "age of crisis," offers both hope and reasons for concern. On the one hand, it is becoming increasingly apparent that contemporary merchant economy may be sustainable and profitable despite constant and continuous crisis and eruptions of violence. Reinvestment of capital into information technology has consolidated merchant power and, for as long as trade and capital flows can circulate without obstructions, there is no reason for the global economy to falter. On the other hand, it is also quite obvious that centralization of merchant power may lead to the continued unarticulated acts of violence and impotent self-destruction in the globally dispersed loci of production. Ironically, such scattered resistance, just like the intense competition among manufacturers, is much more likely to further reinforce the power of merchants in the contemporary global economy than to empower their opponents.

The question of order brings us closer to the second important theme of previous chapters—the relationship between changes in industrial structure and strategy and the sphere of everyday life. As we have seen, any change in spatial and temporal organization of the economy works on both macro and micro levels. It reconfigures locations of particular sectors in the global economy and helps promote certain regional economies at the expense of others. At the same time, it changes distances between home and work, public and private, places of production and places of consumption. In each case that we examined, producers and merchants had found new ways of transposing their conflict onto the private life of their employees and their consumers, as well as new ways of expanding their own power by shifting the boundaries of public and private. The spatial enclosure of manufacturing in the mass production era separated the workplace from the home and created a distinct "private sphere." But it also increased the tendency of employers to intrude into the private life of their workers and to create brand-name products to foster loyalty on the part of their consumers. Conversely, the dispersion of production and the rise of the merchant economy have placed a premium on commodification of privacy of both manufacturers and consumers: under the guise of liberated plurality, they have successfully stimulated the development of franchises based on personal life stories and of niche markets based on extensive databasing of consumer preferences and habits. Finally, the construction of cyberspace has led to the development of "gated communities," both on the Internet and in the "real" world—paradoxically, therefore, expanding the place of make-believe by diminishing the place that we can safely inhabit.

This constant trade-off between the territorial expansion of capitalism and the actual size of private, or personal, space confirms the thesis of Anthony Giddens that time-space distanciation, the stretching of societies through history and geography, transform the form of social organization from the immediacy of "presence-availability" to "system-integration." The greater the distance, argues Giddens, the greater the tendency towards surveillance, standardization and commodification of time and space through schedules and timetables, development of communication and information technologies, and coordination of social and political activities via "authority spheres" detached from the specificity of time and place. The creation of "private authority" spheres that we are witnessing these days shows the impact which time-space distanciation can have on the character of political life. While it does not necessarily shrink the public space—on the contrary, many would argue that development of information technology has enlarged the space available for public discussion—it does change the nature of public discourse by changing the concepts of what is private and what is public, what is hidden and what is revealed, what ought to be discussed and what ought not to be discussed. In short, by changing the material and discursive boundaries of public and private, the spatial reorganization of production and the emergence of merchant economy have changed the nature of politics itself.

Finally, the shifts in Hollywood power lines and the transformations of its architecture have also affected the boundaries between the real and the fantastic, compelling us to reconsider, once again, the main theme of this book: the interplay of space, power, and fantasy, and their role in the creation and sustenance of political and economic order. Namely, there is no doubt that Hollywood—and all the good and bad that it symbolizes—has played an extremely important role in the creation of the new global order. Partly, it is because, as Hollywood's numerous critics are always quick to point out, it has successfully saturated world markets with cultural products that appeal to the lowest common denominator. The global village, to the extent to which it exists, floats in a space produced and delineated by the shared knowledge of *Pocahontas* (1995), Darth Vader, *Baywatch* characters, the *Titanic* romance, and *Rambo* movies. As mentioned, the expansion of the infotainment sector and debates about its political impact have simultaneously expanded the boundaries of a phantasmic global community and shrunk the access to power, wealth, and livable space for the majority of world's population. Even critiques of Hollywood are contributing to the further advancement of this spectral global edifice. The charges of cultural homogenization, in a world which is anything but homogenous, further obfuscate the dissonant aspects of the current political moment, fabricate illusory bonds and threads among sharply divided peoples and regions despite recurrent wars, famine, and financial crisis, and displace discussions about power inequalities onto the issues of culture, play, and entertainment. Similarly, as Lawrence Grossberg notes, political trust in difference and culture as possible sites of resistance seems highly suspect in this "new global economy of culture" which "produces difference as the form of the plane of expression, and money as the substance of the plane of content."[6] In both cases, the scope for political change has been vastly reduced.

But the relationship between Hollywood and global order, fantasy and power, has of late become even more complicated and, perhaps, even more hopeless than this. In his analysis of the fantastic as a literary genre, Tzvetan Todorov defines fantasy as that moment of hesitation in which the main character, and, hence, the reader, have to decide whether a certain event is or is not real. However, Todorov also warns of a paradox: literature itself "bypasses the distinction between real and imaginary" and makes it difficult to sustain the boundary between them.[7] In other words, the acceptance of ambiguity between real and unreal within the text requires that the reader suspend the distinction between reality and literature, herself and the text. And vice versa, it is precisely the fantastic as a genre that creates the possibility of a clear-cut distinction between actual and fictitious. Therefore, writes Todorov, "matters are, in truth, more complex: by the hesitation that it engenders, the fantastic questions precisely the existence of an irreducible opposition between real and unreal. But in order to deny the opposition, we must first acknowledge its terms."[8] Thus, fantastic literature—much like special effects in cinema—thrives on the ambiguity between real and imaginary, while, at the same time, positing them as irrevocably distinct.

So, what happens when the fantastic becomes a gauge by which we measure, examine, and comprehend the reality? What happens when, as Tim Murray notes, the world becomes credible only insofar as it is "like a movie," when the "cinematic 'happenings' of culture—of identity, identification, and politics—are believable only because they are structured like film?"[9] What happens to politics when the "inside" and "outside" of representation, and of media, are no longer easily discernible; when an actor-turned-President builds his political ideology around films that he had once been (or imagined being) a part of; when residents of Sarajevo turn to CNN to learn what is happening in their own, besieged, city; when the plight of Kosovo Albanians is not compared to the plight of Jews in the Second World War but—of course—to those portrayed by Spielberg's *Schindler's List* (1993)?

Perhaps, as Žižek thinks, the very distinction between real and fantastic is a false one, perpetuating an ideological illusion that the real world, the *real* reality, while hidden from us, can somehow still be found, reached, discovered, conquered, and controlled. Perhaps, as Todorov thinks, the achievement of the twentieth century was the transformation of the fantastic into the rule, not the exception. Perhaps, this seemingly unstoppable growth of the spectral space, digital or not, really induces political inter-passivity rather than interactivity, isolation rather than communication, distance rather than intimacy. Perhaps, there is really no way out of *The Truman Show* (1998), and no other reality but *The Matrix*.

Still, I would like to end on a more ambivalent note. The world beyond Hollywood zones, as I said at the outset of this journey, is not free of ideological fantasies, political manipulation, and economic control. Indeed, at this point, there is probably no world beyond Hollywood. But, perhaps, the acceptance of this radical closure—*there is no space but mediated space*—opens up some cracks in the way in which we envision power, our own relationship toward it, and our own possibilities for resistance. The world with no escape is also the world in which the enemy, the other, the evil can no longer be externalized. The world with no exit is also the world which demands utmost political responsibility, even in, or particularly in, the production of fantasies. The world as dependent on everyday life, as contemporary economy appears to be, is also the world vulnerable to even the most irrelevant social practices: if an illicit love affair could exemplify all the weaknesses of the studio system, why not expect that other, personal, transgressions would also have an effect on contemporary politics? The world of seemingly absolute control may also be the world in which control becomes apparently absurd and in which contingencies and inadvertent consequences are finally recognized as possibilities. The cyborgs and other denizens of this closed, claustrophobic, mediated space may prove to be unexpectedly irreverent. As Donna Haraway puts it, in her influential "Manifesto for Cyborgs," written at the height of the Star Wars (Strategic Defense Initiative) era, the key problem with cyborgs is "that they are illegitimate offsprings of militarism and patriarchal capitalism, not to mention state socialism. But illegitimate offsprings are often exceedingly unfaithful to their origins. Their fathers, after all, are inessential."[10]

NOTES

Preface

1. Budd Schulberg, *Moving Pictures, Memories of a Hollywood Prince* (New York: Stein and Day, 1981). Cited in Ronald L. Davis, *The Glamour Factory: Inside Hollywood's Big Studio System* (Dallas: Southern Methodist University Press, 1993), 383.

2. See Stephen Gundle, *Between Hollywood and Moscow: The Italian Communists and the Challenge of Mass Culture, 1943–1991* (Durham: Duke University Press, 2000).

3. See "The New Economy," *Fortune*, 27 June 1994, 40.

4. See Hortense Powdermaker, *Hollywood, the Dream Factory: An Anthropologist Looks at the Movie-Makers* (Boston: Little, Brown, 1950).

5. The question was very much inspired by conversations with Jodi Dean. For her excellent discussion of the contribution of cultural studies to political theory, which revolves precisely around production of the political in this overly mediated age, see Jodi Dean, "Introduction: The Interface of Political Theory and Cultural Studies," in Jodi Dean, ed., *Cultural Studies and Political Theory* (Ithaca: Cornell University Press, 2000), 1–19.

Introduction: Into the Zones

1. Jaye Scholl, "Gold in the Backlot? Questions Arise on What MCA Is Really Worth," *Barron's*, 13 July 1987, 18.

2. Douglas Gomery, *The Hollywood Studio System* (New York: St. Martin's Press, 1986), 150.

3. Suzan Ayscough and Judy Brennan, "Urban Thrills without the Ills," *Daily Variety*, 30 June 1993, 5.

4. Scholl, "Gold in the Backlot," 22.

5. "Universal City Starts Housekeeping: The Complete Municipality That Produces Ten Miles of Film Per Week," *Photoplay*, May 1915, 90.

6. Ibid.

7. Ibid.

8. "Universal's Chameleon City: Most Remarkable Town Ever Built," *Universal Weekly*, 26 September 1914.

9. Ibid.

10. Ibid.

11. Horace B. Davis, "Company Towns," in *Encyclopedia of the Social Sciences* (New York: Macmillan, 1931), quoted in Sharon Zukin, *Landscapes of Power: From Detroit to Disney World* (Berkeley: University of California Press, 1991), 62.

12. Thomas Schatz, *The Genius of the System: Hollywood Filmmaking in the Studio Era* (New York: Pantheon Books, 1988), 20.

13. See "Universal's Chameleon City."

14. "Entertainment and Tourist Destination," PR Newswire, 30 September 1993.

15. Ibid.

16. Ibid.

17. *Universal CityWalk Architecture and Design Fact Sheet*, Press Release, 1993.

18. Ayscough and Brennan, "Urban Thrills without the Ills," 5.

19. Sam Grogg's talk in Charlottesville, Virginia, organized by the Virginia Foundation for the Humanities, April 1994.

20. "Universal CityWalk: An Architect's Dream; A Conversation with Jon Jerde," Universal City Press Release, 1993.

21. Ibid.

22. "Universal CityWalk: A Unique Experience; A Conversation with Tom Gilmore, Vice President and General Manager, Universal CityWalk," Universal City Press Release, 1993.

23. Wyn Wachhorst, *Thomas Alva Edison, an American Myth* (Cambridge: MIT Press, 1981), 199.

24. "Welcome to the Great Indoors," *Time*, 2 August 1993.

25. "The Forum Shops," Caesar's Palace Media Information Kit, 1994.

26. Ibid.

27. For an account of life in Celebration, see Andrew Ross, *The Celebration Chronicles: Life, Liberty, and the Pursuit of Property Values in Disney's New Town* (New York: Ballantine Books, 1999).

28. That exclusion is CityWalk's modus operandi is quite obvious to most of its observers. "As a commodity," writes Josh Stenger, "the 'City' in CityWalk is most fully accessible and most recognizable to the affluent. To be sure, CityWalk's is a semiotics of exclusivity, one that is read most fluently by members of the middle- and upper-middle classes." See Josh Stenger, "Light, Camera, Faction: (Re)Producing 'Los Angeles' at Universal's CityWalk," in David Desser and Garth Jowett, eds., *Hollywood Goes Shopping* (Minneapolis: University of Minnesota Press, 2000), 284.

29. See Stefan Zweig, *Three Masters: Balzac, Dickens, Dostoyevski* (New York: Viking, 1930).

30. See Fredric Jameson, *Postmodernism, or the Cultural Logic of Late Capitalism* (Durham: Duke University Press, 1991).

31. Zukin, *Landscapes of Power*, 5.

32. In her interesting study of colonial and postcolonial spaces in Australia, Jane Jacobs makes an explicit distinction between the study of "cultural politics of space" as opposed to "a reading of textualized landscape." "In their most narrow conceptualization," she writes, "textualized readings over-privilege the built form and the visioned urban plan, which are themselves a mark of power, 'a material manifestation of dominant interests.' . . . I am more concerned with the complicated politics of the production of urban space, than the object produced." See Jane M. Jacobs, *Edge of Empire: Postcolonialism and the City* (London: Routledge, 1996), 9. Similarly, Castells, in his brilliant analysis of the "space of flows" of the network society, also insists that space is a material product of historically determined social relations; it cannot be defined without reference to dominant social practices. See Manuel Castells, *The Information Age: Economy, Society and Culture. Volume I: The Rise of the Network Society* (Oxford: Basil Blackwell, 1996), 376–78 and 410–18. My analysis of Hollywood zones, and my treatment of its architecture, are, likewise, more concerned with the politics behind production of space, than with the reinterpretation of Hollywood's spatial constructs, fascinating though they may be.

33. See Henri Lefebvre, *The Production of Space*, trans. Donald Nicholson-Smith (Oxford: Basil Blackwell, 1991).

34. See Gary Gereffi and Miguel Korzeniewicz, eds., *Commodity Chains and Global Capitalism* (Westport: Greenwood Press, 1994).

35. It is indicative that the first attempt ever to analyze Hollywood as an industry was a series of lectures at Harvard Business School, organized by Joseph P. Kennedy. The lectures were a shrewd strategic move: Kennedy, a banker and a Harvard graduate, was hoping to bring the industry closer to the Eastern establishment, particularly Wall Street. Hence, Kennedy's introductory note stressed the achievements of the industry, while Hollywood moguls did their best to present Hollywood like any other manufacturing sector of their time. See Joseph P. Kennedy, *The Story of the Films; As Told by Leaders of the Industry to the Students of the Graduate School of Business Administration, George F. Baker Foundation, Harvard University. Chicago, A. W. Shaw, 1927* (New York: J. S. Ozer, 1971).

36. See Tom Gunning, "The Whole Town's Gawking: Early Cinema and the Visual Experience of Modernity," *Yale Journal of Criticism* 7, no. 2 (1994): 189–201.

37. Yet another early study of film—Howard Thompson Lewis's *The Motion Picture Industry* (New York: D. Van Nostrand, 1933, reprint by J. S. Ozer, New York, 1971)—devotes most of its attention to negotiations and arbitration between theater owners, distributors, and Hollywood producers. All general overviews of the industry emphasize tensions between exhibitors and producers. Charles Musser in *Before the Nickelodeon: Edwin S. Porter and the Edison Manufacturing Company* (Berkeley: University of California Press, 1991) describes the relationship between producers and exhibitors as constantly troubled given that one side controls the product and the other controls the purse. Therefore, he claims, distributors—the pivotal group between these two forces—have so often held power in the industry. Nonetheless, even the historians most sensitive to this issue never operationalize the tensions between producers and merchants as an explanatory tool for the changes in the industry. When they turn their attention to problems such as the fall of the studio system or the contemporary reorganization of the industry, they adopt the exogenous or endogenous explanations of economic theories and neglect the intra-industrial struggle between producers and merchants.

38. See Alfred Chandler, *The Visible Hand: The Managerial Revolution in American Business* (Cambridge: Belknap Press, 1977); Olivier Zunz, *Making America Corporate, 1870–1920* (Chicago: University of Chicago Press, 1990); and, in particular, Glenn Porter and Harold C. Livesay, *Merchants and Manufacturers: Studies in the Changing Structure of Nineteenth-Century Marketing* (Baltimore: Johns Hopkins University Press, 1971).

39. See Janet Staiger, "The Hollywood Mode of Production to 1930," in David Bordwell, Janet Staiger, and Kristin Thompson, *The Classical Hol-*

lywood Cinema: Film Style and Mode of Production to 1960 (London: Routledge and Kegan Paul, 1985). Also important for this line of analysis were essays in Gorham Kindem, ed., *The American Movie Industry: The Business of Motion Pictures* (Carbondale: Southern Illinois University Press, 1982); in Tino Balio, ed., *The American Film Industry* (Madison: University of Wisconsin Press, 1985); in Janet Staiger, ed., *The Studio System* (New Brunswick: Rutgers University Press, 1995); and in David Bordwell, ed., *Post-Theory: Reconstructing Film Studies* (Madison: University of Wisconsin Press, 1996). See also books by Kristin Thompson, *Exporting Entertainment: America in the World Film Market, 1907–1934* (London: BFI, 1985); Janet Wasko, *Movies and Money: Financing the American Film Industry* (Norwood, N.J.: Ablex, 1982), and David Bordwell, *Making Meaning: Inference and Rhetoric in the Interpretation of Cinema* (Cambridge: Harvard University Press, 1989).

40. See Susan Christopherson and Michael Storper, "The City as Studio; the World as Backlot: The Impact of Vertical Disintegration on the Location of the Motion Picture Industry," *Environment and Planning D: Society and Space* 3 (1986): 305–20; Michael Storper and Susan Christopherson, "Flexible Specialization and Regional Industrial Agglomerations," *Annals of the Association of American Geographers* (March 1987), 104–17; Susan Christopherson and Michael Storper, "The Effects of Flexible Specialization on Industrial Politics and the Labor Market: The Motion Picture Industry," *Industrial and Labor Relations Review* 42 (April 1989): 331–47; Michael Storper, "The Transition to Flexible Specialization in the U.S. Film Industry: External Economies, the Division of Labour, and the Crossing of Industrial Divides," *Cambridge Journal of Economics* 13 (June 1989): 273–305; Michael Storper, "The Limits to Globalization," *Economic Geography* 68 (1992): 60–93; Robert Salais and Michael Storper, "The Four 'Worlds' of Contemporary Industry," *Cambridge Journal of Economics* 16 (1992), 169–93; and Michael Storper, "Flexible Specialization in Hollywood: A Response to Aksoy and Robins," *Cambridge Journal of Economics* 17 (1993): 479–84. More recently, Allen J. Scott has also been working on the geographical concentration of production in the key global culture industries (film, music, publishing). See Allen J. Scott, "French Cinema: Economy, Policy and Place in the Making of a Cultural-Products Industry," *Theory, Culture & Society* 17 (2000): 1–37; "The U.S. Recorded Music Industry: On the Relations Between Organization, Location, and Creativity in the Cultural Economy," *Environment and Planning A* 31 (1999): 1965–1984; and "The Cultural Economy: Geography and the Creative Field," *Media, Culture & Society* 21 (1999): 807–17. Scott, however, much like Storper and Christopherson, also

focuses, almost exclusively, on the production side of the industry and the geographic preconditions for innovation in culture industries.

41. For the original account of "flexible specialization" see Michael J. Piore and Charles F. Sabel, *The Second Industrial Divide: Possibilities for Prosperity* (New York: Basic Books, 1984).

42. Storper, "The Transition to Flexible Specialization in the U.S. Film Industry," 288.

43. Ibid., 285.

44. Ibid., 297.

45. See Mae Dana Huettig, *Economic Control of the Motion Picture Industry: A Study in Industrial Organization* (London: Oxford University Press, 1944).

46. Ibid., 145.

47. Ibid., 6.

48. Mike Davis, *City of Quartz: Excavating Future in Los Angeles* (London: Verso, 1990), 50.

49. Umberto Eco, *Travels in Hyperreality: Essays* (New York: Harcourt Brace Jovanovich, 1986), 8.

50. See Asu Aksoy and Kevin Robins, "Hollywood for the 21st Century: Global Competition for Critical Mass in Image Markets," *Cambridge Journal of Economics* 16 (1992): 1–22.

51. Jameson, *Postmodernism*, x.

52. The term "disorganized capitalism" is an intentional pun on the title of Scott Lash and John Urry's book *The End of Organized Capitalism* (London: Polity, 1987).

53. Baudrillard's views vis-à-vis production and consumption are particularly interesting because he was one of the first theorists who openly challenged the labor theory of value and attempted to confer a certain degree of analytical autonomy to the sphere of consumption. See Jean Baudrillard, *For a Critique of the Political Economy of the Sign*, trans. Charles Levin (St. Louis: Telos Press, 1981). Now, however, when "organized consumption" appears to have achieved actual autonomy, and when market and symbolic exchanges seem entirely separated from the forces of production, Baudrillard's own ideas are coming back to haunt him. In *Transparency of Evil*, he laments that speculation cannot be a surplus value since it is "utterly detached from production and its real conditions: a pure empty form, the purged form of value operating on nothing but its own revolving motion, its own orbital circulation." See Jean Baudrillard, *Transparency of Evil: Essays on Extreme Phenomena*, trans. James Benedict (London: Verso, 1993), 35.

54. Jameson, *Postmodernism*, 315–16.

55. Gunning, "The Whole Town's Gawking," 199.

56. Storper, "Response to Aksoy and Robins," 482.

57. Gary Gereffi, "The Organization of Buyer-Driven Global Commodity Chains," in Gereffi and Korzeniewicz, eds., *Commodity Chains and Global Capitalism*, 95–122.

58. Terence K. Hopkins and Immanuel Wallerstein, "Commodity Chains in the World Economy Prior to 1800," *Review* 10:1 (1986), 157–70. Reprinted in Gereffi and Korzeniewicz, eds. *Commodity Chains and Global Capitalism*, 17–20.

59. Gereffi and Korzeniewicz, eds., *Commodity Chains and Global Capitalism*, 3.

60. Ibid., 97.

61. Ibid.

62. Ibid., 99.

63. See David Harvey, *The Condition of Postmodernity: An Enquiry into the Origins of Cultural Change* (London: Blackwell, 1989).

64. Ibid.

65. For a fascinating account of the changes in cartography on European expansion, see also Jerry Brotton, *Trading Territories: Mapping the Early Modern World* (Ithaca: Cornell University Press, 1998).

66. Harvey, *Condition of Postmodernity*, 233.

67. Ibid., 203–4.

68. John Urry, "Time and Space in Giddens' Social Theory," in Christopher G. A. Bryant and David Jary, eds., *Giddens' Theory of Structuration: A Critical Appreciation* (London: Routledge, 1991), 172.

69. See Moishe Postone, *Time, Labor, and Social Domination: A Reinterpretation of Marx's Critical Theory* (Cambridge: Cambridge University Press, 1993).

70. See Giddens, "Time, Space, and Regionalisation," in Derek Gregory and John Urry, eds., *Social Relations and Spatial Structures* (London: Macmillan, 1985), 265–95.

71. Since Žižek is an extremely prolific writer, and fantasy one of the key concepts of Lacanian psychoanalysis, see, in particular, Slavoj Žižek, *The Sublime Object of Ideology* (London: Verso, 1989) and *The Plague of Fantasies* (London: Verso, 1997).

72. Žižek, *The Sublime Object of Ideology*, 126.

73. Žižek, *The Plague of Fantasies*, 29–30.

74. Žižek, *The Sublime Object of Ideology*, 126.

75. Peter J. Taylor, *Modernities: A Geohistorical Interpretation* (Minneapolis: University of Minnesota Press, 1999).

76. Ibid., 56.

Chapter I: Hollywood in the Studio

1. Wachhorst. *Thomas Alva Edison.*
2. Gomery, *The Hollywood Studio System,* 12.
3. For detailed overviews of Hollywood's performance in foreign markets in the inter-war period, see Ian Jarvie, *Hollywood's Overseas Campaign: The North Atlantic Movie Trade, 1920–1950* (New York: Cambridge University Press, 1992); Thompson, *Exporting Entertainment;* and Andrew Higson and Richard Maltby, eds., *"Film Europe" and "Film America": Cinema, Commerce, and Cultural Exchange, 1920–1939* (Exeter: University of Exeter Press, 1999).
4. See Schatz, *The Genius of the System,* but especially Bordwell, Staiger, and Thompson, *The Classical Hollywood Cinema.*
5. Terry Pristin, "Old Hollywood Lots Disappearing: Preservationists Hope to Rewrite Ending at Studios," *Los Angeles Times,* 22 March 1989, 1.
6. Frederic Raphael, "A Writer Stalks the Hollywood Myth," *New York Times,* 6 January 1985, Section 2, 1.
7. Kevin Robins and Frank Webster, "Cybernetic Capitalism: Information, Technology, Everyday Life," in Vincent Mosco and Janet Wasko, eds., *The Political Economy of Information* (Madison: University of Wisconsin Press, 1988), 49.
8. Harvey, *Condition of Postmodernity,* 125–40.
9. See William Lazonick, *Competitive Advantage on the Shop Floor* (Cambridge: Harvard University Press, 1990).
10. See Chandler, *The Visible Hand.*
11. See Piore and Sabel, *The Second Industrial Divide.*
12. See Herman M. Schwartz, *States versus Markets: History, Geography, and the Development of the International Political Economy* (New York: St. Martin's Press, 1994).
13. Indeed, Douglas Gomery is quite explicit on this point. "The studio system," wrote Gomery, "was so successful that only forces outside its control could significantly disrupt it." See Gomery, *The Hollywood Studio System,* 22. As mentioned in the previous chapter, Michael Storper and Susan Christopherson also assume that the Hollywood studio system ended because of exogenous shocks.
14. Although the Little Three did not own theaters, they were equally affected by the Supreme Court decision due to their close relationship with the exhibition circuit of the Big Five.

15. See Storper, "The Transition to Flexible Specialization in the U.S. Film Industry."

16. See Tino Balio, *History of American Cinema: Grand Design, Hollywood as a Modern Business Enterprise,* vol. 5 (New York: Charles Scribner's Sons, 1993).

17. See Christopher Anderson, *Hollywood TV: The Studio System in the Fifties* (Austin: University of Texas Press, 1994) for a nuanced account of the evolving symbiotic relationship between Hollywood studios and TV networks in the 1950s.

18. Thomas H. Guback, "Hollywood's International Market," in Balio, ed., *The American Film Industry,* 477.

19. United States, Congress, House, Committee on Education and Labor, *Impact of Imports and Exports on American Employment, Hearings before the Subcommittee on the Impact of Imports and Exports on American Employment of the Committee on Education and Labor, House of Representatives,* 87th Congress, 1st and 2d Session (Washington: U.S. Government Printing Office, 1961–1962).

20. See Chandler, *The Visible Hand.*

21. The merchants controlled the distribution of generic goods sold in bulk through the broad network of personal contacts in an otherwise disorganized and geographically dispersed market. Manufacturers, on the other hand, long remained men "of limited horizons who knew business conditions only in [their] immediate geographic area." See Zunz, *Making America Corporate,* 13.

22. See Harvey, *Condition of Postmodernity;* Robins and Webster, "Cybernetic Capitalism"; and a nice collection of essays on transition from outwork to factory system in Sanford M. Jacoby, ed., *Masters to Managers: Historical and Comparative Perspectives on American Employers* (New York: Columbia University Press, 1991).

23. See W. Hawkins Ferry, "Albert Kahn, 1869–1942," in Albert Kahn, *The Legacy of Albert Kahn* (Detroit: Detroit Institute of Arts, 1970), 23.

24. See L. H. Bucknell, Introduction to C. G. Holme, ed., *Industrial Architecture* (London: Studio Publication, 1935), 13.

25. See Samuel S. Marquis, "I Have Known Henry Ford for Twenty Years," in John B. Rae, ed., *Henry Ford* (Englewood Cliffs, N.J.: Prentice Hall, 1969), 83.

26. See Keith Sward, "Embattled Autocrat," in Rae, *Henry Ford,* 124.

27. Samuel Levin, "The Ford Profit-Sharing Plan, 1914–1920. The Growth of the Plan," *Personnel Journal* 6 (1927); quoted in David M. G. Raff, "Ford Welfare Capitalism," in Jacoby, *Masters to Managers.*

28. John R. Commons, *Industrial Goodwill* (New York: McGraw Hill, 1919), 129.

29. Carroll R. Daugherty, *Labor Problems in American Industry* (Madison: Houghton Mifflin, 1944), 593.

30. Commons, *Industrial Goodwill*, 322.

31. Daugherty, *Labor Problems in American Industry*, 613.

32. Susan Strasser, *Satisfaction Guaranteed: The Making of the American Mass Market* (New York: Pantheon Books, 1989), 19.

33. Ibid.

34. Ibid., 28.

35. Gordon S. Watkins, "The Motion Picture Industry," *Annals of the American Academy of Political and Social Science* 254 (November 1947), vii.

36. See Balio, *Grand Design*.

37. Lary May, *Screening Out the Past: The Birth of Mass Culture and the Motion Picture Industry* (Chicago: University of Chicago Press, 1983), 238.

38. Robert C. Allen, "Vitascope/Cinematographe: Initial Patterns of American Film Industrial Practice," in Kindem, ed., *The American Movie Industry*, 3–11.

39. See Douglas Gomery, *Shared Pleasures: A History of Movie Presentation in the United States* (Madison: University of Wisconsin Press, 1992).

40. Theodore Huff, "Hollywood's Predecessor," *Films in Review*, February 1951, 17.

41. Eileen Bowser, *History of American Cinema: The Transformation of Cinema, 1907–1915*, vol. 2 (New York: Charles Scribner's Sons, 1990).

42. Ibid.

43. "Scientific Nature Faking," *Colliers* 43 (3 July 1909): 13. Reprinted in Kalton C. Lahue, *Motion Picture Pioneer: The Selig Polyscope Company* (South Brunswick: A. S. Barnes, 1973), 51–53.

44. Robert G. Duncan, "The Ince Studios," *Picture-Play Magazine*, December 1915, 25.

45. Ibid.

46. G. P. Von Harleman, "Motion Picture Studios of California," *The Moving Picture World*, 10 March 1917, 1604.

47. "Completeness of Studios Adds to Business Efficiency; Inner Views of the Industry Reveal Real Acumen," *The Motion Picture* 4: 6, 4.

48. Richard Koszarski, *History of American Cinema: An Evening's Entertainment*, vol. 3 (New York: Charles Scribner's Sons, 1990), 100.

49. Von Harleman, "Motion Picture Studios of California," 1604.

50. Ibid., 1608.

51. Halsey, Stuart & Company, "The Motion Picture Industry as a Basis for Bond Financing, May 27, 1927," in Balio, *The American Film Industry*, 205. Also quoted in Catherine E. Kerr, "Incorporating the Star: The Intersection of Business and Aesthetic Strategies in Early American Film," *Business History Review* 64 (Autumn 1990): 383–410.

52. Christine Gledhill, Introduction to Christine Gledhill, ed., *Stardom: Industry of Desire* (London: Routledge, 1991), xiv.

53. See May, *Screening Out the Past*.

54. Richard De Cordova, *Picture Personalities: The Emergence of the Star System in America* (Urbana: University of Illinois Press, 1990), 102, 108.

55. Schatz, *The Genius of the System*, 20.

56. Terry Ramsey, "The Rise and Place of the Motion Picture," *Annals of the American Academy of Political and Social Science* 254 (November 1947): 1–11.

57. Huettig, *Economic Control of the Motion Picture Industry*, 32–33.

58. Ibid., 37.

59. Ibid., 38.

60. Ibid., 39.

61. Murray Ross, *Stars and Strikes: Unionization of Hollywood* (New York: Columbia University Press, 1941), 103.

62. Lewis, *The Motion Picture Industry*, 180.

63. Simon N. Whitney, "Antitrust Policies and the Motion Picture Industry," in Kindem, ed., *The American Movie Industry*, 161–204.

64. See Lewis, *The Motion Picture Industry*; Raymond Moley, *The Hays Office* (Indianapolis: Bobbs-Merrill Company, 1945); and Koszarski, *History of American Cinema: An Evening's Entertainment*.

65. See Lizabeth Cohen, *Making a New Deal: Industrial Workers in Chicago, 1919–1939* (Cambridge: Cambridge University Press, 1990).

66. Benjamin B. Hampton, *A History of the Movies* (New York: Covici, Friede, 1931), 283–84.

67. Balio, *Grand Design*, 70.

68. See Lewis, *The Motion Picture Industry*.

69. David A. Cook, *A History of Narrative Cinema* (New York: W. W. Norton, 1990), 229.

70. Michael Conant, *Anti-Trust in the Motion Picture Industry: Economic and Legal Analysis* (Berkeley: University of California Press, 1960), 29.

71. Janet Wasko writes: "According to various figures, the cost of sound installation for each theater ranged from $8,000 to $15,000 in 1927, $5,000 to $12,000 in 1928, and $5,000 and $7,000 in 1929. Other estimates have

been made of the total cost of sound conversion for the entire industry; the MPPDA declared at the time that it would cost around 1/2 billion, while Gomery later estimated $30 million." See Janet Wasko, *Movies and Money*, 49.

72. Ibid.

73. See Conant, *Anti-Trust in the Motion Picture Industry*, 41.

74. Ibid.

75. One of the greatest inventions of the upscale toy consumption in the 1980s, Alexander dolls are precious porcelain dolls with real hair that come together with books explaining the doll's entire life, friends, and families, naturally linked to other dolls in the series. Enormously successful, and available only through mail order or in the most exclusive toy stores such as FAO Schwarz, Alexander dolls have been marketed primarily to grandparents—the only family members who could presumably afford the average cost of $200 to $300 per doll and fully appreciate the narrative that came with them.

76. See Balio, *Grand Design*; Ross, *Stars and Strikes*.

77. Moley, *The Hays Office*, 207.

78. Ibid., 7.

79. Ibid.

80. See Powdermaker, *Hollywood, the Dream Factory*, 39.

81. *Variety*, August 16, 1940, quoted in Larry Ceplair and Steven Englund, *The Inquisition in Hollywood: Politics in the Film Community, 1930–1960* (Berkeley: University of California Press, 1983), 157.

Chapter II: Hollywood on Location

1. Lori Holladay, executive director of the Greater Cincinnati Film Commission, addressing filmmakers in the commission's press material from 1994.

2. Chris Carter, executive producer of *The X-Files* in an interview with Mark Leiren Young, "X-Philes," *Hollywood Reporter*, British Columbia Special Issue, 26 September 1995, S-8.

3. "Canada Goes Hollywood," *Los Angeles Times*, 7 December 1986, Calendar Section, 20.

4. *On Location Israel*, Israel Film Center, Ministry of Industry and Trade, 1992, 41.

5. In their recent work on the interplay between culture, power, and place, anthropologists Akhil Gupta and James Ferguson have suggested

that contemporary challenges to spatially territorialized notions of culture should lead us to ask not how local relates to global, or what is so distinct about "the local," but, rather, how are the perceptions of locality, culture, and community discursively and historically constructed. In other words, instead of wondering whether or not "the local" is really being threatened by "the global" (in our case Hollywood), we should be wondering about the ways in which both "the global" and "the local" are being produced. See Akhil Gupta and James Ferguson, "Culture, Power, Place: Ethnography at the End of an Era," in Akhil Gupta and James Ferguson, eds., *Culture, Power, Place: Explorations in Critical Anthropology* (Durham: Duke University Press, 1997), 1–29.

6. In January 1999, the Directors Guild of America and the Screen Actors Guild ordered an investigative report on runaway production in the U.S. film industry from Monitor Company, a management-consulting firm founded by Michael Porter of Harvard Business School. The study attempted to quantify the extent of runaway production in Hollywood and to discern its major causes. The major finding of the study was that "in 1998, of the 1,075 U.S. developed film and television productions in the study's scope identified by Monitor Company, 285 (27% of the total) were economic runaways, a 185% increase from 100 (14% of total) in 1990. When these productions moved abroad, a \$10.3 billion economic loss (lost direct production spending plus the multiplied effects of lost spending and tax revenues) resulted for the U.S. in 1998 alone. This amount is five times the \$2.0 billion runaway loss in 1990." See Monitor Company, *U.S. Runaway Film and Television Production Study Report,* 1999, 2.

7. For more information on the Film and Television Action Committee check their website at http://www.ftac.net.

8. For nice overviews of these debates see Joseph Grunwald and Kenneth Flamm, eds., *The Global Factory: Foreign Assembly in International Trade* (Washington, D.C.: Brookings Institution, 1985); Mira Wilkins, *The Maturing of Multinational Enterprise: American Business Abroad from 1914 to 1970* (Cambridge: Harvard University Press, 1974); and Raymond Vernon, *Storm over the Multinationals: The Real Issues* (Cambridge: Harvard University Press, 1977).

9. This position was taken by a number of Third World countries in the postcolonial period leading to a series of expropriations and threats of expropriations in the late 1960s and the early 1970s.

10. Raymond Vernon's product cycle theory had clear implications for the increasing intra-industry trade and transnationalization of capital in

the 1950s: as products move downward on the product cycle curve, argued Vernon, the production moves to more competitive locations abroad. See original Vernon's article, "International Investment and International Trade in the Product Cycle," *Quarterly Journal of Economics* 80 (May 1966): 190–207, and his book *Sovereignty at Bay, the Multinational Spread of U.S. Enterprises* (New York: Basic Books, 1971).

11. See Mira Wilkins and Frank Ernest Hill, *American Business Abroad: Ford on Six Continents* (Detroit: Wayne State University Press, 1964).

12. Ibid., 407.

13. Piore and Sabel, *The Second Industrial Divide*, 197.

14. Erica Shoenberger, "Competition, Time, and Space in Industrial Change," in Gereffi and Korzeniewicz, eds., *Global Commodity Chains*, 51–66.

15. Piore and Sabel, *The Second Industrial Divide*, 200–202. See also Wilkins, *The Maturing of Multinational Enterprise*, 395–97.

16. Ross, *Stars and Strikes*, 137.

17. See Balio, *Grand Design*.

18. See Robert S. Sennett, *Setting the Scene: The Great Hollywood Art Directors* (New York: Henry N. Abrams, 1994).

19. U.S. Congress, House, Committee on Education and Labor, *Impact of Imports and Exports on American Employment, Hearings*, 523 and Table 14, 532.

20. Director Billy Wilder said in an interview with the *New York Times:* "The Yugoslav and Spanish armies are the busiest armies in the world today. They will fight for any movie company from any country." *New York Times*, 19 November 1961.

21. Ian Jarvie shows that in 1947 Hollywood faced trade barriers in countries as diverse as Brazil, Chile, Netherlands, Lebanon, United Kingdom. See Jarvie, *Hollywood's Overseas Campaign*, 409.

22. See Margaret Dickinson and Sarah Street, *Cinema and State: The Film Industry and the Government, 1927–84* (London: BFI, 1985), 189.

23. U.S. Congress, House, Committee on Education and Labor, *Impact of Imports and Exports on American Employment, Hearings*, Table 13, 531.

24. See Dickinson and Street, *Cinema and State.*

25. Alexander Walker, *Hollywood, England: The British Film Industry in the Sixties* (London: Harrap, 1974), 475.

26. The unions claimed that the average monthly employment in the industry declined from 21,775 in 1946 to 11,175 in the first months of 1959. U.S. Congress, House, Committee on Education and Labor, *Impact of Imports and Exports on American Employment, Hearings*, 521.

27. Ibid., 466.

28. Ibid., 522–23.

29. Matthew Bernstein notes in his detailed biography of *Cleopatra*'s producer, Walter Wanger, *Walter Wanger, Hollywood Independent* (Berkeley: University of California Press, 1994), the convergence of the collapse of the studio system and the *Cleopatra* debacle in the near-bankruptcy of 20th Century Fox. "The studio," writes Bernstein, "set forth the notion, which countless historians and biographers repeat, that *Cleopatra* ruined Fox. But in truth, Fox did itself in, and the film was its most convenient scapegoat" (343). By the time of the film's shooting in Italy, all the prerogatives of the studio system that had made 20th Century Fox into one of Hollywood's most successful companies, had already fallen apart. The lack of a shootable script, turf battles within the management, and location shooting exposed all the pitfalls of Hollywood's "frenzied transition" in the post-studio era. Unable or unwilling to follow any of the ground rules of the studio filmmaking, and yet still bureaucratically bound to the studio, protagonists of the *Cleopatra* saga found themselves at odds with each other and with the vanishing studio system itself. For other entertaining and illustrative descriptions of *Cleopatra* and its impact see Dick Sheppard, *Elizabeth: The Life and Career of Elizabeth Taylor* (New York: Doubleday, 1974); Michael Medved and Harry Medved, *The Hollywood Hall of Shame: The Most Expensive Flops in Movie History* (New York: Perigee, 1984); and John Gregory Dunne, *The Studio* (New York: Farrar, Straus & Giroux, 1968).

30. Indeed, as Michael Conant writes, the Paramount decision only increased the competition on the production side of the industry and brought new barriers to entry into distribution part of the industry. "Barriers to the entry of new distributors contrived by the defendants," writes Conant, "were augmented by the high costs of establishing and operating a system of distribution exchanges. It is estimated that the weekly operating costs of a nation-wide distribution system were $80,000 to $125,000 in 1945. By 1946, the leading firms had all curtailed their own production and hence began to bid more actively to distribute independent films in order to keep their facilities operating at greater capacity. Furthermore, distribution overhead increased from 20 to 35 percent in 1946. All these factors were barriers to the entry of new distributors, though the number of independent producers had risen greatly." See Conant, *Anti-Trust in the Motion Picture Industry*, 48–49.

31. See Harvey, *Condition of Postmodernity*, 222.

32. According to Kanter's assessment of transformations in American corporations, there is now more "detachment of what was once 'inside' (for example employees being replaced by contingent workers, and staff

departments being spun-off as independent contractors) and more 'attachment' to what was once 'outside' (closer, more committed relationships with suppliers, customers and even competitors)." Rosabeth Moss Kanter, "The Future of Bureaucracy and Hierarchy in Organizational Theory: A Report from the Field," in Pierre Bourdieu and James S. Coleman, eds., *Social Theory for a Changing Society* (Boulder: Westview Press, 1991), 63–87.

33. The group of investors who came to dominate the motion picture industry included Charles Bluhdorn, the man who owned Gulf and Western Corporation and a great part of the Dominican Republic; Steve Ross, a self-made owner of Kinney Corporation, a parking lot and funeral parlor company in New York; Kirk Kerkorian, a Las Vegas gambling and casino tsar; and Lou Chesler, head of the Seven Arts production company, with established links with the Mafia and diversified interests in the Bahamas.

34. Paramount became a part of Charles Bluhdorn's Gulf and Western; Warner Bros. was absorbed by Ross's Kinney Corporation and then became Warner Communications; Kirk Kerkorian bought MGM; Transamerica Corporation purchased United Artists; Universal was acquired by Lew Wasserman's MCA Corporation. Even 20th Century Fox and Columbia, officially independent until the early 1980s, were mostly governed by Wall Street investment bankers.

35. The most atrocious change took place at MGM. Having made most of his fortune in gambling, the studio's new owner Kirk Kerkorian decided to use the MGM logo and "brand name" to build a hotel in Las Vegas. The plans called for a twenty-five-floor tower with suites named after MGM's most famous stars and public rooms named after the studio's most popular movies. In order to finance his "franchising" operations, Kerkorian literally destroyed the studio. The newly appointed head of the studio Jim Aubrey stopped production on films such as Michelangelo Antonioni's *Zabriskie Point* (1970), Fred Zinneman's adaptation of Andre Malraux's *Man's Fate* and David Lean's *Ryan's Daughter* (1970); he sold off huge parts of the studio lot, overseas theaters, and music subsidiaries; he closed down the distribution offices and pre-sold the distribution rights to MGM projects to United Artists. Kerkorian's speculations continued well into the 1980s. In 1981, Kerkorian bought United Artists, and then, in a complicated swap deal, he sold the studio to Ted Turner, while retaining the rights to the MGM logo. Turner, for his part, sold back the entire studio but kept the library which now feeds his TNT channel. The culmination of this sad and ironic transformation of the former "Tiffany" of the studios was the 1994 opening of Kerkorian's new MGM hotel in Vegas. The hotel includes a "studio tour" in its garden, while the original company—with no production facilities of its own—

struggled in court with its penultimate owner, Italian speculator Giancarlo Paretti.

36. "So You Wanna Be in Pictures," *Business Week*, August 22, 1988, 102–3.

37. David G. Holmes, "Lending to the Motion Picture Industry," *Journal of Commercial Bank Lending*, June 1990, 28–38.

38. Approximately one third of the box office goes to theater owners, and the distributor and producer split the rest. But since the producer is also responsible for production costs, deferred salaries, and percentages for the talent and the crew, the "net" profit is usually minimal. Thus, if a movie flopped, partners were at best promised to get their investment back since the producer was expected to pay them back; if the movie was a success, the investors and producers were the last to see a profit since the studio/distributor held most of it.

39. Benjamin J. Stein, "Glitz By Association," *Barron's*, 27 April 1987, 14–16.

40. Peter Biskind, "Synergetic," *Sight and Sound*, 1 (June 1991): 8.

41. On British tax-law SP/79 from 1979 which stimulated arrangements based on lease-back deals with the production company acting as a seller, the bank or financial intermediary as a lessor, and the distribution company as a lessee, see "The Taxing Question of Film Finance," *Euromoney*, June 1983, 28–29, 31.

42. Terry Ogisu, "Japanese Conglomerate Seeks Rising Presence in Hollywood Prod'n Scene," *Daily Variety*, 15 June 1977, 64.

43. Peter Besas, *Behind the Spanish Lens* (Denver: Arden Press, 1985), 54–55.

44. John Hyde, "How Foreign Distribution Works," *Variety*, 19 February 1986, 18, 336.

45. Philip L. Zweig, "Lights! Camera! Pinstripes!" *Institutional Investor*, September 1987, 171–78.

46. Lisa Gubernick and Kathleen Healy, "Where Others Fear to Tread," *Forbes*, 18 April 1988, 38–39.

47. Alan Citron, "Major Talent Agency Launches Financing Unit," *Los Angeles Times*, 12 July 1991, D2. An interesting touch to the establishment of the financing unit at ICM was that it was headed by Frans J. Afman. Another interesting element was the fact that talent agencies moved into financing at the time when the studios such as Disney, Columbia, and Paramount tried to back out of the "packages."

48. See David Puttnam with Neil Watson, *Movies and Money* (New York: Alfred A. Knopf, 1998) and Andrew Yule, *Fast Fade: David Puttnam, Columbia Pictures, and the Battle for Hollywood* (New York: Delta, 1989).

49. See Claudia Eller, "Disney Getting Back to Basics," *Daily Variety*, 30 January 1991, 8.

50. David Morley and Kevin Robins discuss both of these views in their *Spaces of Identity* (London: Routledge, 1995). For the selection of thoughts on the resurgence of Medievalism see Stephen J. Korbin, "Back to the Future: Neomedievalism and the Postmodern World Economy," paper presented at the 1996 Annual Meeting of the International Studies Association, San Diego, California, 17 April 1996.

51. An excellent overview of the links between liberal economic theory and geography can be found in Ron Martin and Peter Sunley, "Paul Krugman's Geographical Economics and Its Implications for Regional Development Theory: A Critical Assessment," *Economic Geography* 72, no. 3 (July 1996): 259–93.

52. See Harvey, *Condition of Postmodernity*.

53. See Roland Robertson, "Social Theory, Cultural Relativity, and the Problem of Globality," in Anthony D. King, ed., *Culture, Globalization, and the World System* (London: Macmillan, 1991), 69–90. Another interesting volume, although written from a more explicitly geographic/architectural perspective, is Leslie Budd and Sam Whimster, eds., *Global Finance and Urban Living: A Study of Metropolitan Change* (London: Routledge, 1992). A few other anthologies seem worth mentioning: Rob Wilson and Wilam Dissanayake, eds., *Global/Local: Cultural Production and the Transnational Imaginary* (Durham: Duke University Press, 1996); Smadar Lavie and Ted Swedenburg, eds., *Displacement, Diaspora, and Geographies of Identity* (Durham: Duke University Press, 1996); and Fredric Jameson and Masao Miyoshi, eds., *Cultures of Globalization* (Durham: Duke University Press, 1998).

54. Scott Lash and John Urry, *Economies of Signs and Space* (London: Sage, 1994).

55. Lefebvre, *The Production of Space*, 355–56, 365–67.

56. See Motion Picture Association, "MPAA Average Negative Costs and Marketing Costs of New Features," *U.S. Economic Review* (1991) for statistics between 1980 and 1991. See also Jeffrey Daniels, "Studio Pic Costs Up 14 Percent," *Hollywood Reporter*, 8 March 1995.

57. See Jeanie Kasindorf, "Payback Time," *New York*, 27 January 1992, 36–40; Stan Berkowitz and David Lees, "What Price Romance? Why Movies Cost What They Cost," *Esquire Film Quarterly*, July 1982; Richard Natale, "The Bucks Don't Stop Here," *US*, 24 December 1970; Richard Natale, "The Price Club," *American Film* 14 (June 1989): 42–44+; Pat Dowell, "Shooting Words," *American Film* 16 (July 1991): 26–30+;

Will Tusher, "Studios Seek Alternatives to Script Bidding Frenzy," *Daily Variety*, 17 May 1990, 1, 27; Ronald Grover, "Fat Times for Studios, Fatter Times for Stars," *Business Week*, 24 July 1989.

58. *Variety*, 6 May 1987.

59. Will Tusher, "High Labor Costs Hold Key to Runaway Filming," *Daily Variety*, 5 June 1990, 3, 17.

60. Vernon Scott, "Runaway Production," *BC Cycle*, 25 January 1988.

61. Jube Shiver, "State Study Cites Costs, Red Tape for Loss of Film Work," *Los Angeles Times*, 8 February 1989, Part 4, 1.

62. See Jack Kyser, "Business Opportunities in the Entertainment Industry," and "Selected Facts about the Economic Impact of the Motion Picture, Television and Commercial Production Industries in California," Special Reports of the Economic Development Corporation, Los Angeles County, 1993.

63. See Monitor Company, *U.S. Runaway Film and Television Production Study Report.*

64. Morgan Gendel, "Hollywood's Runaways," *Los Angeles Times*, 9 December 1986, Part 6, 1.

65. Stephen Farber, "Australia Becomes a Stand-In for Hollywood," *New York Times*, 16 May 1988, D10. For more elaborate analyses of the Hollywood-Australian film relations, see Toby Miller, *Technologies of Truth: Cultural Citizenship and the Popular Media (Visible Evidence, 1)* (Minneapolis: University of Minnesota Press, 1998), and Stuart Cunningham, Toby Miller, and David Rowe, eds., *Contemporary Australian Television (Communication and Culture)* (Sydney: New South Wales University Press, 1995).

66. Interviews with Brian Unger, IATSE, New York, February 1993; and Andrea Meyer, IATSE, Los Angeles, February 1994.

67. Sharon Bernstein, "Union Strategy in the Battle for Independents," *Los Angeles Times*, 3 January 1991, F1.

68. Sharon Bernstein, "Learning How to Flex Their Muscles," *Los Angeles Times*, 4 January 1991, F14.

69. Harry Bernstein, "Labor: Hollywood Seeks Job-Saving Compromise," *Los Angeles Times*, 4 February 1987, Part 4, 1.

70. Kyser, "Selected Facts about the Economic Impact of the Motion Picture, Television and Commercial Production Industries in California," 3.

71. Will Tusher, "AMPTP Proxy Counter Says H'woods Real Problem Is 'Forced-Away' Production," *Daily Variety*, 12 December 1986, 1, 58.

72. For North Carolina developmental politics (fascinating in its own right) see Jack D. Fleer, *North Carolina Government and Politics*

(Lincoln: University of Nebraska Press, 1994); Paul Luebke, *Tar Heel Politics 2000* (Chapel Hill: University of North Carolina Press, 1998), and, particularly, Philip J. Wood, *Southern Capitalism: The Political Economy of North Carolina* (Durham: Duke University Press, 1986).

73. Catherine Hinman, "Florida's Push for More Films Appears to Sag," *Orlando Sentinel Tribune,* 26 November 1990, A6.

74. Leslie Halpern, "Sunny Side Up," *Hollywood Reporter,* Florida Special Issue, 1993.

75. Joachim Hirsch, "From the Fordist to the Post-Fordist State"; Bob Jessop, "The Welfare State in Transition"; and Hans Joachim Schabedoth, "Neo-Conservatism and Modernization Policy in West Germany"—all in Bob Jessop, Hans Kastendiek, Klaus Nielsen, and Ove K. Pedersen, eds., *The Politics of Flexibility: Restructuring State and Industry in Britain, Germany, and Scandinavia* (London: Edgar Elgar, 1991).

76. Anatole Dauman, "Lettre aux 'majors' d'Hollywood . . . et à leurs zélateurs francais," *Le Monde Diplomatique,* 28 December 1995 (trans. A. Hozic).

77. Nagisa Oshima, *Cinema, Censorship, and the State: The Writings of Nagisa Oshima* (Cambridge: MIT Press, 1992), 10.

78. See Justin Wyatt, *High Concept: Movies and Marketing in Hollywood* (Austin: University of Texas Press, 1994).

79. "Market Research for Film Sells; Parables for Believers, Skeptics," *Variety,* 12 May 1976, 162, 168.

80. Time Warner, *Building Global Brands,* Annual Report, 1995, 2.

81. Actors started their push into merchandising in the late 1970s and the early 1980s. Elizabeth Taylor's statement, however, can be considered as a watershed since it was the most open acknowledgment of self-commodification up to that point. See Greil Marcus, *Lipstick Traces: A Secret History of the Twentieth Century* (Cambridge: Harvard University Press, 1989), 106. By the mid 1980s, actors were not the only ones trying to make a profit out of their own life-stories. The integration of cable companies and Hollywood studios, and particularly the creation of Fox TV—once again a product of Barry Diller's genius—introduced a new concept into the entertainment industry: "Reality TV." The latter denotes programs based on real-life stories and covers a variety of genres and sub-genres—from shows such as *America's Most Wanted* to talk shows and numerous made-for-TV films based on "private" lives of "private" personalities whose vicissitudes had suddenly become a focus of attention. Although film production companies mostly resisted the trend of making films based on such direct translation of life into movies, they

were not completely immune to the trend either. For a more detailed account of the relationship between *Cleopatra*, Reality TV, and the merchandising of both Hollywood and movies, see Aida A. Hozic, "Hollywood Goes on Sale: Or What Do the Violet Eyes of Elizabeth Taylor Have to Do with 'Cinema of Attraction'?" in Desser and Jowett, *Hollywood Goes Shopping*, 312–22.

82. For a very nice overview of the U.S. efforts in the area of intellectual property rights see Susan K. Sell, "Intellectual Property Protection and Antitrust in Developing World: Crisis, Coercion, and Choice," *International Organization* 49, no. 2 (1995): 315–49.

83. Walter Benjamin, "The Work of Art in the Age of Mechanical Reproduction," in Walter Benjamin, *Illuminations: Essays and Reflections* (New York: Schocken Books, 1968), 217–52.

84. Ibid., 233.

Chapter III: Hollywood in Cyberspace

1. As mentioned in the chapter about the Hollywood studio system, throughout the 1920s, Hollywood studios were feverishly purchasing theater chains and borrowing money on Wall Street. Their debts increased even more in the course of the conversion to sound at the end of that decade. The overextension pushed the studios onto the brink of financial disaster in the early 1930s, aggravated their relationship with independent theater owners, and drew the attention of the U.S. Department of Justice, which resulted in the forced divestment of the studios from their theaters in 1949.

2. For fine analyses of "private authority," see Claire A. Cutler's articles "Locating 'Authority' in the Global Political Economy," *International Studies Quarterly* (1999): 59–81; "Artifice, Ideology, and Paradox: The Public/Private Distinction in International Law," *Review of International Political Economy* 4 (1997): 261–85; and a volume edited by Claire Cutler, Virginia Haufler, and Tony Porter, *Private Authority and International Affairs* (Albany: State University of New York Press, 1999). See also Susan Strange's book, *The Retreat of the State: The Diffusion of Power in the World Economy* (Cambridge: Cambridge University Press, 1996).

3. Rob Sabin, "The Movies' Digital Future Is in Sight and It Works," *New York Times*, 26 November 2000, Arts Section, Web Edition.

4. John Seabrook, "Why Is the Force Still with Us? Letter from Skywalker Ranch," *New Yorker*, 6 January 1997, 44.

5. The citation is from a caption for a photograph of Mr. Spielberg at the Department of Defense official website. See http://www.defenselink.mil/photos/Aug1999/990811-D-2987S-042.html. Accessed 29 January 2001.

6. See, in particular, the report by Michael Oden, Ann Markusen, Dan Flaming, Jonathan Feldman, James Raffel and Catherine Hill, *Post Cold War Frontiers: Defense Downsizing and Conversion in Los Angeles* (New Brunswick, N.J.: Rutgers University, Project on Regional and Industrial Economics, Working Paper No. 105, 1996). According to more recent newspaper accounts, the aerospace and electronics equipment industries lost 135,000 jobs between 1988 and 1997, while the entertainment industry created 144,000 jobs. See Andrew Pollack, "Aerospace Engineers Are Turning to Hollywood," *New York Times*, 10 October 1997; Daniel B. Wood, "California as a 21st Century Economy," *Christian Science Monitor*, 29 August 1997, 1, 9; a series of articles titled "The Hollywood Economy" in the *Los Angeles Times*, 18–20 January 1998, and a special issue of the *Nation* on Hollywood, 3 April 2000, particularly an article by James Der Derian, "Virtuous War and Hollywood."

7. In 1997, at an already described annual Location Expo (Los Angeles, February 1997), Department of Defense featured a seminar entitled "Working with the Military: Opening Doors to Closed Bases." At the initiative of the Los Angeles Film Development Office, filmmakers got a chance to discuss the possibilities of expanded usage of military bases with representatives of the Pentagon. See "Blowing It," *Hollywood Reporter*, 5 March 1997.

8. See Joseph S. Nye and William A. Owens Jr., "America's Information Edge," *Foreign Affairs*, March/April 1996, 20–37.

9. Morley and Robins, *Spaces of Identity*, 11.

10. This, of course, is not to say that there were no contacts or collaborations between the U.S. Army, the U.S. government, and the film industry before the advent of digital technology. On the contrary: even the American motion-picture pioneers were fascinated with warfare. As Charles Musser writes, "The sinking of the [battleship] *Maine* and the Spanish–American war [of 1898] were a boon to the American film industry, as cinema regained a wider audience." See Musser, *Before the Nickelodeon*, 126. Much later, in the 1940s, write Koppes and Black, the U.S. government,

> convinced that movies had extraordinary power to mobilize public opinion for war, carried out an intensive, unprecedented effort to mold the content of Hollywood feature films. Officials of the Of-

fice of War Information, the government's propaganda agency, issued a constantly updated manual instructing the studios in how
to assist the war effort, sat in on story conferences with Hollywood's top brass, reviewed the screenplays of every major studio
(except the recalcitrant Paramount), pressured the movie makers
to change scripts and even scrap pictures when they found objec-
tionable material, and sometimes wrote dialogue for key speeches.

> Clayton R. Koppes and Gregory D. Black,
> *Hollywood Goes to War: How Politics, Profits*
> *and Propaganda Shaped World War II Movies*
> (Berkeley: University of California Press, 1987), vii.

The cooperation between the government and Hollywood producers continued through the 1950s and, after a relatively brief interlude
of anti-war films prompted by the Vietnam War, it resurfaced—in a tacit
form—during the Reagan and Clinton presidency. However, the acknowledgment that films can be a powerful propaganda tool or even the
recognition of Hollywood's political importance are quite different from
the contemporary technological convergence between the military-
industrial complex and the film industry, or from the celebration of Hollywood as the engine of economic growth. The intimacy of the current
relationship resembles Paul Virilio's perceptive writings on the "fatal" in-
terdependence between technologies of cinema and warfare much more
than any historical accounts (or textual analysis) of film as propaganda.
See Paul Virilio, *War and Cinema: The Logistics of Perception* (London:
Verso, 1989).

11. See Kenneth Flamm, *Creating the Computer: Government, Industry, and High Technology* (Washington, D.C.: Brookings Institution, 1988).

12. The two most important challenges to neo-classical economic theory over the past two decades have come from within its own ranks. Rediscovery of Schumpeter's theory of economic growth based on innovation and entrepreneurship, on the one hand, and the rise of the new
institutional economics on the other, have refined the view that competition, pure and simple, is the sufficient incentive for technological
change. The most influential works on technological innovation and development in this period have relied on one or the other or some combination of these perspectives. See, for example, Richard Nelson and
Samuel Winter, *An Evolutionary Theory of Economic Change* (Cambridge: Belknap, 1982); Giovanni Dosi, *Technical Change and Industrial
Transformation* (London: Macmillan, 1984); Piore and Sabel, *The Second
Industrial Divide*; Porter, *Competitive Advantage*; Michael Best, *The*

New Competition: Institutions of Industrial Restructuring (Cambridge: Polity Press, 1990); and William Lazonick, *Business Organization and the Myth of the Market Economy* (Cambridge: Cambridge University Press, 1991).

13. The seminal critical work which viewed technological development as a result of (labor replacing) social choice was David Noble's work on numerically controlled machines. See David F. Noble, "Social Choice in Machine Design," *Politics and Society* 8 (1978): 313–47; and David F. Noble, *Forces of Production: A Social History of Industrial Automation* (New York: Alfred A. Knopf, 1984). For excellent introductions to the critique of information technology see Jennifer Daryl Slack and Fred Fejes, *The Ideology of the Information Age* (Norwood, N.J.: Ablex, 1987); Mosco and Wasko, *Political Economy of Information;* Les Levidow and Kevin Robins, eds., *Cyborg Worlds: The Military Information Society* (London: Free Association Books, 1989); Lash and Urry, *Economies of Sign and Space;* and Gene I. Rochlin, *Trapped in the Net: The Unanticipated Consequences of Computerization* (Princeton: Princeton University Press, 1997).

14. In the 1960s, the exodus of production and the overall crisis of the studio system forced Hollywood studios to close down their special effects departments. Their employees, who had long nurtured the tightest apprenticeship system in Hollywood, either left the industry or started their own independent companies. The practice was mostly continued in alternative, low-budget productions where special effects, as in old monster movies, represented an inexpensive substitute for actors and stars. Apart from Ed Wood, whose films have now acquired a new lease on life thanks to the renewed cult status of effects, the most important figure of low-budget production was Roger Corman. Corman and his numerous filmmaking progeny built a little empire with their low-cost film manufacturing, consistent avoidance of stars, and an ingenious creation of a special-effects library. The latter allowed them to carry the same footage from one project to another and to produce dozens of movies around the same special effects. Thus, inadvertently, Corman paved the way for contemporary digital-effects industry and reinvigorated the hopes of Hollywood producers. Thanks to Corman, they were led to believe that they could regain their lost status in the industry by replacing stars with special effects, locations with computers, and extensive hours of shooting with old footage of the already filmed effects. See Roger Corman and Jim Jerome, *How I Made a Hundred Movies in Hollywood and Never Lost a Dime* (New York: Doubleday, 1990).

15. For a history of special effects and a discussion of Spielberg's and Lucas's contributions, see John Brosnan, *Movie Magic: The Story of Special Effects in the Cinema* (London: Abacus Books, 1977); Ron Fry and Pamela Fourzan, *The Saga of Special Effects* (Englewood Cliffs, N.J.: Prentice Hall, 1977); Dennis Saleh, *Science Fiction Gold: Film Classics of the 50s* (New York: McGraw Hill, 1979); John Culhane, *Special Effects in the Movies: How They Do It* (New York: Ballantine Books, 1981); L. B. Abbott, *Special Effects: Wire, Tape, and Rubber Band Style* (Hollywood: ASC Press, 1984); Thomas G. Smith, *Industrial Light and Magic: The Art of Special Effects* (New York: Ballantine Books, 1986); Douglas Brode, *The Films of Steven Spielberg* (New York: Carol Publishing Group, 1995).

16. ILM created all of the most important digital effects in the motion picture industry since 1985—from the first-ever digital image in *Young Sherlock Holmes* (1985) to the liquid robot in *Terminator 2* (1991), a field of running dinosaurs in *Jurassic Park* (1993), and Tom Hanks's adventures through American history in *Forrest Gump* (1994). The company was also (and still is) a "motherboard" for a majority of special-effects firms in the American film industry—PIXAR, Digital Domain, Boss, Apogee, etc., all started out as ILM spin-offs.

17. "Working It," *Hollywood Reporter,* Animation Special Issue, 23 January 1996, S64+.

18. The most active organization for the protection of authors' rights in Hollywood is the Artists Rights Foundation. For the complete description, a list of sponsors, and recent activities, visit their website at http://www.artistsrights.org.

19. See John Geirland and Eva Sonesh-Kedar, *Digital Babylon: How the Geeks, the Suits, and the Ponytails Fought to Bring Hollywood to the Internet* (New York: Arcade, 1999).

20. This is the "central heresy" of Levidow and Robins's *Cyborg Worlds.*

21. A detailed and fascinating account of these links can be found in Howard Rheingold's *Virtual Reality* (New York: Simon and Schuster, 1991).

22. Council of Economic Advisors, *Economic Report of the President* (Lanham, Md.: Bernan, February 1995).

23. See Oden et al., *Post Cold War Frontiers;* and Michael Storper, "Competitiveness Policy Options: The Technology-Regions Connections," *Growth and Change* 26 (Spring 1995): 285–308.

24. Council of Economic Advisors, *Economic Report of the President,* 164.

25. The issue was approached from several different directions. In the view of the more traditional economists, the fundamental problem was the issue of "private appropriability," i.e., the ability of firms to accumu-

late extra profits through technological breakthroughs. Such profits, it was assumed, could not be achieved if the government was the main consumer of new technologies. Hence, dependence on the government, according to this view, would lead, in due time, to a slowdown in innovation. A good overview of this argument can be found in Lars Magnusson, ed., *Evolutionary and Neo-Schumpeterian Approaches to Economics* (Boston: Kluwer Academic, 1994). More popular and influential were numerous books and articles about industrial policy in the U.S. and Japan which argued that Japan was superior in producing "applicable" high-tech gadgets because of its government-led ("administrative guidance") market orientation in research and development. See, for instance, Chalmers Johnson, Laura D'Andrea Tyson, and John Zysman, eds., *Politics and Productivity: The Real Story Why Japan Works* (Cambridge: Ballinger, 1989); Stephen S. Cohen and John Zysman, eds., *Manufacturing Matters: The Myth of the Post-Industrial Economy* (New York: Basic Books, 1987); Clyde V. Prestowitz Jr., *Trading Places: How We Allowed Japan to Take the Lead* (New York: Basic Books, 1988); Laura D'Andrea Tyson, *Who's Bashing Whom? Trade Conflicts in High Technology Industries* (Washington, D.C.: Institute for International Economics, 1993). Similar arguments were also made by defense economists and geographers. See Peter Hall and Ann Markusen, eds., *Silicon Landscapes* (Boston: Allen and Unwin, 1985); Ann Markusen, Peter Hall, and Amy Glasmeier, *High Tech America: The What, How, Where, and Why of the Sunrise Industries* (Boston: Allen and Unwin, 1986); Patricia MacCorquodale, Martha W. Gilliland, Jeffrey P. Kash, and Andrew Jameton, eds., *Engineers and Economic Conversion: From the Military to the Marketplace* (New York: Springer-Verlag, 1993).

26. See Lev Manovich, *The Language of New Media* (Cambridge: MIT Press, 2001).

27. Ibid., 253.

28. Ibid., 252.

29. Ibid., 258.

30. Justin Wyatt, "The Stigma of X: Adult Cinema and the Institution of the MPAA Ratings System," in Matthew Bernstein, ed., *Controlling Hollywood: Censorship and Regulation in the Studio Era* (New Brunswick: Rutgers University Press, 1999), 238–63.

31. The transformation of Times Square and 42nd Street in New York from the land of pornography into an urban Disneyland is just another architectural sign of mainstream Hollywood's resilience in the face of ongoing culture wars.

32. See Charles Lyons, *The New Censors: Movies and the Culture Wars* (Philadelphia: Temple University Press, 1997).

33. Cox News Service, "Ted Turner Urges TV Violence Ratings," *St. Petersburg Times*, 26 June 1993, 1A.

34. Willard D. Rowland Jr., "Television Violence Redux: The Continuing Mythology of Effects," in Martin Barker and Julian Petley, eds., *Ill Effects: The Media/Violence Debate* (London: Routledge, 1997), 118.

35. Ibid., 119.

36. For a brilliant discussion of the link between the defunding of public art and the commercialization of documentary filmmaking, see Patricia Zimmermann's book *States of Emergency—Documentaries, Wars, Democracies* (Minneapolis: University of Minnesota Press, 2000).

37. See Taylor, *Modernities*.

38. Robert W. Cox, "Structural Issues of Global Governance: Implications for Europe," in Stephen Gill, ed., *Gramsci, Historical Materialism, and International Relations* (Cambridge: Cambridge University Press, 1993), 264.

39. As Giovanni Arrighi puts it, hegemony "is the additional power that accrues to a dominant group in virtue of its capacity to pose on a universal plane all the issues around which conflict rages." See Giovanni Arrighi, "The Three Hegemonies of Historical Capitalism," also in Gill, ed., *Gramsci, Historical Materialism, and International Relations*, 148–85.

40. See Mark Rupert, *Producing Hegemony: The Politics of Mass Production and American Global Power* (Cambridge: Cambridge University Press, 1995).

41. Hannah Arendt, *The Human Condition* (Chicago: University of Chicago Press, 1958), 69.

42. May, *Screening Out the Past*, 238.

43. See Wolfgang Streeck and Philippe C. Schmitter, eds., *Private Interest Government: Beyond Market and State* (London: Sage, 1985).

44. Nye and Owens, "America's Information Edge," 20.

45. See Steven Brand, *The MIT Media Lab: Inventing the Future at MIT* (New York: Viking Penguin, 1987) and Nicholas Negroponte, *Being Digital* (New York: Alfred A. Knopf, 1995).

46. For additional information visit http://www.media.mit.edu/MediaLab.

47. Michael Stern, "Making Culture into Nature," in Annette Kuhn, ed., *Alien Zone: Cultural Theory and Contemporary Science Fiction Cinema* (London: Verso, 1990), 69.

48. Ibid., 70.

49. Michael Sorkin, "See You in Disneyland," in Michael Sorkin, ed., *Variations on a Theme Park: The New American City and the End of Public Spaces* (New York: Hill and Wang, 1992), 228.

50. See Dale Hrabi, "Will the 'New' Times Square Be New Enough," *Wired*, vol. 3, no. 8, August, 1995, 128+.

51. Indeed, the attention that Disney places on education may in and of itself be a sign of the extent to which social engineering is the key component of new urbanism. For description of the school, although somewhat less problematized than this author would have wished, see Ross, *The Celebration Chronicles.*

52. See Scott Bukatman, *Terminal Identity: The Virtual Subject in Postmodern Science Fiction* (Durham: Duke University Press, 1993).

53. See Cutler, "Locating 'Authority'" and "Artifice, Ideology, and Paradox" for her detailed accounts of "law merchant."

54. See Strange, *Retreat of the State.*

Conclusion: Beyond the Zones

1. See Hans Magnus Enzensberger, *Europe, Europe* (New York: Pantheon, 1989).

2. See Charles Tilly, *Coercion, Capital, and European States,* A.D. *990–1992* (Oxford: Basil Blackwell, 1990), 17.

3. See Jan de Vries, *Economy of Europe in an Age of Crisis, 1600–1750* (Cambridge: Cambridge University Press, 1976).

4. See "Distribution's Emerging Role," *Industrial Distribution,* May 1994, 39–46.

5. See Louis W. Stern and Frederick D. Sturdivant, "Customer-Driven Distribution Systems," *Harvard Business Review,* May–June 1987, 34–40.

6. Lawrence Grossberg, "The Space of Culture; The Power of Space," in Iain Chambers and Lidia Curti, eds., *The Post-Colonial Question* (London: Routledge, 1996), 169.

7. See Tzvetan Todorov, *The Fantastic: A Structural Approach to a Literary Genre* (Ithaca: Cornell University Press, 1975), 167.

8. Ibid., 168.

9. Tim Murray, *Like a Film: Ideological Fantasy on Screen, Camera, and Canvas* (London: Routledge, 1993), 5.

10. Donna Haraway, "A Manifesto for Cyborgs," *Socialist Review* 80: 65–70.

BIBLIOGRAPHY

Abbott, L. B. *Special Effects: Wire, Tape, and Rubber Band Style*. Hollywood: ASC Press, 1984.

Aksoy, Asu, and Kevin Robins. "Hollywood for the 21st Century: Global Competition for Critical Mass in Image Markets." *Cambridge Journal of Economics* 16 (1992): 1–22.

Allen, Robert C. "Vitascope/Cinematographe: Initial Patterns of American Film Industrial Practice." In *The American Movie Industry*, edited by Gorham Kindem, 3–11. Carbondale: University of Southern Illinois Press, 1982.

Anderson, Christopher. *Hollywood TV: The Studio System in the Fifties*. Austin: University of Texas Press, 1994.

Appadurai, Arjun. *Modernity at Large: Cultural Dimensions of Globalization*. Minneapolis: University of Minnesota Press, 1996.

Arendt, Hannah. *The Human Condition*. Chicago: University of Chicago Press, 1958.

Arrighi, Giovanni. "The Three Hegemonies of Historical Capitalism." In *Gramsci, Historical Materialism, and International Relations*, edited by Stephen Gill, 148–85. Cambridge: Cambridge University Press, 1993.

Balio, Tino. *History of American Cinema: Grand Design, Hollywood as a Modern Business Enterprise*. Vol. 5. New York: Charles Scribner's Sons, 1993.

——, ed. *The American Film Industry*. Madison: University of Wisconsin Press, 1985.

Baudrillard, Jean. *For a Critique of the Political Economy of the Sign*. Translated by Charles Levin. St. Louis: Telos Press, 1981.

———. *Transparency of Evil: Essays on Extreme Phenomena*. Translated by James Benedict. London: Verso, 1993.

Benjamin, Walter. "The Work of Art in the Age of Mechanical Reproduction." In Walter Benjamin, *Illuminations: Essays and Reflections*, edited by Hannah Arendt, 217–52. New York: Schocken Books, 1968.

Bernstein, Matthew. *Walter Wanger, Hollywood Independent*. Berkeley: University of California Press, 1994.

Besas, Peter. *Behind the Spanish Lens*. Denver: Arden Press, 1985.

Best, Michael. *The New Competition: Institutions of Industrial Restructuring*. Cambridge: Polity Press, 1990.

Bordwell, David. *Making Meaning: Inference and Rhetoric in the Interpretation of Cinema*. Cambridge: Harvard University Press, 1989.

———, ed. *Post-Theory: Reconstructing Film Studies*. Madison: University of Wisconsin Press, 1996.

Bordwell, David, Janet Staiger, and Kristin Thompson. *The Classical Hollywood Cinema: Film Style and Mode of Production to 1960*. London: Routledge and Kegan Paul, 1985.

Bowser, Eileen. *History of American Cinema: The Transformation of Cinema, 1907–1915*. Vol. 2. New York: Charles Scribner's Sons, 1990.

Brand, Steven. *The MIT Media Lab: Inventing the Future at MIT*. New York: Viking Penguin, 1987.

Brode, Douglas. *The Films of Steven Spielberg*. New York: Carol Publishing Group, 1995.

Brosnan, John. *Movie Magic: The Story of Special Effects in the Cinema*. London: Abacus Books, 1977.

Brotton, Jerry. *Trading Territories: Mapping the Early Modern World*. Ithaca: Cornell University Press, 1998.

Bucknell, L. H. Introduction to *Industrial Architecture*, edited by C. G. Holme. London: Studio Publication, 1935.

Budd, Leslie, and Sam Whimster, eds. *Global Finance and Urban Living: A Study of Metropolitan Change*. London: Routledge, 1992.

Bukatman, Scott. *Terminal Identity: The Virtual Subject in Postmodern Science Fiction*. Durham: Duke University Press, 1993.

Castells, Manuel. *The Information Age: Economy, Society, and Culture. Volume I: The Rise of the Network Society*. Oxford: Basil Blackwell, 1996.

Ceplair, Larry, and Steven Englund. *The Inquisition in Hollywood: Politics in the Film Community, 1930–1960*. Berkeley: University of California Press, 1983.

Chandler, Alfred. *The Visible Hand: The Managerial Revolution in American Business*. Cambridge: Belknap Press, 1977.

Christopherson, Susan, and Michael Storper. "The City as Studio; the World as Backlot: The Impact of Vertical Disintegration on the Location of the Motion Picture Industry." *Environment and Planning D: Society and Space* 3 (1986): 305–20.

——. "The Effects of Flexible Specialization on Industrial Politics and the Labor Market: The Motion Picture Industry." *Industrial and Labor Relations Review* 42 (April 1989): 331–47.

Cohen, Lizabeth. *Making a New Deal: Industrial Workers in Chicago, 1919–1939*. Cambridge: Cambridge University Press, 1990.

Cohen, Stephen S., and John Zysman, eds. *Manufacturing Matters: The Myth of the Post-Industrial Economy*. New York: Basic Books, 1987.

Commons, John R. *Industrial Goodwill*. New York: McGraw Hill, 1919.

Conant, Michael. *Anti-Trust in the Motion Picture Industry: Economic and Legal Analysis*. Berkeley: University of California Press, 1960.

Cook, David A. *A History of Narrative Cinema*. New York: W. W. Norton, 1990.

Corman, Roger, and Jim Jerome. *How I Made a Hundred Movies in Hollywood and Never Lost a Dime*. New York: Doubleday, 1990.

Council of Economic Advisors. *Economic Report of the President*. Lanham, Md.: Bernan, February 1995.

Cox, Robert W. "Structural Issues of Global Governance: Implications for Europe." In *Gramsci, Historical Materialism, and International Relations*, edited by Stephen Gill. Cambridge: Cambridge University Press, 1993.

Culhane, John. *Special Effects in the Movies: How They Do It*. New York: Ballantine Books, 1981.

Cunningham, Stuart, Toby Miller, and David Rowe, eds. *Contemporary Australian Television (Communication and Culture)*. New South Wales University Press, 1995.

Cutler, Claire A. "Artifice, Ideology, and Paradox: The Public/Private Distinction in International Law." *Review of International Political Economy* 4 (1997): 261–85.

——."Locating 'Authority' in the Global Political Economy." *International Studies Quarterly* (1999): 59–81.

Cutler, Claire A., Virginia Haufler, and Tony Porter, eds. *Private Authority and International Affairs*. Albany: State University of New York Press, 1999.

Daugherty, Carroll R. *Labor Problems in American Industry*. Madison: Houghton Mifflin, 1944.

Davis, B. Horace. "Company Towns." In *Encyclopedia of the Social Sciences*. New York: Macmillan, 1931.

Davis, Mike. *City of Quartz: Excavating Future in Los Angeles*. London: Verso, 1990.

Davis, Ronald L. *The Glamour Factory: Inside Hollywood's Big Studio System*. Dallas: Southern Methodist University Press, 1993.

Dean, Jodi, ed., *Cultural Studies and Political Theory*. Ithaca: Cornell University Press, 2000.

De Cordova, Richard. *Picture Personalities: The Emergence of the Star System in America*. Urbana: University of Illinois Press, 1990.

Desser, David, and Garth Jowett, eds. *Hollywood Goes Shopping*. Minneapolis: University of Minnesota Press, 2000.

de Vries, Jan. *Economy of Europe in an Age of Crisis, 1600–1750*. Cambridge: Cambridge University Press, 1976.

Dickinson, Margaret, and Sarah Street, *Cinema and State: The Film Industry and the Government, 1927–84*. London: BFI, 1985.

Dosi, Giovanni. *Technical Change and Industrial Transformation*. London: Macmillan, 1984.

Dunne, John Gregory. *The Studio*. New York: Farrar, Straus & Giroux, 1968.

Eco, Umberto. *Travels in Hyperreality: Essays*. New York: Harcourt Brace Jovanovich, 1986.

Enzensberger, Hans Magnus. *Europe, Europe*. Translated by Martin Chalmers. New York: Pantheon, 1989.

Ferry, W. Hawkins. "Albert Kahn, 1869–1942." In *The Legacy of Albert Kahn*, by Albert Kahn. Detroit: Detroit Institute of Arts, 1970.

Flamm, Kenneth. *Creating the Computer: Government, Industry, and High Technology*. Washington, D.C.: Brookings Institution, 1988.

Fleer, Jack D. *North Carolina Government and Politics*. Lincoln: University of Nebraska Press, 1994.

Fry, Ron, and Pamela Fourzan. *The Saga of Special Effects*. Englewood Cliffs, N.J.: Prentice Hall, 1977.

Geirland, John, and Eva Sonesh-Kedar. *Digital Babylon: How the Geeks, the Suits, and the Ponytails Fought to Bring Hollywood to the Internet*. New York: Arcade, 1999.

Gereffi, Gary. "The Organization of Buyer-Driven Global Commodity Chains." In *Commodity Chains and Global Capitalism*, edited by Gary Gereffi and Miguel Korzeniewicz, 95–122. Westport, Conn.: Greenwood Press, 1994; London: Praeger, 1994.

Gereffi, Gary, and Miguel Korzeniewicz, eds. *Commodity Chains and Global Capitalism*. Westport, Conn.: Greenwood Press, 1994; London: Praeger, 1994.

Gereffi, Gary, Miguel Korzeniewicz, and Roberto P. Korzeniewicz. "Introduction." In *Commodity Chains and Global Capitalism*, edited by Gary Gereffi and Miguel Korzeniewicz, 1–14. Westport, Conn.: Greenwood Press, 1994; London: Praeger, 1994.

Giddens, Anthony. "Time, Space, and Regionalisation." In *Social Relations and Spatial Structures*, edited by Derek Gregory and John Urry, 265–95. London: Macmillan, 1985.

Gledhill, Christine. Introduction to *Stardom: Industry of Desire*, edited by Christine Gledhill. London: Routledge, 1991.

Gomery, Douglas. *The Hollywood Studio System*. New York: St. Martin's Press, 1986.

———. *Shared Pleasures: A History of Movie Presentation in the United States*. Madison: University of Wisconsin Press, 1992.

Gregory, Derek. *Geographical Imaginations*. Cambridge: Blackwell, 1994.

Gregory, Derek, and John Urry, eds. *Social Relations and Spatial Structures*. London: Macmillan, 1985.

Grossberg, Lawrence. "The Space of Culture; The Power of Space." In *The Post-Colonial Question*, edited by Iain Chambers and Lidia Curti. London: Routledge, 1996.

Grunwald, Joseph, and Kenneth Flamm, eds. *The Global Factory: Foreign Assembly in International Trade*. Washington, D.C.: Brookings Institution, 1985.

Guback, Thomas H. "Hollywood's International Market." In *The American Film Industry*, edited by Tino Balio. Madison: University of Wisconsin Press, 1985.

Gundle, Stephen. *Between Hollywood and Moscow: The Italian Communists and the Challenge of Mass Culture, 1943–1991*. Durham: Duke University Press, 2000.

Gunning, Tom. "The Whole Town's Gawking: Early Cinema and the Visual Experience of Modernity." *Yale Journal of Criticism* 7, no. 2 (1994): 189–201.

Gupta, Akhil, and James Ferguson. "Culture, Power, Place: Ethnography at the End of an Era," 1–29. In *Culture, Power, Place: Explorations in Critical Anthropology*, edited by Akhil Gupta and James Ferguson. Durham: Duke University Press, 1997.

Hall, Peter, and Ann Markusen, eds. *Silicon Landscapes*. Boston: Allen and Unwin, 1985.

Hampton, Benjamin B. *A History of the Movies*. New York: Covici, Friede, 1931.

Haraway, Donna. "A Manifesto for Cyborgs." *Socialist Review* 80:65–70.

Harvey, David. *The Condition of Postmodernity: An Enquiry into the Origins of Cultural Change*. London: Blackwell, 1989.

Higson, Andrew, and Richard Maltby, eds. *"Film Europe" and "Film America": Cinema, Commerce, and Cultural Exchange, 1920–1939*. Exeter: University of Exeter Press, 1999.

Hirsch, Joachim. "From the Fordist to the Post-Fordist State." In *The Politics of Flexibility: Restructuring State and Industry in Britain, Germany and Scandinavia*, edited by Bob Jessop, Hans Kastendiek, Klaus Nielsen, and Ove K. Pedersen. London: Edgar Elgar, 1991.

Hopkins, Terrence K., and Immanuel Wallerstein. "Commodity Chains in the World Economy Prior to 1800." In *Commodity Chains and Global Capitalism*, edited by Gary Gereffi and Miguel Korzeniewicz, 17–20. Westport, Conn.: Greenwood Press, 1994; London: Praeger, 1994.

Hozic, Aida A. "Hollywood Goes on Sale: Or What Do the Violet Eyes of Elizabeth Taylor Have to Do with 'Cinema of Attraction'?" In *Hollywood Goes Shopping*, edited by David Desser and Garth Jowett, 312–22. Minneapolis: University of Minnesota Press, 2000.

Huettig, Mae Dana. *Economic Control of the Motion Picture Industry: A Study in Industrial Organization.* London: Oxford University Press, 1944.

Jacobs, Jane M. *Edge of Empire: Postcolonialism and the City.* London: Routledge, 1996.

Jacoby, Sanford M., ed. *Masters to Managers: Historical and Comparative Perspectives on American Employers.* New York: Columbia University Press, 1991.

Jameson, Fredric. *Postmodernism, or the Cultural Logic of Late Capitalism.* Durham: Duke University Press, 1991.

Jameson, Fredric, and Masao Miyoshi, eds. *Cultures of Globalization.* Durham: Duke University Press, 1998.

Jarvie, Ian. *Hollywood's Overseas Campaign: The North Atlantic Movie Trade, 1920–1950.* New York: Cambridge University Press, 1992.

Jessop, Bob. "The Welfare State in Transition." In *The Politics of Flexibility: Restructuring State and Industry in Britain, Germany and Scandinavia,* edited by Bob Jessop, Hans Kastendiek, Klaus Nielsen, and Ove K. Pedersen. London: Edgar Elgar, 1991.

Jessop, Bob, Hans Kastendiek, Klaus Nielsen, and Ove K. Pedersen, eds. *The Politics of Flexibility: Restructuring State and Industry in Britain, Germany, and Scandinavia.* London: Edgar Elgar, 1991.

Johnson, Chalmers, Laura D'Andrea Tyson, and John Zysman, eds. *Politics and Productivity: The Real Story of Why Japan Works.* Cambridge: Ballinger, 1989.

Kanter, Rosabeth Moss. "The Future of Bureaucracy and Hierarchy in Organizational Theory: A Report from the Field," 63–87. In *Social Theory for a Changing Society,* edited by Pierre Bourdieu and James S. Coleman. Boulder: Westview Press, 1991.

——. *World Class: Thriving Locally in the Global Economy.* New York: Simon & Schuster, 1995.

Katznelson, Ira. *Marxism and the City.* Oxford: Clarendon Press, 1992.

Kennedy, Joseph P. *The Story of the Films; As Told by Leaders of the Industry to the Students of the Graduate School of Business Adminis-*

tration, George F. Baker Foundation, Harvard University. Chicago, A. W. Shaw, 1927. New York: J. S. Ozer, 1971.

Kerr, Catherine E. "Incorporating the Star: The Intersection of Business and Aesthetic Strategies in Early American Film." *Business History Review* 64 (Autumn 1990): 383–410.

Kindem, Gorham, ed. *The American Movie Industry: The Business of Motion Pictures.* Carbondale: University of Southern Illinois Press, 1982.

Koppes, Clayton R., and Gregory D. Black. *Hollywood Goes to War: How Politics, Profits, and Propaganda Shaped World War II Movies.* Berkeley, University of California Press, 1987.

Korbin, Stephen J. "Back to the Future: Neomedievalism and the Post Modern World Economy." Paper presented at the 1996 Annual Meeting of the International Studies Association, San Diego, California, April 17, 1996.

Koszarski, Richard. *History of American Cinema: An Evening's Entertainment.* Vol. 3. New York: Charles Scribner's Sons, 1990.

Kristeva, Julia. *Strangers to Ourselves.* Translated by Leon S. Roudiez. New York: Columbia University Press, 1991.

Lahue, Kalton C. *Motion Picture Pioneer: The Selig Polyscope Company.* South Brunswick: A. S. Barnes, 1973.

Lash, Scott, and John Urry. *Economies of Signs and Space.* London: Sage, 1994.

——. *The End of Organized Capitalism.* London: Polity, 1987.

Lavie, Smadar, and Ted Swedenburg, eds. *Displacement, Diaspora, and Geographies of Identity.* Durham: Duke University Press, 1996.

Lazonick, William. *Business Organization and the Myth of the Market Economy.* Cambridge: Cambridge University Press, 1991.

——. *Competitive Advantage on the Shop Floor.* Cambridge: Harvard University Press, 1990.

Lefebvre, Henri. *The Production of Space.* Translated by Donald Nicholson-Smith. Oxford: Basil Blackwell, 1991.

Levidow, Les, and Kevin Robins, eds. *Cyborg Worlds: The Military Information Society.* London: Free Association Books, 1989.

Levin, Samuel. "The Ford Profit-Sharing Plan, 1914–1920. The Growth of the Plan." *Personnel Journal* 6 (1927).

Lewis, Howard Thompson. *The Motion Picture Industry.* New York: D. Van Nostrand, 1933. Reprinted by J. S. Ozer, N.Y., 1971.

Luebke, Paul. *Tar Heel Politics 2000.* Chapel Hill: University of North Carolina Press, 1998.

Lyons, Charles. *The New Censors: Movies and the Culture Wars.* Philadelphia: Temple University Press, 1997.

MacCorquodale, Patricia, Martha W. Gilliland, Jeffrey P. Kash, and Andrew Jameton, eds. *Engineers and Economic Conversion: From the Military to the Marketplace.* New York: Springer-Verlag, 1993.

Magnusson, Lars, ed. *Evolutionary and Neo-Schumpeterian Approaches to Economics.* Boston: Kluwer Academic Publishers, 1994.

Manovich, Lev. *The Language of New Media.* Cambridge: MIT Press, 2001.

Marcus, Greil. *Lipstick Traces: A Secret History of the Twentieth Century.* Cambridge: Harvard University Press, 1989.

Markusen, Ann, Peter Hall, and Amy Glasmeier. *High Tech America: The What, How, Where, and Why of the Sunrise Industries.* Boston: Allen and Unwin, 1986.

Marquis, Samuel S. "I Have Known Henry Ford for Twenty Years." In *Henry Ford,* edited by John B. Rae. Englewood Cliffs, N.J.: Prentice Hall, 1969.

Martin, Ron, and Peter Sunley, "Paul Krugman's Geographical Economics and Its Implications for Regional Development Theory: A Critical Assessment," *Economic Geography* 72, no. 3 (July 1996): 259–93.

May, Lary. *Screening Out the Past: The Birth of Mass Culture and the Motion Picture Industry.* Chicago: University of Chicago Press, 1983.

Medved, Michael, and Harry Medved. *The Hollywood Hall of Shame: The Most Expensive Flops in Movie History.* New York: Perigee, 1984.

Miller, Toby. *Technologies of Truth: Cultural Citizenship and the Popular Media (Visible Evidence, 1).* Minneapolis: University of Minnesota Press, 1998.

Moley, Raymond. *The Hays Office.* Indianapolis: Bobbs-Merrill, 1945.

Morley, David, and Kevin Robins. *Spaces of Identity.* London: Routledge, 1995.

Mosco, Vincent, and Janet Wasko, eds. *The Political Economy of Information.* Madison: University of Wisconsin Press, 1988.

Murray, Tim. *Like a Film: Ideological Fantasy on Screen, Camera, and Canvas.* London: Routledge, 1993.

Musser, Charles. *Before the Nickelodeon: Edwin S. Porter and the Edison Manufacturing Company.* Berkeley: University of California Press, 1991.

Negroponte, Nicholas. *Being Digital.* New York: Alfred A. Knopf, 1995.

Nelson, Richard, and Samuel Winter. *An Evolutionary Theory of Economic Change.* Cambridge: Belknap, 1982.

Noble, David F. *Forces of Production: A Social History of Industrial Automation.* New York: Alfred A. Knopf, 1984.

——."Social Choice in Machine Design." *Politics and Society* 8 (1978): 313–47.

Nye, Joseph S., and William A. Owens Jr. "America's Information Edge," 20–37. *Foreign Affairs*. March/April 1996.

Oden, Michael, Ann Markusen, Dan Flaming, Jonathan Feldman, James Raffel, and Catherine Hill. *Post Cold War Frontiers: Defense Downsizing and Conversion in Los Angeles*. New Brunswick, N.J.: Rutgers University, Project on Regional and Industrial Economics, Working Paper No. 105, 1996.

Oshima, Nagisa. *Cinema, Censorship, and the State: The Writings of Nagisa Oshima*. Edited by Annette Michelson; translated by Dawn Lawson. Cambridge: MIT Press, 1992.

Piore, Michael J., and Charles F. Sabel. *The Second Industrial Divide: Possibilities for Prosperity*. New York: Basic Books, 1984.

Porter, Glenn, and Harold C. Livesay. *Merchants and Manufacturers: Studies in the Changing Structure of Nineteenth-Century Marketing*. Baltimore: Johns Hopkins University Press, 1971.

Porter, Michael. *Competitive Advantage: Creating and Sustaining Superior Performance*. New York: Free Press, 1985.

——. *The Competitive Advantage of Nations*. New York: Free Press, 1990.

——, ed. *Competition in Global Industries*. Boston: Harvard Business School Press, 1986.

Postone, Moishe. *Time, Labor, and Social Domination: A Reinterpretation of Marx's Critical Theory*. Cambridge: Cambridge University Press, 1993.

Powdermaker, Hortense. *Hollywood, the Dream Factory: An Anthropologist Looks at the Movie-Makers*. Boston: Little, Brown, 1950.

Prestowitz, Clyde V., Jr. *Trading Places: How We Allowed Japan to Take the Lead*. New York: Basic Books, 1988.

Puttnam, David, with Neil Watson. *Movies and Money*. New York: Alfred A. Knopf, 1998.

Rae, John B., ed. *Henry Ford*. Englewood Cliffs, N.J.: Prentice Hall, 1969.

Raff, David M. G. "Ford Welfare Capitalism." In *Masters to Managers*, edited by Sanford M. Jacoby. New York: Columbia University Press, 1991.

Ramsey, Terry. "The Rise and Place of the Motion Picture." *Annals of the American Academy of Political and Social Science* 254 (November 1947): 1–11.

Rheingold, Howard. *Virtual Reality*. New York: Simon and Schuster, 1991.

Robertson, Roland. "Social Theory, Cultural Relativity, and the Problem of Globality." In *Culture, Globalization, and the World System*, edited by Anthony D. King, 69–90. London: Macmillan, 1991.

Robins, Kevin, and Frank Webster. "Cybernetic Capitalism: Information, Technology, Everyday Life." In *The Political Economy of Information*, edited by Vincent Mosco and Janet Wasko, 44–75. Madison: University of Wisconsin Press, 1988.

Rochlin, Gene I. *Trapped in the Net: The Unanticipated Consequences of Computerization*. Princeton: Princeton University Press, 1997.

Ross, Andrew. *The Celebration Chronicles: Life, Liberty, and the Pursuit of Property Values in Disney's New Town*. New York: Ballantine Books, 1999.

Ross, Murray. *Stars and Strikes: Unionization of Hollywood*. New York: Columbia University Press, 1941.

Rowland, Willard D., Jr. "Television Violence Redux: The Continuing Mythology of Effects." In *Ill Effects: The Media/Violence Debate*, edited by Martin Barker and Julian Petley. London: Routledge, 1997.

Rupert, Mark. *Producing Hegemony: The Politics of Mass Production and American Global Power*. Cambridge: Cambridge University Press, 1995.

Salais, Robert, and Michael Storper. "The Four 'Worlds' of Contemporary Industry." *Cambridge Journal of Economics* 16 (1992): 169–93.

Saleh, Dennis. *Science Fiction Gold: Film Classics of the 50s*. New York: McGraw Hill, 1979.

Saxenian, Anna Lee. *Regional Advantage: Culture and Competition in Silicon Valley and Route 128*. Cambridge: Harvard University Press, 1994.

Schabedoth, Hans Joachim. "Neo-Conservatism and Modernization Policy in West Germany." In *The Politics of Flexibility: Restructuring State and Industry in Britain, Germany and Scandinavia*, edited by Bob Jessop, Hans Kastendiek, Klaus Nielsen, and Ove K. Pedersen. London: Edgar Elgar, 1991.

Schatz, Thomas. *The Genius of the System: Hollywood Filmmaking in the Studio Era*. New York: Pantheon Books, 1988.

Schulberg, Budd. *Moving Pictures, Memories of a Hollywood Prince*. New York: Stein and Day, 1981.

Schwartz, Herman M. *States versus Markets: History, Geography, and the Development of the International Political Economy*. New York: St. Martin's Press, 1994.

Scott, Allen J. "The Cultural Economy: Geography and the Creative Field." *Media, Culture & Society* 21 (1999): 807–17.

——. "French Cinema: Economy, Policy and Place in the Making of a Cultural-Products Industry." *Theory, Culture & Society* 17 (2000): 1–37.

——. "The U.S. Recorded Music Industry: On the Relations Between Organization, Location, and Creativity in the Cultural Economy." *Environment and Planning A* 31 (1999): 1965–1984.

Scott, Allen J., and Michael Storper. *Production, Work, Territory: The Geographical Anatomy of Industrial Capitalism*. Boston: Allen and Unwin, 1986.

Sell, Susan K. "Intellectual Property Protection and Antitrust in Developing World: Crisis, Coercion, and Choice." *International Organization* 49, no. 2 (1995): 315–49.

Sennett, Robert S. *Setting the Scene: The Great Hollywood Art Directors.* New York: Henry N. Abrams, 1994.

Sheppard, Dick. *Elizabeth: The Life and Career of Elizabeth Taylor.* New York: Doubleday, 1974.

Shoenberger, Erica. "Competition, Time, and Space in Industrial Change," In *Commodity Chains and Global Capitalism*, edited by Gary Gereffi and Miguel Korzeniewicz, 51–66. Westport, Conn.: Greenwood Press; London: Praeger, 1994.

Slack, Jennifer Daryl, and Fred Fejes. *The Ideology of the Information Age.* Norwood, N.J.: Ablex, 1987.

Smith, Thomas G. *Industrial Light and Magic: The Art of Special Effects.* New York: Ballantine Books, 1986.

Soja, Edward. *Postmodern Geographies: The Reassertion of Space in Critical Social Theory.* London: Verso, 1989.

Sorkin, Michael. "See You in Disneyland." In *Variations on a Theme Park: The New American City and the End of Public Spaces*, edited by Michael Sorkin. New York: Hill and Wang, 1992.

Staiger, Janet. "Dividing Labor for Production Control: Thomas Ince and the Rise of the Studio System." In *The American Movie Industry*, edited by Gorham Kindem, 94–103. Carbondale: University of Southern Illinois Press, 1982.

———, ed. *The Studio System.* New Brunswick: Rutgers University Press, 1995.

Stenger, Josh. "Lights, Camera, Faction: (Re)Producing 'Los Angeles' at Universal's CityWalk." In *Hollywood Goes Shopping*, edited by David Desser and Garth Jowett. Minneapolis: University of Minnesota Press, 2000, 277–308.

Stern, Michael. "Making Culture into Nature." In *Alien Zone: Cultural Theory and Contemporary Science Fiction Cinema*, edited by Annette Kuhn. London: Verso, 1990.

Storper, Michael. "Competitiveness Policy Options: The Technology-Regions Connections." *Growth and Change* 26 (Spring 1995): 285–308.

———. "Flexible Specialization in Hollywood: A Response to Aksoy and Robins." *Cambridge Journal of Economics* 17 (1993): 479–84.

———. "The Limits to Globalization." *Economic Geography* 68 (1992): 60–93.

———. "The Transition to Flexible Specialization in the U.S. Film Industry: External Economies, the Division of Labour, and the Crossing of Industrial Divides." *Cambridge Journal of Economics* 13 (June 1989): 273–305.

Storper, Michael, and Susan Christopherson. "Flexible Specialization and Regional Industrial Agglomerations." *Annals of the Association of American Geographers* (March 1987), 104–17.

Strange, Susan. *The Retreat of the State: The Diffusion of Power in the World Economy.* Cambridge: Cambridge University Press, 1996.

Strasser, Susan. *Satisfaction Guaranteed: The Making of the American Mass Market.* New York: Pantheon Books, 1989.

Streeck, Wolfgang, and Philippe C. Schmitter, eds. *Private Interest Government: Beyond Market and State.* London: Sage, 1985.

Sward, Keith. "Embattled Autocrat." In *Henry Ford,* edited by John B. Rae. New Jersey: Prentice Hall, 1969.

Taylor, Peter J. *Modernities: A Geohistorical Interpretation.* Minneapolis: University of Minnesota Press, 1999.

Thompson, Kristin. *Exporting Entertainment: America in the World Film Market, 1907–1934.* London: BFI, 1985.

Tilly, Charles. *Coercion, Capital, and European States, A.D. 990–1992.* Oxford: Basil Blackwell, 1990.

Todorov, Tzvetan. *The Fantastic: A Structural Approach to a Literary Genre.* Translated by Richard Howard. Ithaca: Cornell University Press, 1975.

Tyson, Laura D'Andrea. *Who's Bashing Whom? Trade Conflicts in High Technology Industries.* Washington, D.C.: Institute for International Economics, 1993.

United States. Congress. House. Committee on Education and Labor, *Impact of Imports and Exports on American Employment, Hearings before the Subcommittee on the Impact of Imports and Exports on American Employment of the Committee on Education and Labor, House of Representatives,* 87th Congress, 1st and 2d Sessions. Washington, D.C.: U.S. Government Printing Office, 1961–1962.

Urry, John. "Time and Space in Giddens' Social Theory," 160–75. In *Giddens' Theory of Structuration: A Critical Appreciation,* edited by Christopher G. A. Bryant and David Jary. London: Routledge, 1991.

Vernon, Raymond. "International Investment and International Trade in the Product Cycle." *Quarterly Journal of Economics* 80(May 1966): 190–207.

——. *Sovereignty at Bay, the Multinational Spread of U.S. Enterprises.* New York: Basic Books, 1971.

——. *Storm over the Multinationals: The Real Issues.* Cambridge: Harvard University Press, 1977.

Virilio, Paul. *War and Cinema: The Logistics of Perception.* Translated by Patrick Camiller. London: Verso, 1989.

Wachhorst, Wyn. *Thomas Alva Edison, an American Myth.* Cambridge: MIT Press, 1981.

Walker, Alexander. *Hollywood, England: The British Film Industry in the Sixties*. London: Harrap, 1974.

Wasko, Janet. *Movies and Money: Financing the American Film Industry*. Norwood, N.J.: Ablex, 1982.

Watkins, Gordon S. "The Motion Picture Industry." *Annals of the American Academy of Political and Social Science* 254 (November 1947): vii.

Whitney, Simon N. "Antitrust Policies and the Motion Picture Industry." In *The American Film Industry*, edited by Gorham Kindem, 161–204. Carbondale: University of Southern Illinois Press, 1982.

Wilkins, Mira. *The Maturing of Multinational Enterprise: American Business Abroad from 1914 to 1970*. Cambridge: Harvard University Press, 1974.

Wilkins, Mira, and Frank Ernest Hill. *American Business Abroad: Ford on Six Continents*. Detroit: Wayne State University Press, 1964.

Wilson, Rob, and Wilam Dissanayake, eds. *Global/Local: Cultural Production and the Transnational Imaginary*. Durham: Duke University Press, 1996.

Winter, John Anthony. *Industrial Architecture: A Survey of Factory Building*. London: Studio Vista, 1970.

Wood, Philip J. *Southern Capitalism: The Political Economy of North Carolina*. Durham: Duke University Press, 1986.

Wyatt, Justin. *High Concept: Movies and Marketing in Hollywood*. Austin: University of Texas Press, 1994.

———. "The Stigma of X: Adult Cinema and the Institution of the MPAA Ratings System," in *Controlling Hollywood: Censorship and Regulation in the Studio Era*, edited by Matthew Bernstein. New Brunswick: Rutgers University Press, 1999.

Yule, Andrew. *Fast Fade: David Puttnam, Columbia Pictures, and the Battle for Hollywood*. New York: Delta, 1989.

Zimmermann, Patricia. *States of Emergency—Documentaries, Wars, Democracies*. Minneapolis: University of Minnesota Press, 2000.

Žižek, Slavoj. *The Plague of Fantasies*. London: Verso, 1997.

———. *The Sublime Object of Ideology*. London: Verso, 1989.

Zukin, Sharon. *Landscapes of Power: From Detroit to Disney World*. Berkeley: University of California Press, 1991.

Zunz, Olivier. *Making America Corporate, 1870–1920*. Chicago: University of Chicago Press, 1990.

Zweig, Stefan. *Three Masters: Balzac, Dickens, Dostoyevski*. New York: Viking, 1930.

INDEX